THE BOYS *of* FAIRY TOWN

THE BOYS *of* FAIRY TOWN

SODOMITES, FEMALE IMPERSONATORS, THIRD-SEXERS, PANSIES, QUEERS, AND SEX MORONS IN CHICAGO'S FIRST CENTURY

JIM ELLEDGE

CHICAGO
REVIEW
PRESS

Published by Chicago Review Press Incorporated
814 North Franklin Street
Chicago, Illinois 60610
978-1-61373-935-8

Library of Congress Cataloging-in-Publication Data
Names: Elledge, Jim, 1950– author.
Title: The boys of fairy town : sodomites, female impersonators,
    third-sexers, pansies, queers, and sex morons in Chicago's first century /
    Jim Elledge.
Description: Chicago, Ill. : Chicago Review Press, [2018] | Includes
    bibliographical references and index.
Identifiers: LCCN 2017058268 (print) | LCCN 2017060444 (ebook) | ISBN
    9781613739365 (PDF edition) | ISBN 9781613739389 (EPUB edition) | ISBN
    9781613739372 (Kindle edition) | ISBN 9781613739358 (cloth edition)
Subjects: LCSH: Gays—Illinois—Chicago—History—19th century. |
    Gays—Illinois—Chicago—History—20th century.
Classification: LCC HQ76.3.U52 (ebook) | LCC HQ76.3.U52 I4445 2018 (print) |
    DDC 306.76/60977311—dc23
LC record available at https://lccn.loc.gov/2017058268

Cover design: John Yates at Stealworks
Cover photo: Tony Jackson (standing) and unknown friend. *The William Russell
    Jazz Collection at the Historic New Orleans Collection, acquisition made
    possible by the Clarisse Claiborne Grima Fund, 92-48-L.242*
Back cover photo: A John D. Hagenhofer photograph of his friends Mickey and
    Heine "going batey." *Courtesy of Gerber/Hart Library and Archives*
Typesetting: Nord Compo

Printed in the United States of America
5 4 3 2 1

For David

Fairy Town, Fairy Town—
that's where all the boys go down.
Even the chief of police is queer.
Whoops! my dear.
Whoops! my dear.

When the Navy comes to town,
that's when all the boys turn brown.
The Fagots all dish.
The Mentes all fish
in Fairy Town.

Contents

List of Illustrations

Acknowledgments

SOME OF THE CHAPTERS in this book initially appeared as essays in various publications, sometimes in much different versions, and I would like to thank the editors and publishers of the following for including my work in their pages: *Five Points* for "Frankie Jaxon & Chicago's Jazz-Age Pansy Craze"; the *Gay and Lesbian Review Worldwide* for "Eugen Sandow's Gift to Gay Men" and "Lovers' Quarrel, 1890s Style"; Praeger, a division of ABC-Clio, for "'Artfully Dressed in Women's Clothing': Drag Queens on Chicago's Burlesque Stage, an Account from the Summer of 1909" and "'It Is Just Something Greek; That's All': Eugen Sandow—Queer Father of Modern Body Building" in *Queers in American Popular Culture*; and the *Windy City Times* for "Chicago's Man-Girl Trial" and "When 'the Love That Dare Not Speak Its Name' Did."

The universities where I've taught have supported my work financially, and had it not been for that support, *The Boys of Fairy Town* would not have been written. At Kennesaw State University, I would like to thank Tommy and Beth Holder, the Center for Excellence in Teaching and Learning for its Incentive Fund for Scholarship, and Rich Vengroff, then dean of the College of Humanities and Social Sciences, for stipends. I also want to thank the Provost's Faculty Development Grant and Toni Oliviero, then dean of the School of Liberal Arts and Sciences, for stipends at Pratt Institute.

The financial support I was given allowed me to conduct research at a number of institutions, to whose staff—many nameless to me—I also owe a great deal of thanks. To that end, I'd like to thank the many individuals at the following for their help: the Special Collections of the Regenstein Library, University of Chicago; the Newberry Library, Chicago; the Harold Washington Library Center, Chicago; the Chicago History Museum; the Special Collections and University Archives of the Daley Library, University of Illinois at Chicago;

the Gerber/Hart Library and Archives, Chicago; the Vivian G. Harsh Research Collection, Woodson Regional Library, Chicago; the Historic New Orleans Collection; ONE National Gay & Lesbian Archives, USC Libraries, University of Southern California, Los Angeles; and the Kinsey Institute for Research in Sex, Gender, and Reproduction, Indiana University, Bloomington.

Finally many thanks to my agent, Adriann Ranta Zurhellen, at Foundry Literary + Media, and to copyeditor Julia Loy and editors Yuval Taylor and Devon Freeny at Chicago Review Press. Their intelligence and creativity makes "work" a pleasure.

Introduction

From Sodomite
to Sex Moron

She—Sometimes you appear really manly
and sometimes you are effeminate.
How do you account for it?

He—I suppose it is hereditary. Half of my
ancestors were men and the other half
were women.

"FAIRY TOWN" WAS NOT AN ACTUAL NEIGHBORHOOD in Chicago
as Greektown or Little Italy are. It was, more or less, an idea, a concept, that
grew from the Windy City's queer men's need for a place where they felt safe
enough to be themselves, where they might live, and where they might find
entertainment, support, and friendship—and perhaps even love. "Fairy Town"
had many different geographical centers during the period this book covers:
the Near North Side's Towertown, the South Side's Bronzeville, the neighborhood along West Madison Street on the Near West Side, Bryant's Block in
the Loop, and even a small but no less important area of a few blocks near
the University of Chicago. I'm sure there were other pockets in the city where
queer men built lives for themselves, and each would be a "Fairy Town" too.

The Boys of Fairy Town traces queer life in Chicago from a few years
after Chicago's incorporation as a city in 1837 until the mid-1940s—practi-
cally speaking, its first century as a city. For much of that period, the homosexual, as we define him today, didn't exist. Although the word *homosexual*

was coined in 1869, it wouldn't appear in print in the United States until 1892, when Dr. James G. Kiernan, a Chicago physician, used it in one of his medical essays, "Responsibility in Sexual Perversion." Afterward, physicians, some legal authorities, professors and graduate students in sociology and psychology, and a few especially well-read individuals would begin to use the word, but it wouldn't find its way into the mainstream until the late 1920s, and even then it would be used rather sporadically.

There were many terms other than *homosexual* that society applied to men who were sexually and romantically attracted to other men. Through many of the labels, the larger society tried to identify the otherness that it found in its midst—what we now call *sexual orientation*—but some of the other terms came from within the queer subculture as it tried to understand itself.

One of the first terms to be used in Chicago was *sodomite*. Chicagoans knew the sodomite existed and might agree that he was a criminal and even a sinner, but if asked to define what a sodomite actually was or what he did, the typical man or woman on the street would hem and haw, perhaps mutter something about the Bible and a crime against nature or the love that dare not speak its name, and then let it drop. The sodomite rarely rose from the shadowy realm in which he lived into the general population's consciousness. When he did, his appearance was only occasional and quite brief, typically when he was caught in flagrante delicto and arrested by a police officer, and his detention was reported in one of Chicago's newspapers.

The other terms that were used over and over again in a vain attempt to describe him, such as *degenerate* or *pervert*, were just as vague, just as imprecise, as *sodomite*—and just as useless in identifying him. He was a vague figure because society had not yet identified any visible, physical feature that it could associate with him and so set him apart from a nonsodomite man. He didn't wear a particular type of clothing, nor did he have particular mannerisms. A man could be extremely effeminate, be called a sissy, and even laughed at behind his back, but no one would presume he was interested in men sexually. Because he couldn't be defined or described, the sodomite blended seamlessly and unrecognized into the mainstream, and as long as he didn't get caught sexually engaged with another man, he was virtually invisible to Chicagoans.

The only individuals who would have been aware of the sodomite in any substantial way were those who were acquainted with Chicago's thriving underworld, such as the "sporting man" who was a dedicated denizen of Chicago's nightlife or the police officer on the beat who monitored that nightlife. Most Chicagoans didn't know that some brothels, which nominally operated for the benefit of non-queer men, also kept a young man or two on the premises to satisfy the needs of men interested in bedding another man. Most Chicagoans were also unaware that, in certain parts of the city, a few brothels existed that were exclusively dedicated to male-male sexual contact.

But not long after the beginning of the twentieth century, the veil that had long hidden Chicago's man-loving men from society's scrutiny would begin to lift. In early 1910 a group of civic-minded businessmen, university professors, and religious leaders talked then mayor Fred A. Busse into forming a commission that would investigate vice in Chicago in order to figure out how to get rid of it. *Vice* encompassed male/female prostitution, gambling, drug and alcohol abuse, and so on. Unexpectedly, one of Chicago Vice Commission's investigators stumbled onto a large number of public places, such as saloons and cafés, that either catered exclusively to queer men or at least welcomed them and their cash. He learned that queer men hobnobbed with others like themselves not just for romantic and sexual relationships but for entertainment and camaraderie as well.

One of the most important aspects of the investigator's discovery is the fact that he described these men. The men he had come across often dressed in female clothing, he reported, wore makeup, and called themselves and their friends, whom they referred to as "sisters," by female nicknames. Society would soon declare that these men had turned their gender identity upside down—or "inverted" it—a notion that gave rise to one of the labels for them: *invert*. They were also called *female impersonators*.

Typically, inverts didn't seek out other inverts for sexual or romantic relationships but set their sights on what many of them thought of as "normal" men—those who were, in essence, the exact opposite of the invert except for the fact that they, too, had sex with men and sometimes exchanged sexual favors for cash. Like the sodomite, "normal" men looked and acted like any non-queer man in Chicago, and so they too fit seamlessly into, and went unrecognized by, society. The investigator did learn, however, that they had a way of recognizing each other, often wearing red neckties to signal to others in the know that they were queer.

In the mid-1910s a politically conservative movement began to develop in the United States in response to the threat of World War I, which was then looming on the horizon. Politically liberal Chicagoans strained against the confines of that conservatism and embraced bohemianism, a liberal artistic and political movement that had begun in Europe and then crossed the Atlantic. At the same time, young, white Chicagoans were becoming devotees of the new music craze, jazz. *Jazz* was an umbrella term that, in its early days, included ragtime, the blues, and other African American styles of music.

By 1920 Prohibition had been ratified, and it outlawed the "manufacture, transportation and sale of intoxicating liquors." Nevertheless, huge numbers of Chicagoans ignored the new law and patronized speakeasies and the scores of cabarets that served alcohol on the sly and staged jazz performances. Young, socially liberal women whom society called *flappers* and their male counterparts, labeled *sheiks*, crowded the cabarets where jazz was performed. For the most part, they could not have cared less about politics, but they were devoted to having a good time, drinking heavily, and dancing to jazz.

The confluence of the bohemian movement, the jazz-related culture (which came to be known as the Jazz Age or the Roaring Twenties), and Prohibition set the stage for the very visible appearance of queer men in a new guise: the "pansy" or the "fairy." While some pansies appropriated a few telltale signs of effeminacy, they weren't female impersonators per se. They expressed themselves visually as part male (their clothing) and part female (the dabs of makeup they might wear and their longish, sometimes bleached hair, as well as effeminate mannerisms). The pansy was not merely visible to Chicagoans in certain quarters of the city, he was also a transgressive and, unlike the sodomite, an easily identifiable figure.

Pansies and fairies were not afraid to appear in public in many neighborhoods—on the sidewalk, in a lecture hall, or in a speakeasy—because the bohemians had accepted them. Flappers and sheiks, whose chief slogan was "free love," couldn't reject queer men, because like them they clashed with society's predominant sexual taboos. If, by mainstream standards, queer men were deviant, they were no more deviant by those same socially sanctioned standards than the young women who bobbed their hair, raised the hemlines of their dresses, demanded equal rights, and lost their virginity before marriage—or the young men who stood beside them, cheering them on. With their liberal sociopolitical agenda, the bohemians had to accept queer men too. Besides, accepting queer men into the fold was another way for bohemians, flappers, and sheiks to thumb their noses at their families, specifically, and, more generally, at society.

Thus, queer men owned businesses, patronized the same establishments as non-queer men, found roles in Chicago's cabaret productions, made records for Chicago's budding music industry, and even appeared in comic strips printed in Chicago's newspapers. Female impersonators became as visible as pansies, a large number of them finding jobs in drag shows staged at various cabarets. The period in which the pansy and female impersonator enjoyed so much visibility wasn't unique to Chicago but blossomed in major urban centers across the country. Historians refer to this phenomenon as the Pansy Craze.

Of course, to say that the pansy was free from societal restraints and what we today would call *homophobia* is simplifying a very complex situation. The public as a whole was divided about them. One queer man recalled how the non-queer men he knew at the Subway, one of Chicago's many queer-friendly bars, reacted to the pansies among them: "Some of my friends said, 'I get a kick out of kidding with them'; others said, 'I feel sorry for them.' Most of them say, 'I would kick the shit out of them if they tried to make me.'" The pansy's freedom was limited to particular neighborhoods and to specific activities. If he went beyond those parameters, he could face arrest or brutality from non-queer men. Yet queer men had become so much a part of the fabric of Chicago life that when two male investigators for the Juvenile Protective Association checked into the Sterling Hotel at 1859 West Madison Street to investigate a prostitution ring there, the desk clerk thought that they might be having a sexual tryst and, without a thought, asked them, "Two rooms, boys, or one?"

And, of course, the hubbub that filled cabarets and speakeasies allowed "normal" men to duck unnoticed in and out of the queer subculture. Queer men called those who offered their sexual favors to female impersonators and fairies in exchange for money by a new label, *trade*. They gave those who blackmailed their clients a specific label too: *dirt*.

Unfortunately, the Pansy Craze was short lived. On October 29, 1929, the US stock market crashed after months of plummeting stock prices, and the country was sunk into the worst financial depression it had ever known. A devastating poverty swallowed up Chicago. Following the repeal of Prohibition a few years later, the Illinois state legislature put a stranglehold of regulations on the cabarets, and the city fathers took the opportunity to send police to raid and board them up. Although much of the effort by the police was supposed to be a backstop against the Mafia, which had bought up or otherwise controlled many of the more lucrative hot spots in Chicago, they also took the opportunity to obliterate queer presence as much as possible.

As Adolph Hitler's Nazis rose to power in the mid-1930s and as the threat of a new war loomed on the horizon, a second wave of sociopolitical conservatism, which was even stronger than the earlier one, swept across the country. At the same time, a plague of sex murders, mostly of little girls and women, erupted in Chicago and the rest of the country, causing a great deal of anxiety. FBI director J. Edgar Hoover and his minions blamed the assaults on what they referred to as the *sex moron*, a shadowy figure who was immediately associated with queer men, and a homophobic frenzy ensued. By the end of the 1930s, virtually any sexual assault or murder not immediately recognized as the work of a non-queer man, or any such crime that was sensational in nature, was blamed on the sex moron/queer man.

Terrified of being rounded up singularly or en masse and feeling extremely persecuted with no hope of relief, much of Chicago's queer subculture sank into what can only be called a pit of despair, and they fled into a figurative underground, trying to escape detection by police and the very harsh prison sentences they would receive if convicted of "a crime against nature." Those men who dared to gather together in public often had no choice but to meet in dingy bars in the grittiest backstreets and alleys in Chicago, where at any moment they might be subjected to a police raid, arrest, and either a fine or a jail term or both. When most people think of the history of queer men, it's this period of extreme homophobia that comes to mind—the "post-pansy panic," as one historian has called it.

During the period that *The Boys of Fairy Town* covers, queer men were a very diverse group, ranging from the well-to-do to the homeless, from the quite old to the very young, from the super butch to the flaming fem, from African Americans to those of European descent. Except for one or two of the men included in *The Boys of Fairy Town* (Alfred Kinsey, and perhaps Henry Gerber) they are all virtually unknown today. A few achieved some acclaim or notoriety during their lives, but the rest were little more than a name in a newspaper article or a line in a census report. They run the gamut of queer "types" too: sodomites, dandies, inverts, psychic hermaphrodites, "normal" men, female impersonators, third-sexers, sissies, mollycoddles, girl-men, bitches, belles, pansies, fairies, gardenia boys, lily bearers, perverts, queers, queens, trade, dirt, temperamentals, fags, gays, homosexuals, homos, and sex morons.

In writing *The Boys of Fairy Town*, I wanted to give a personal view of how gay men lived in Chicago during its first century or so, to focus on lives rather than on what is usually considered history. In some chapters I highlight a single person's life, like Henry Gerber in chapter 11, but in others I deal with the lives of several men at once, as with the young man known as "Herman" and his friends in chapter 14.

I open *The Boys of Fairy Town* with "Took Him Home with Me, and Love Him Better Than Ever," in which I investigate the life of John Wing, a newspaper reporter who arrived in Chicago from a small town in New York at the close of the Civil War. An avid diarist from a very early age, his journals are full of details about his numerous love affairs with other boys when he was a teenager in New York and, as a man, with other men in Chicago. His diaries offer the first autobiographical account of a queer man in Chicago and give a distinct view of his emotional and sexual life. It seemed to me that his story, being the oldest and most complete, was the best to open the book.

I close *The Boys of Fairy Town* with "Thank God I Got Only 60 Days and a Small Fine," a chapter in which I recount the research into homosexuality that noted sexologist Alfred C. Kinsey conducted in Chicago. His investigation into male sexuality, which would be published as *Sexual Behavior of the Human Male* (1948), owed a great deal to the queer men he met, interviewed, befriended, and even bedded there. The ideas that they expressed to him, and the conclusions he drew from them, helped to create a movement that would emerge nationally a few decades later as the gay liberation movement.

Between newspaper reporter John Wing and sexologist Alfred Kinsey, I report on the lives of dozens of men who lived and loved in Chicago, from Dr. Richard Murphy, who was accused of being a sodomite by his political rival in 1843, to the beginning of what would be dubbed the "post-pansy panic," which began in 1937 and which by 1943 had a stranglehold on the United States. To me, the century of life in Chicago that I depict is the most fascinating of any, especially when it comes to queer life. It's a century in which many queer men were at first invisible, then quite visible, then invisible again but hunted down by the authorities; one in which the labels that defined them constantly shifted as their sense of themselves and how they dealt with their sexuality evolved; and one that today is virtually unknown to most people, queer or not.

The other men whose lives I portray include but are not limited to:

- Eugen Sandow, the father of modern bodybuilding, whose debut at the Trocadero Music Hall in the Loop became the talk of the town, not only because of his near-nude performances onstage but also because of the hanky-panky associated with his private salons offstage after his last curtain call
- Guy T. Olmstead, a post office employee who shot his male lover in the back in broad daylight for rejecting him, who was arrested on the spot, and who had himself castrated in a futile attempt to rid himself of his homosexuality
- Quincy de Lang and George Quinn, female impersonators who performed a striptease act at Riverview Amusement Park so expertly and so convincingly that the city fathers had them arrested after one of their performances because they were sure that de Lang and Quinn turned young men in their audiences queer
- Edward Clasby, who founded and directed the Seven Arts Club, through which he sponsored highbrow lectures on, for example, James Joyce's *Ulysses* as well as staged drag shows, and who was arrested with other members of the club in the vestibule of a bordello infamous throughout Chicago for its male prostitutes
- Frances Carrick, a female impersonator who became a cause célèbre when she was taken into custody for murder and the public discovered that she had legally married not only another man but also a woman—and lived with both in the same apartment at the same time
- The Sepia Mae West, the Sepia Gloria Swanson, the Sepia Joan Crawford, Valda Gray, Petite Swanson, Nancy Kelly, Jean LaRue, Nina Mae McKinney, Peaches Browning, Doris White, Frances Dee, and Dixie Lee—all female impersonators and superstars in the South Side's hottest nightspots
- Recording artist Frankie Jaxon, a powerhouse of energy onstage and off who adopted a female persona on most of his records and whose hit "Willie the Weeper" was rerecorded by Cab Calloway as "Minnie the Moocher," with heterosexualized lyrics

- "Shorty," a hobo who was struck with wanderlust and set out for a life on the road but who ended up headquartered in Chicago, where he bedded other men and teenagers
- "Harold," Bill Kirkland, Edward Stevens, "Herman," Alexander Stahl, "Carl," "J.B.," "Mr. H.," "Ted," and a host of other young men who worked as male prostitutes before, during, and after the Great Depression because they couldn't find legitimate jobs—and because they liked it

Through the lives of such men, we can readily see the political and social currents with which they struggled, what strategies they developed to cope with or to curtail those currents, and what the results were. Many of the men were quite successful in leading lives that, by anyone's standards, were meaningful and happy, but others were not so lucky.

The fact that there was a large queer presence—visible or not—in Chicago before the Great Chicago Fire of 1871 and that it grew by leaps and bounds, becoming quite visible by the mid-1920s, shouldn't come as a surprise to anyone, and yet it usually does. What we've been told for so long—that *all* queer men, regardless of when they lived, had miserable, isolated, and utterly desperate lives; that *all* queer men were terrified by the threat of their sexual activities being discovered; that *all* queer men found it impossible to control their lusts, and so they were forced to hunt for release in public restrooms and parks; that *all* queer men secretly dressed in women's clothes because they had been raised as momma's boys; and many, many other things—are lies.

If *The Boys of Fairy Town* achieves no other end, I hope that it will dispel the myth of the desperate and isolated pre-Stonewall queer man and will reveal queer life in Chicago as it really was: at times hidden, at other times very visible, but ever present, amazingly diverse, very complex, and remarkably durable.

1 | Took Him Home with Me, and Love Him Better Than Ever

> Monday is a sort of dull day with me always—not because of my having any[thing] to do with the females—because the good lord knows that I do nothing of a kind.

TRUTH BE TOLD, John Wing was a sodomite.

He was also a devoted diarist, having begun keeping a journal when he was thirteen. He grew into a man with fine features and "fair" complexion. He was five feet, seven and a half inches tall, his light blue eyes were piercing, and his mustache was as dark brown as his hair, neatly trimmed, and thick. He dressed to the nines in top hat and coat and had a penchant for diamond stickpins—and for younger men. "Diamonds are my delight," Wing wrote in his diary on Saturday, September 23, 1865, and then added, "diamond pins or diamond friends, in the shape of whole soulded boys."

Born in 1844 and raised on a farm just outside of Pulaski, New York, Wing dropped out of school at sixteen to become a "printer's devil," performing menial tasks for a local newspaper, the *Pulaski Democrat*. Over the next five years, he worked on the staffs of three newspapers and as a teacher at two schools—all in upstate New York. He also read every book he could get his hands on and began building his personal library. As the Civil War wound down, Wing decided to go west to seek his fortune. He had just turned

1

twenty-one years old when he boarded a steamship that sailed through the Great Lakes, stopping at Cleveland and Detroit, where he looked for employment—unsuccessfully, as it turned out.

Wing returned to the ship and traveled to Chicago, arriving on June 4, 1865, a sweltering Sunday two months after Robert E. Lee surrendered to Ulysses S. Grant at Appomattox Court House. As he walked down the gangplank, Wing carried a valise of clothing in one hand and a parcel of his diaries in the other. His library was in crates. He found lodgings in a rooming house, and the next day he called on the editor of the *Chicago Tribune* and asked him for a job as a reporter. He was hired on the spot and would live in Chicago for the rest of his life. At first he boarded in various rooming houses, but by 1866 he began living in hotels, among them Brigg's House at the northeast corner of Wells and Randolph Streets and the Shepard Building at the southeast corner of Dearborn and Monroe Streets.

Considered by historians to have been a "largely male frontier city" in the mid-1860s, Chicago was, nevertheless, beginning to metamorphose into a major urban center. Its population was rapidly growing and would soon reach a quarter of a million inhabitants, due in large part to both its preeminence as a hub in the network of railroads that would soon crisscross the nation and its leadership in the meatpacking industry. The Union Stock Yard, which opened the year Wing arrived, was one of Chicago's first major industries, providing thousands of jobs to residents and shoving the Windy City into the forefront of the nation's economy.

Despite its rough-and-tumble reputation, Chicago was also becoming well known for its array of entertainment venues. At one extreme it had scores of saloons and bordellos catering to homebred toughs and tourists alike, and Under the Willow, at the northwest corner of Monroe and Wells, was the most famous of all. Behind its walls men could find any sexual experience imaginable, from the everyday to the queer, from the normal to the debauched. It was well known that a few "male prostitutes rented cubicles" there and made themselves available to clients.

At the other extreme were the more legitimate but no less popular forms of entertainment. Uranus H. Crosby's newly erected and elegant opera house opened its debut season with Verdi's *Il Trovatore*, drawing hundreds to its performances, but Wing, who loved theater almost as much as he loved books and "whole souled boys," was attracted to Col. Wood's Theatre and Museum and its more popular fare, such as John Buckstone's *Leap Year; or, The Ladies' Privilege*, one of Col. Wood's hits. Wing kept mum in his diary about any saloon or bordello visits he may have made.

During his first few weeks in Chicago, Wing put his nose to the grindstone, often ending the day exhausted by the demands of his seven-days-a-week job of reporting on a variety of Chicago events, from goings-on at the police court to the high jinks at political conventions. To augment his salary, he wrote actual news stories in which he would add favorable mentions of items available in specific stores or services available in specific establishments, neither of which had anything to do with the news stories. He received generous kickbacks from the proprietors for the publicity and admitted to writing many.

Then on Monday, July 3, a month after he first set foot in Chicago, Wing had a brief respite from his humdrum day. He "fell in with a bully little boy" whom he talked up for quite some time in hopes of making a date to meet later. Because he never recorded the boy's age, Wing might appear to have been a pedophile targeting a child, but Wing used *boy* and *boys* to refer to anyone to whom he was attracted regardless of the man's actual age—a convention that had been popular among queer men across the United States and in Europe long before Wing arrived in Chicago.

Because no labels had yet been coined for the relationships that grew up between them, queer men created their own from what was at hand. According to historian Jonathan Katz, they might describe their bond as one between a "'youth' and an 'old man,' or a 'boy' and a 'man,'" ignoring the actual ages of the individuals involved, or they might use labels from family life—"child/parent, father/son, brother/brother, uncle/nephew"—as a way to understand that a strong bond existed between men, between men and boys, or between boys and boys. The bond that the labels suggested legitimized their relationship. Walt Whitman used both types of labels in his romantic relationships, calling Harry Stafford, who was twenty-two years old, "my darling boy" and using *son* when addressing Tom Sawyer, Lewy Brown, and Peter Doyle.

The practice found its way into the popular culture of the time in a camouflaged form. While Wing was out seeking bedmates in Chicago, Horatio Alger, who was a Unitarian minister in Brewster, Massachusetts, was denounced for having sexual liaisons with teenagers in his church, and he quickly relocated to New York. Strapped for cash, he made a successful career and earned a great deal of money from writing his Ragged Dick and Tattered Tom series of novels. In them a wealthy older man takes a destitute teenager under his wing, and through the younger one's hard work and determination—as well as the guidance and patronage of the older man—the younger becomes the epitome of the American success story. The homoeroticism of their relationship lies just under the surface of each of the novels but went virtually unrecognized by non-queer readers. Interestingly while in New York, Alger informally adopted three teenage boys.

Although he was only twenty-one when he reached Chicago, Wing adopted the convention in his diaries, using the generic *boy* for his pickups and, when he was especially enthralled by someone, the more effusive "bully boy." He once even used *boy* when he described himself as "a lucky boy." As Paul Gehl has shown, Wing reported in the first volumes of his diaries that he was "the younger partner" in several same-sex sexual relationships during his adolescence and young adulthood, but in Chicago he took on the label of "the elder" partner in his romantic dalliances, even if his paramour was in fact older than he.

Wing never revealed where he met the "boy" on July 3, only that he chatted with him, hoping it would lead to something in the future. It never did. In fact, Wing recorded a number of other dead-end experiences in his diary, as well as several that resulted in one-night stands. On Monday, September 11, 1865, for example, Wing "fell in love with a little beauty," but he "got the mitten," nineteenth-century slang for getting dumped. Upset over the outcome, he had a "d—d poor bed" alone that night. Even when he was able to bed someone, his pickups rarely remained the entire night.

On October 4 Wing made the acquaintance of Johnny Maier. Wing succinctly, and with only a bare hint of emotion, described their first night: "Saw a boy with whom I fell in love, and chased him up. Found him and got him all right. Engaged a room"—that is, he rented a hotel room for the two of them—"and he and I retired. He is a bully fellow, but got up in the night and dug," nineteenth-century slang for slipping out without a word.

Hearing Maier leave, Wing followed him to a pool hall, where Maier began drinking heavily. Instead of returning to the hotel room for which he had paid two dollars for the night, Wing went home, dejected. The next day he wrote in his diary about his "*enamorata* of last night," and by using the feminine ending *a*, instead of the masculine *o*, he may have been hinting about Maier's sexual preferences. Unfortunately, Wing didn't bother to explain in the diary entry why he didn't just take Maier back to his place, rather than the hotel, after they met.

Along with his many one-night stands, Wing sustained a relationship for several days with a young man whom he happened to meet on Wednesday, August 23, 1865. After finishing a reporting job, Wing returned to his office at the newspaper, where, he wrote in his diary, "I run against a boy dressed in military clothes, whose countenance was so familiar that I stepped up to him, and succeeded in making his acquaintance by telling him that I must have met him in the south. Invited him to call at the office in the evening, which he did."

The "boy" was Tommy Phelan, and in his diary entry for the next day, Wing describes his budding interest in Phelan. "When my newly found soldier boy came to the office last evening," Wing reported, "I was charmed by his noble bearing, and the intelligence and refinement which he displayed. Took him to the theatre, and soon became charmed with his society." Phelan captivated Wing with his uniform and his story of having been a prisoner in Andersonville, the Confederate-run prison in Georgia for captured Union soldiers.

They slept together for the first time that Wednesday night and then again the next night. On Friday morning Wing "went to work, somewhat played out by" his sexual "excess" with Phelan, "who persisted in doing" some sexual act that so enthralled Wing that he swore he would "never forget" it. He wondered in an aside if Phelan learned it from his army buddies. It was common knowledge among queer men that some soldiers engaged in sexual relationships with one another and with civilians.

Later that Friday Wing took Phelan to a photographer's studio and had his picture taken as a keepsake. Although their relationship seemed to be going well, Phelan had met a servant girl and asked her out. He told Wing that although he would be seeing the girl that evening, he would spend the night with Wing, not her. But by the next morning, Phelan still hadn't returned.

Wing had a difficult time concentrating at work on Saturday, presumably troubled by his lover's unexpected absence. When Phelan reappeared in the evening, he admitted to Wing that had tried to get the girl in bed but she rejected his advances, and that he decided to spend the night out on his own and not to notify Wing of the change in his plan. Despite the distress that Phelan caused him, Wing welcomed him into his bed that night and reported that he had another enjoyable time. The next morning Phelan rose before Wing and

Fig. 1. John Wing (left, 1844–1917) had photographs of his most favored "bully boys" taken as keepsakes. In this one, taken two years before he moved to Chicago, he is with another young man named John. *Newberry Library, John M. Wing Collection, uncataloged*

left, vowing to return later that afternoon. When Wing finally roused himself from bed, he discovered that a ring he owned was missing. He didn't want to believe that Phelan had stolen it and rationalized to himself that Phelan had only borrowed it. Four o'clock came and went, then five o'clock, which was quickly followed by six, and Phelan hadn't returned. Wing gave up hoping that he would see him, or the ring, again.

Stealing Wing's ring was not the end of Phelan's surprises. On Monday morning Wing "found to my great horror that my soldier boy had given me crabs, and worse than that, head lice. Found my corpus alive with vermin, and shuddered at the thought. Resorted to ample potations of anquinnin"— probably quinine—"and everything else, not forgetting to use a fine toothed comb. O! Horror!!"

Wing was undoubtedly feeling betrayed and perhaps even a little foolish by now, having been wronged not once but three times by Phelan and in such a short amount of time, and yet he again rationalized Phelan's behavior. By the next day, Wing had forgiven him for the robbery, for the crabs and lice, and for lying about returning at four o'clock. "I love the boy," he wrote in his diary and tried to explain why:

> There is an indescribable something about him fascinating in the extreme. The present devotion to myself, professing the most ardent love, and still so refined and the hero of so many battles and prisons. Perhaps he did not take the ring—and he, a homeless wanderer—is not to blame for giving me the horrible vermin! I will trust him, and believe that he did not take the ring.

A few days passed, and Wing still hadn't heard a word from Phelan. Then on Friday evening, September 1, as Wing was busy at work in his office, Phelan unexpectedly appeared at his door, wearing

> a horrible old suit of . . . citizen's clothes. He says that he has been to Washington and back; that he had no place to stay but at the soldier's rest. The dear fellow! Took him home with me, and love him better than ever. He declairs [sic] that he did not take the ring, and feels terribly that I should accuse him of it. The poor boy is an enigma—I cannot make him out.

If they had sex that night, Wing didn't mention it in his diary, in sharp contrast to his bragging about the sexual escapade he had had with Phelan only a week earlier.

The next day Phelan told Wing that he planned to leave Chicago and head to Milwaukee, and he admitted with a dramatic flair that he didn't have any prospects once he arrived there. He was hinting to Wing that he was available to be kept, if Wing would only say the word, but the fire that he had once ignited in the newspaper man had burned itself out during the time in which Phelan had disappeared. While he was away, Wing was evidently able to put their relationship into some sort of context. Phelan, he seems to have realized, was trouble, and Wing wrote an equally dramatic, and perhaps disingenuous, response in his diary to Phelan's leaving: "O, that I could help him."

Phelan left Chicago as he had planned, and Wing never saw him again. Wing admitted in his diary that he was exhausted from his busy work schedule at the newspaper and from worrying about Phelan's poverty and "strange behavior," but he never explained which of Phelan's behaviors were odd to him. It may have been stealing Wing's ring, or infesting Wing with crabs and lice, or trying to bed the servant girl, or any number of things that Wing had forgotten to mention in his diary.

Robert Williams, editor of Wing's Chicago diaries, has pieced together some of Tommy Phelan's history. Williams reports that if Phelan gave Wing his real name, he may have been Charles T. Phelan, who had enlisted in the Union army on September 26, 1861, when he was eighteen years old. Confederate forces captured him and confined him to the prison at Andersonville. After his last encounter with Wing, he returned to his native New York, not Milwaukee, and enrolled in the Eastman Commercial College in Poughkeepsie. He graduated in December 1865 and the following year sailed to Cuba, where he remained for a year. After he returned to the United States, he married a woman in 1868, and according to the 1870 census, lived in Manhattan.

Wing's summary of his and Phelan's relationship and Williams's investigation into the former soldier's life suggest several important things about Phelan—and about the queer subculture in Chicago in the mid-1860s. Although Wing repeatedly called Phelan a *boy* in his diary, Phelan was actually a year older than Wing. He may have been a small or otherwise young-looking man and never told Wing his actual age, allowing Wing to think he was younger than he actually was. More likely, Wing used *boy* as a hierarchical marker, as

Whitman and others had done. Wing had money, a place to live, and a station in life. Because he was successful, Wing was a "man," as society at the time defined the term. In contrast, Phelan was destitute, homeless, and without a career or any hope of one for the near future. His only resource was his body. Because he had not yet achieved manhood as illustrated by Wing and been approved by society, Phelan was a "boy."

Regardless, Phelan was quite experienced in sex between men and seems to have been more practiced than Wing in ways to satisfy his lovers. Wing suggested that their sexual activities, which left him exhausted, were intense, and he relished the former soldier's bag of tricks. It's possible that by the time he met Wing, Phelan may have had a substantial record of sex-for-pay experiences with other financially well-off men.

In Chicago, as well as in most other major urban centers, a number of teenagers and young men who may or may not have actually enjoyed sexual contact with other men nevertheless engaged in it for financial gain. Although Wing never reported in his diaries that he had given Phelan cash, he paid for Phelan's meals at restaurants, for his admission at theaters, and so forth, and Phelan probably pawned or fenced the ring he stole from Wing.

Tommy Phelan could potentially represent at least three models of male same-sex behavior evident in Chicago in the mid-1800s. The fact that Phelan wanted to bed the servant girl and, a few years later, married a woman is key. Perhaps his sexual desire focused not only on men but also on women. Perhaps he camouflaged his real sexual interests in men by having occasional sexual contacts with women, including marrying one. Or perhaps his only real sexual interest was female, but he found certain men willing, even eager, to pay him with a variety of currencies for his sexual favors, and for a time he relied on their attraction to him to make do. These three behaviors will exist in Chicago's queer subculture for the next century—and well beyond.

Regardless of what Phelan's motives were, Wing didn't grieve over losing him for long. In less than a week after saying good-bye to Phelan, Wing met Joe Irwin, who appears to have been the exact opposite of Tommy Phelan. Irwin was "a stylish boy, and a perfect gentleman. He has a fine position in the bank of Montreal," where he lived. Irwin and Wing slept together for some of the time that Irwin was visiting Chicago, but their relationship ended once Irwin's business in the United States was finished and he returned to Canada. Wing easily found other men to bed. Billy Bissel—"a brick—a *roue*!

How the night passed, let memory only know. It was happiness, bliss. He is my beau-ideal"—followed Irwin, and Jack Mattoon followed Bissel, but Mattoon disappointed Wing, who confided to his diary, "We did not have much of a time."

Although he never seems to have been interested in analyzing why he was sexually drawn only to other men, Wing did once mention off-handedly in his diary what might be called his sexual identity: "Monday is a sort of dull day with me always—not because of my having any[thing] to do with the females—because the good lord knows that I do nothing of a kind." He did once admit, however, that he briefly had a girlfriend, Fran Churchill, in 1863, when he was nineteen, and he claimed that she was "'the only girl I ever loved.'" By putting quotation marks around the phrase, he may have meant to indicate he was being ironic, that theirs was a platonic love, not a romantic, much less an erotic, one. His diary entries for his first year in Chicago alone mention nearly twenty young men with whom he either slept or struck up conversations in hopes of a later sexual tryst but mention nothing romantic or sexual about girls or young women.

The concept of sexual orientation didn't exist widely during the 1800s, and neither the word *homosexual* nor the word *heterosexual* would be in use, except by a few physicians and legal experts, before the turn of the century. Because the concepts didn't exist, society judged *all* sexual activities acceptable or legitimate "by whether they served reproduction" or not, and because of "that standard," all "nonprocreative different-sex erotic acts," such as using a condom during intercourse, "were just as perverted as same-sex erotic acts," such as anal intercourse.

For queer men of the nineteenth century, the sexual relationship they sought fell by definition under *sodomy*, a word that Chicagoans knew long before Wing settled among them, although what a sodomite actually was would have been nearly impossible for most of them to define.

In June 1843 "Long" John Wentworth, owner and publisher of the *Chicago Democrat*, the Windy City's first newspaper, was running for the US House of Representatives. To give himself a lead in the election, he published an editorial in the *Democrat* in which he accused his rival Dr. Richard Murphy of sodomy. Murphy appears not to have ever married and so may have been queer, but Wentworth gave no evidence of it. He simply made the accusation. This is the first reference in print to queer men existing in Chicago. It's unclear whether or not Wentworth's strategy actually helped his bid for the post or not, but he did win the election.

Other references to the sodomite began to appear. In February 1864, the year before Wing arrived in Chicago, a man named Foly was arrested and pleaded guilty to the crime of sodomy, a case reported in the *Chicago Tribune*. Four days later his lawyer argued to quash the motion. On March 8 the judge overruled Foly's lawyer, and the case went to trial. Despite the fact that Foly had pleaded guilty to the charge, the jury acquitted him of the crime on March 18, and the police released him. In August 1868, three years after Wing arrived in Chicago, the Reverend David Teed, the married father of three and pastor of the Methodist Episcopal Church in Evanston, a suburb of Chicago, was arrested for committing sodomy with a boy under his care at a camp meeting. His bail was set at $1,000. In September he was acquitted. He remained with the church for a very short time, until he began earning his living by selling real estate. Whether church members forced him out of the ministry or he left of his own accord is unknown.

Two years later a reporter for Chicago's *Inter Ocean* wrote that a police officer had arrested two men, Andrew Larsen and Albert Borgen, whom he had caught engaged in a "crime against nature so inexpressibly vile" that there were no laws against it, and so the authorities could only charge them with vagrancy and fine each man twenty-five dollars. The reporter seems to have been so aghast by them and their actions that he could find no words to describe them adequately—not even *sodomites* captured their particular activities for him—and he resorted to calling them simply "*things*." For the next few decades, arrests of men in Chicago involved in sodomy would grow slowly but steadily. These included Barney Jennings in 1881, Thomas Walsh in 1888, and Michael Palas twice in 1890, first on September 3 and then again on September 30.

Undoubtedly, Wing never mentioned his sexual proclivities to others. While a public scandal surrounding his love interests would have branded him a sodomite and probably resulted in his being unable to work as a journalist in Chicago, he also might have faced life in prison if he had been brought to court and convicted of a crime against nature. In Chicago and throughout Illinois, a man who was convicted of sodomy could be imprisoned for life, the penalty until 1874, when the length of a prison term for someone convicted of a crime against nature was limited to ten years.

Luckily for Wing, it was quite common in the 1800s for one man to offer to share his bed with another who happened to have nowhere to sleep. It was so common and acceptable that no one would have raised an eyebrow over it. The man without a bed may have needed one for many reasons. He may have been a visitor to Chicago who couldn't find a room in a hotel or boardinghouse, he may have lost his home to some disaster and needed a place to sleep, or he may have simply been too poor to afford a room—or any number of other reasons. This convention allowed men like Wing to bring other men home with them for sexual contact under the eyes of their landlords and neighbors without raising any suspicion. To those not knowing his real intention, he would simply appear generous, sharing his good fortune of having a bed and a safe place to sleep with someone in need.

By the time he arrived in Chicago, Wing had already been sexually and romantically involved with a number of boys who lived in or around Pulaski. Most were schoolboys who attended the Pulaski Academy, as Wing did. In his earlier diary entries, those for 1858 through 1861, when he was between thirteen and sixteen years old, Wing is circumspect about his sexual relationships, using ambiguous language to camouflage his sexual activity. On April 30, 1858, for example, Wing and his schoolmate George W. Porter spent the night together, and Wing wrote in his diary, "Porter and I went and took a walk he come in my Room at night nice time [*sic*]." Not long after, Porter disappeared from Wing's diary, because Wing's father, a very successful farmer, needed his son's help tending the crops. Wing had to postpone his schooling for a number of months, which seemed like an eternity to the teenager. Instead of reports about his relationship with Porter, he filled his diary with complaints about his loneliness.

By May 20, 1859, Wing had returned to school and Porter reappeared in his life—and his diary. The boys picked up their relationship where they had left off. Wing noted, "Geo W Porter went home with me and staid [*sic*] all night we had lots of fun." His renewed fling with Porter lasted through the end of the month, when he wrote, "I and Porter etc." *Etc.* hides their sexual contact. The next day, Porter left town, and on the day after, Wing reported his distress over the other boy's departure, forgetting in his despair to camouflage his feelings: "He has gone! The [?] has ended—but alas: not my love. for Him my heart is secretly worshipping."

Nearly two weeks later, he began writing letters to Porter. Wing would keep in contact with Porter for the next few years, not just exchanging letters but thinking intensely about him. "Have been thinking about Porter all day," he confessed to his diary, and then he exclaimed, "Oh I want to see him." His feeling about Porter were so intense, in fact, that Porter appeared in his dreams: "I dreamed of seeing Geo. Porter. Oh." *Oh* suggests sexual contact, as *etc.* had earlier in the diary.

Despite his feelings for Porter, other boys also sparked Wing's libido. Shortly after November 18, 1859, Wing met another sixteen-year-old, Charles D. Gurley, who would become the chief focus of his romantic fervor for the next year or so. After Gurley, Wing fell for a boy named Lony, and after him a young man Wing would call simply "Ex." The rest of the volumes of his boyhood diaries reveal a similar string of juvenile paramours. It appears that no adults at Pulaski Academy thought twice about the many boys who spent the night in Wing's room. In the nineteenth century it was not uncommon for men to share their beds with other, perhaps less fortunate men, which helped protect Wing from detection, humiliation, and punishment even during his youth.

Wing remained in Chicago for all of his adult life, but his diaries end with the volume covering 1866. Wing may have decided to stop keeping a journal at that point, though it's also possible that later volumes were lost during the Great Chicago Fire of 1871. He continued to build his collection of books, and it later developed into a library of hundreds of volumes, which he bequeathed, along with nearly $250,000, to the Newberry Library when he died in 1917. He traveled extensively throughout Europe, remained a "bachelor by the Grace of God" to the end of his life, and very likely continued to pick up young men who caught his eye, sharing his bed with them.

2 | The Most Effeminate Type of Sex Perversions

The audience disturbed me a little bit. All those guys watching.

CHICAGO USUALLY SIZZLES DURING THE DOG DAYS, but during the night of Wednesday, August 8, 1888, the temperature dropped to a cool seventy-two degrees. It would have been what midwesterners call "a good night for sleeping," but the racket from the "ordinary-looking two-story frame house" at 140 West Monroe Street in the Loop was keeping those who lived nearby awake. Tired of tossing and turning, one of the neighbors finally dragged himself out of bed and trundled off to the Desplaines Street police station nine blocks away. He complained about the loud fracas that came from the house and had been keeping him and his neighbors awake night after night. The sergeant at the front desk sent several plainclothesmen to the address to investigate the goings-on there, but he was already certain he knew what they'd find—so certain, in fact, that he sent a paddy wagon to the house without waiting for the plainclothesmen to summon one.

When the paddy wagon arrived, neighbors began to pour from their homes, and a crowd formed. A few minutes later, at nearly ten o'clock in the evening, the police led a group of two women and four men out the door of 140 West Monroe Street. One of the men was wearing nothing more than "a woman's night dress," and the neighbors made a loud to-do—they "hooted and yelled"—as the police hustled the cross-dressed young man through the mob to the paddy wagon.

Once the police got the six to the station, the women identified themselves as "Mamie Conley and Mamie Moore," while the men called themselves "Charles Steward, Fred Harris, Fred Allen, and George Wilson." Wilson, the man in women's clothing, claimed he was a female impersonator who had appeared on many of Chicago's stages. All of the men wore "powder on their faces," and two of them answered to women's nicknames: "Steward was known as Marguerite and Wilson was called Lillie." Wilson acted and looked so much like a woman that the police matron was about to lock him up with the female prisoners when the desk sergeant stopped her. The six were charged with "disorderly conduct," a catchall phrase that covered the arrest of prostitutes and virtually anyone doing anything outside of the era's very narrow idea of what was sexually acceptable.

The little wooden house on West Monroe wasn't Chicago's only house of prostitution with male inmates. "Boy houses" that catered to queer men were scattered around the Loop and adjacent neighborhoods, and following the lead of one of the first bordellos in Chicago, Under the Willow, many of the brothels that were open for non-queer men "also retained a young man or two for their homosexual clientele." The immediate area surrounding the intersection of Randolph and Dearborn Streets became known as "Bryant's Block," after real estate investor J. W. Bryant, who owned property there. Bryant's Block was notorious for its houses that offered their male clients "nameless ecstacies [sic]" with young men. They could also find willing bedmates in any of the "twenty-seven panel houses" along the block of South Clark Street bounded by Harrison Street on the north and Polk Street on the south. Cafés that served as little more than queer bordellos also existed and were known especially for the intermingling of the races, as Chicago physician James G. Kiernan discovered:

> The method of negro perverts who solicit men in certain Chicago cafés is usually fellatio, although paederasty by the customer is permitted. At one time a resort of these people existed under a Chicago dime museum. Lately, as shown by some recent arrests, certain cafés patronized by both negroes and whites, are the seat of male solicitation.

Paederasty (or *pederasty*) was a term sometimes used as a synonym for *homo-sexuality* and at other times for *anal intercourse*. *Resort* referred to a business or establishment for entertainment or relaxation.

At the same time, a number of resorts catering to queer men had opened, including very public "dancehalls attached to saloons, and presided over by an invert, as are all the waiters and musicians. . . . Singing and dancing in turns by certain favorite performers are the features of these gatherings with much gossip and drinking at the small tables ranged along the four walls of the room." Like the cafés that Kiernan described, male prostitutes, often female impersonators, trolled the venues.

William Healy, the first director of Chicago's Juvenile Psychopathic Institute, reported the case history of a boy, one of his clients, who had been enticed from his family in Indiana to one of the houses in Bryant's Block "by bad influences." Back in his hometown, after graduating from school, the boy had found a job as a performer, and the "men he worked with" gave him the female nickname "Hattie." He began fantasizing about becoming a female impersonator, and he not only "had a dress made [for him] by some women friends," but he also "began wearing effeminate types of men's garments." He was so convincing in his imitation of a woman that he was "once arrested by a policeman who was sure that he was a woman in disguise"—that is, he was a biological woman impersonating a man. "About this time," as Healy put it, "he was made acquainted with the most effeminate type of sex perversions, and fell at once in with them." Shortly thereafter he traveled to Chicago, where he found work in one of the houses in the Loop and was eventually taken into custody by police "for the most flagrant female impersonations."

At about the same time, another boy, known simply as "H-9," began working in a similar house in Chicago. At fourteen he had begun engaging in "mutual masturbation and fellatio with a boy friend and attempted sodomy with him." At first H-9 simply enjoyed the sex, but then he began to fall in love with his friend. Hoping to help their son make something of his life, his father tried to persuade him to find work in a local pharmacy, while his mother wanted him to become a man of the cloth. His parents' nagging became too much for him to handle, and H-9 ran away to Chicago. No sooner had he arrived than he learned he could sell his body to men for a considerable amount of money, and he found work in a "peg house," another term for a male brothel.

H-9 was nineteen when he arrived in Chicago and worked in the peg house for two years before he decided to return to his undisclosed hometown in Indiana and take classes at the university there. A short time after moving back into his parents' house, "his father insisted that he get married" to "one of his second cousins" to whom he'd been betrothed as a child. Shortly after the minister pronounced them man and wife, H-9 ran away again, but returned in three days, ready "to settle down, become as masculine as possible, and be a good husband." Although he thought intercourse with a woman was "disgusting," he and his wife conceived a child almost immediately. The life of a married man and a soon-to-be father didn't sit well with him, however, and within a few months, he ran away again, for the third time, and returned to Chicago and to prostitution.

Despite the many brothels that made young men available to their clients, male prostitutes often decided to make their living through other venues. Some female impersonators who performed on the stages of Chicago's theaters continued their masquerade long after their role onstage ended, as reports reveal:

> Their disguise is so perfect, they are enabled to sit at tables with men between the acts, and solicit for drinks the same as prostitutes.
>
> Two of these "female impersonators" were recently seen in one of the most notorious saloons of —— street. These "supposed" women solicited for drinks, and afterwards invited the men to rooms over the saloon for pervert practices.

Female impersonators weren't the only ones trying to pick up men in the audience during and after their performances. Masculine-looking and -acting men drifted through the crowds at risqué shows on the lookout for another man or boy interested in sex, some of whom were undoubtedly selling their sexual favors. At an unnamed burlesque theater in a neighborhood along West Madison Street, probably Chicago's most notorious vice district, an investigator with the Juvenile Protective Association, who just happened to take in the salacious acts there, discovered to his amazement "the almost unbelievable situation of little boys, as young even as ten years of age," there "for the purpose of soliciting men for homosexual practices." The word *soliciting* suggests the boys traded sex for cash. The Haymarket Theater and the La Salle Theater, also located in the West Madison Street neighborhood, were two of the best-known joints where the sexual titillation onstage might invite male-male sexual contact offstage.

Another was the Park Theatre, at 335 State Street. It offered a different fare for the man on the make. One vice crusader declared that the "whole theatre is an exhibition which would be more in place in Sodom and Gomorrah than in Chicago" because it presented "jaded sex circuses"—nineteenth-century slang for live sex shows—to those who had paid the cost of admission and "who wanted to watch as well as those who wished to join in."

Despite such public venues available to them, many queer men chose to hunt for bedmates in more secluded, albeit still public, places. Lincoln Park or Bughouse Square were two of the most popular. While very public during the day, the parks' atmosphere changed drastically late at night. The occasional dull, gaslit streetlamps of the late nineteenth and early twentieth centuries sporadically dotting the parks didn't illuminate them as brightly as streetlights do now, and the parks' shrubs and trees often afforded men a barrier behind which they might, if they chose, satisfy themselves sexually with one another.

Since the 1890s, Bughouse Square, officially called Washington Park, had been a meeting place where the politically minded, often left-leaning, stood on soap boxes and ranted against city, state, and federal laws or, in fact, about anything that may have been on their mind—political, social, or personal. The small park's popularity as a forum for political diatribes may have been due, at least in part, to its being only a few steps west of the Dill Pickle Club, headquarters for many of Chicago's left-leaning bohemians and queer men. The radicals among its clientele could easily move from the discussions behind the Pickle's protective walls to the open air. Interestingly, the speeches that drew the most applause were about sex.

Although Bughouse Square's reputation as a magnet for radical thinkers had developed early and spread widely across Chicago, few Chicagoans knew about its second and far more nefarious use. Long after the politically minded left Bughouse Square and settled into bed, queer men arrived and strolled up and down its lanes looking for sex partners until the wee hours of the morning. Many were drawn there after having spent a few hours in the many nearby "cafes, bars, baths, and other homosexual places." At least some of the men were interested in selling their sexual favors to others who were willing to pay for their services, and reports from the time suggest that the prostitutes doing business there did not cross-dress.

Many men opted to take their newfound sex mates, whether prostitutes or not, to semipublic places. Those who first made contact with one another at Bughouse Square might go to the rooming house where one or the other lived or to one of the bathhouses in the area: Jack's at North Dearborn and Walton Streets, the Lafayette on North Wabash Avenue, and on North Clark Street the Lincoln Baths. In the semipublic bathhouse, they could engage in sex in the communal areas or in one of the rooms that were available to rent. Since at least the early 1800s, bathhouse trysts were common among men, as Lord Byron noted when he called those bathhouses that he patronized in the Middle East "palaces of sherbet and sodomy."

Queer American novelist Xavier Mayne (the pseudonym of Edward Irenaeus Prime-Stevenson) offered a peek into how the baths accommodated queer men:

> A special factor in homosexual uses of vapor-bath establishments in larger cities is the fact that in America these are kept open and much patronized during all hours. . . . Indeed, some are never closed at all. . . . In most such baths, each client has always a separate dressing room, usually with a couch. What "goes on" is under the guest's own lock and key, and without surveillance.

Pioneer sexologist Magnus Hirschfeld quoted a queer man he had met in Denver who revealed that "Turkish baths . . . serve as gathering spots" for men "in New York, Boston, Philadelphia, and Chicago" and mentioned an important bath "in Chicago on P—— Street." He explained the popularity of the bathhouses where queer men could enjoy sexual trysts with other men:

> In general, one can say that the Turkish baths in America are a . . . secure place for homosexuals. The price of admission of one dollar is high enough to keep out the average male prostitute. The people you meet there do not go in order to blackmail. Naturally, not all the visitors are necessarily homosexual.

"Visiting Urnings do not hesitate to go to the Turkish baths," he added—*Urning* was a term coined by Hirschfeld, synonymous with *homosexual*—"while the locals have to be more careful" so as not be caught in compromising situations by other locals, who probably would know them.

Bathhouses weren't the only semipublic places that queer men used for their sexual assignations. Chicago had its share of "certain smart clubs" that were "rather exclusive and aristocratic" and were becoming "well-known for their homosexual atmosphere." These sites were inviting to queer men because they typically disguised themselves as "athletic societies, chess-clubs or dramatic societies." One of the most important of these was the Chicago Athletic Club located on Michigan Avenue in the Loop. Behind its walls of respectable heterosexuality, men indulged in sexual activities that included "adolescent boys and young men" who would have sex with the club's members for a price. A private facility that rented rooms to members, most of whom were among Chicago's professional elite, including "a doctor, a university professor and a major stockholder in the Chicago Stock Yards," the club quickly earned the reputation of being nothing more than a hotel for "wealthy gay men."

Two of the Chicago Athletic Club's most prominent members, writer George Ade and businessman Orson Collins Wells, must have been more than a little surprised when one of Ade's most trusted friends and his former roommate, cartoonist William Herman Schmedtgen, painted their portrait. In *A Caricature of Ade and Wells*, Schmedtgen depicted Ade wearing a suit with a red necktie and carrying a fan with the logo of the Chicago Athletic Club on it while Wells is depicted in a woman's dress. As close to Ade as Schmedtgen was, the implication of Schmedtgen's "caricature"—not only that Ade and Wells were queer, and Wells a female impersonator at that, but also that they were probably a couple—was never questioned. Underscoring the painting's queer elements, the painting hung in a men's-only inn in the Loop, Chaplin and Gore's Saloon and Restaurant, for many years.

Galen Moon corroborated the "homosexual atmosphere" of the Chicago Athletic Club. At fourteen years old, Moon left an orphanage in New Orleans where he'd been living and made his way north to the Windy City. He landed a job at the Chicago Athletic Club, working in its kitchens. Little did he know that the chef of the club pimped out the teenagers who worked for him to the wealthy male members who either lived at the club or rented rooms by the week. One day the chef told the unsuspecting Moon to put on "a busboy's jacket and deliver room service to one of the residents, a Dr. S."

Once in Dr. S.'s room, Moon realized the physician was hungry for more than the food, and he and the older man "had sex." As time passed, Dr. S. introduced the fourteen-year-old to other men living at the club, and

Fig. 2. The secret of George Ade (left, 1866–1944) and businessman Orson Collins Wells (1859–1940) was revealed by William Henry Schmedtgen in his painting *A Caricature of Ade and Wells* (1912). *Chicago History Museum, ICHi-62439*

Moon transformed the one-night stands he was having with the physician into a profitable business. Eventually Dr. S. told Moon that he could earn "$100 a night" by putting on a sex circus with another teenager whom the doctor knew.

A few days later, Dr. S. took Moon and the second boy to the "Officer's Club, a private lounge" that catered to "military officers." Inside the lounge someone had built a "glass enclosure" that included a bed. Moon and the other boy ended up performing there once a week for five weeks. At first Moon bragged that the voyeurs—"40 or 50 men"—didn't bother him a bit but, in fact, excited him. Later he admitted that briefly, initially, "the audience disturbed me . . . a little bit. All these guys watching." A thrifty adolescent, Moon put his earnings into a savings account that, by the end of the five weeks, amounted to over $10,000 in today's money.

The Chicago Athletic Club wasn't the only establishment that served as a stronghold for queer men in Chicago. A man who called himself "Daniel O" revealed his experiences as a young man at another athletic establishment, one which he refused to identify by name. "I worked in a men's club for a year and then had an argument," he said, and quit. "They always kept after me for sex," but he was unwilling. Like the Chicago Athletic Club, the establishment where Daniel O worked provided a safe, private space where its queer members could engage in same-sex sexual activities behind closed doors.

While there's no evidence that members of the private Hamilton Club of Chicago used its premises for rendezvous with male prostitutes or other men, some of its staff certainly did. Another young man revealed that when he was sixteen years old, he worked there as a bellhop and had sexual relationships with other employees of the club, boys his own age and young men in their twenties.

At the same time that some queer men were visiting public or semipublic places, such as parks and streets or theaters and clubs, others who either couldn't afford a club's membership or a bathhouse's entrance fee or who were concerned that they might be seen entering or leaving such establishments looked for alternatives. In 1879 the Chicago Daily Tribune published a letter to the editor signed by "Decency." The letter began with a generalized comment about the obscure haunts under Chicago's bridges where men gathered for sexual activities, but then Decency pointedly focused on one of them, the Randolph Street Bridge. The men who "infested" the area where the bridge met the bank of the Chicago River and formed a cave-like structure, Decency claimed, were so deviant that they would not have been welcomed "even in Sodom." While still technically a public site, the bridge hid the men from being noticed by any passersby.

Apparently taking its cue from Decency's letter, a few days later another Chicago newspaper, the *Daily Inter Ocean*, printed a lengthy exposé of the netherworld of the Randolph Street Bridge. The reporter began his article by acknowledging that it was no secret that many large urban centers were full of queer men, and he mentioned that Paris, London, and New York had "beasts" who were "filth in men's clothing . . . whose very touch would contaminate one who came in contact with them." He never labeled the men who gathered under the bridge but was confident that his readers would know what they were. He also never mentioned whether or not male prostitutes visited the bridge's underside. However, he did demand that the police step in and round up the "beasts."

Then the reporter got down to the nitty-gritty. He had gone to the Randolph Street Bridge and asked the attendant to guide him to the cavity where the bridge and the bank of the Chicago River met so that he could see for himself "how low men will sink." The attendant lit a lantern and led the reporter from street level down a flight of stairs, around a corner, and into an area where they came upon several men clustered together. As soon as the lantern's light fell on them, one man bolted past the reporter, ran up the stairs onto Randolph Street, and escaped into the night. The others, taken aback by being caught in flagrante delicto, were stunned at first and couldn't move a muscle, but then they too scurried up the stairs and disappeared.

Unsure about what he had just witnessed, the reporter asked the attendant, "And what do these dregs of filth come here for?" as they climbed the stairs toward Randolph Street. The attendant answered vaguely that they visited the bridge for "engagements." Mulling the attendant's answer over for a few seconds, the reporter then asked if the attendant knew any of the men they had just interrupted, and without hesitation the attendant told the reporter that one, the best dressed of the lot, a "sleek-looking fellow, with white vest and silk hat," was a physician. The reporter was taken aback but then regained his composure and wondered aloud if the men congregated under the bridge often. Again the attendant didn't hesitate for a moment. "Almost every night," he replied, "from nine to eleven o'clock."

The attendant explained that only men, no women, met men there, perhaps half a dozen or so every night of the week, and that no real crime, except for two robberies, had ever happened there as far as he knew. The number of men who visited the underbelly of the bridge had risen substantially over the previous year, and from the attendant's descriptions of them, it's apparent that the men came from all levels of society. Whether some of the men who gathered there were prostitutes remains unclear, but as with the sexual activities in both Lincoln Park and Bughouse Square, it's likely that at least a few men slipped under the bridge in hopes of making some money.

Occasionally the reporter described the men he saw as "dregs of filth" and "outcasts," suggesting the morally, as well as the financially, bankrupt. At other times he depicted them wearing "fine suits, a white vest, a silk hat," and carrying "a cane"—the description of the well-to-do dandy. Within a few years, the *Chicago Daily Tribune* began to educate its readers about the dandy, a "foppish and effeminate youth" who was often called "a regular Miss Nancy" because of the cologne he wore and his genteel voice. He was an oddball figure in rough-and-tumble Chicago, and his only link to the queer subculture in Chicago was the bridge attendant's observation of him.

Most notable in the reporter's article is the fact that the men the reporter observed weren't female impersonators. The bridge attendant's assurance that he had never seen a "woman" beneath the bridge confirms this fact. Had any of the men cross-dressed, the attendant would surely have noted it, and because he doesn't, his report confirms the existence of a group of masculine-appearing men who sought out sexual contact with other masculine-appearing men. The article also suggests that some sort of network probably existed—perhaps simply word of mouth from one friend or one pickup to another, perhaps graffiti on public toilet walls—that informed men about the well-hidden spot where they might engage in sexual activities with others like themselves. The *Inter Ocean*'s article is the first mention of such men in Chicago and of one of their regular meeting places.

The Randolph Street Bridge was only one of the many bridges in Chicago that concerned Decency, but even after the *Inter Ocean*'s detailed report of the nighttime activities beneath the bridge and the article's very loud call for police intervention, the authorities ignored it. Month after month passed, and no other report about the nefarious activities under the bridge appeared.

Then, almost a year after the *Inter Ocean*'s exposé, one of Chicago's police officers, Frederick De Celle, suddenly began to focus his attention on the "band of dissolute characters who" continued in their "habit of meeting beneath" the Randolph Street Bridge. He interrupted their sexual trysts, rounded them up, and hauled them off to the station house. The hidden spot suddenly became the focus of numerous newspaper reports.

On Friday, May 14, 1880, Officer De Celle caught "two filthy wretches"—Charles Gibson and Frank Bush—under the bridge. Whether filthy was meant to describe the men's lack of hygiene or morals is unknown, but each received a fifty-day jail sentence. Two weeks later De Celle discovered William Herod and another man beneath the bridge. After securing Herod, De Celle tried to take the second man into custody, but they got into a fight, and the second man leaped into the river and was presumed drowned.

On June 21 De Celle caught two "old men," Jerry Bromley and Jacob Johnson, committing "an unmentionable crime." They weren't sentenced to jail, but each received a $100 fine. De Celle was very busy eight days later, when he made two separate arrests in one evening. He detained Albert Glickauf for "attempting to commit a crime against nature," and the court fined Glickauf $700. Glikauf's partner went unnamed and perhaps escaped. Later that night De Celle interrupted three men "engaged in disgusting practices": John Robinson, a "stone-cutter"; William Upton, a "house servant"; and W. W. Wardwell, a "commission merchant." Compared to Glickauf they got off easy, with $25 fines each.

Three weeks later De Celle took Edward Rastop into custody for "committing a nameless crime." Rastop, a thirty-year-old immigrant from Norway, received a fine of $100. Because he was unemployed, he couldn't pay and was sent to jail. During questioning, he "confessed that he had" engaged in sex with other men beneath the Randolph Street Bridge "for a long time—since the war." That would mean that the bridge had been a site for sexual contact in Chicago at least since the mid-1860s, when John Wing arrived in Chicago. Rastop would have been about thirteen years old when he began visiting the bridge.

Reports of De Celle's crusade stopped being published in the newspapers as suddenly and as unexpectedly as they had begun. Perhaps the eleven arrests he made had sated his need for cleaning out "the professors of a nameless vice," as one newspaper report called the bridge's habitués, and De Celle moved on to do his part in eradicating some other social ill. But Decency's letter, the *Inter Ocean*'s exposé, and De Celle's war on the bridge's nighttime visitors helped to give at least some visibility in the press to the burgeoning notoriety afforded Chicago's queer denizens of out-of-the-way resorts, darkened parks, and the even darker underbellies of at least some of the city's bridges. It's no wonder, then, that Chicago was gaining a reputation as something of a hotspot of queer sexual activity, as noted from as far away as Utah. "Chicago," an 1891 article in the *Deseret Weekly* declared in disgust, "is not far removed from what the cities of the plain were in former days."

3 | We Never Liked His Species

Erotic imagery calculated to arouse male members of the audience.

THANKSGIVING WAS ONLY THREE DAYS AWAY WHEN, in 1892, two young men set out on a shoplifting spree in Chicago's Loop. The temperature was near freezing, the sky gray, and their breaths turned into clouds as they made their way through the lunch-hour crowds. An hour or so later, police stopped the pair as they drifted through Mandel Brothers, a huge department store located at State and Madison Streets. The very next day, the two men found their story—and names—plastered on the front page of the single most widely read newspaper in the Windy City, the *Chicago Daily Tribune*, to the guffaws of some and the raised eyebrows of others.

The shoplifters, identified in the *Tribune* as James Janes and Frank Smith, had begun their shopping excursion at two other department stores that were popular rivals of Mandel Brothers. They had first stopped off at the Fair on Dearborn Street between State and Adams, and then at the Leader, half a block east of the Fair. They then walked north on State to Mandell Brothers. They brought with them a cardboard box measuring twenty-four by ten by ten inches. Because it was secured with a string tied tightly around it, the box appeared to be a parcel that contained items that they had already bought. Each of the men held one side of the box, and it swayed ever so slightly between them.

When they entered Mandel Brothers, Janes and Smith made a beeline to the Ladies' Department, a move that caught the attention of the store's floorwalkers and counter clerks. As the young men combed through the women's clothes, someone called the police. As it turned out, Janes and Smith were female impersonators, and they were on the lookout for a few new accessories to give their drag a little oomph.

In fact, both men were already well known to the police, although not by the monikers they were using that Monday afternoon. *James Janes*, a combination of male and female names, was as appropriate a nom de theatre for a female impersonator—a male body adorned with female clothing and accruements—as possible. *Smith*, a far less imaginative alias, had been ubiquitous for years for masquerades of all types, mostly nefarious ones.

Once the police stopped Janes and Smith, it only took them a few seconds to discover that the box the men carried between them wasn't at all what it appeared to be. The top had hinges and a spring so sensitive that whenever Janes or Smith placed even the lightest of objects onto it, the item would fall, disappearing into the box as perfectly as a magician's trick.

When the police opened the box, they found women's "gloves and silk stockings" and various unmentionables, and labels on the items showed the two had been very busy that afternoon at the Fair and the Leader. After nabbing articles from both stores, they had continued pilfering at Mandel Brothers, and after Mandel Brothers they planned to slip across the street to Marshall Field's and ransack it too.

The police handcuffed the two men and led them off to jail. With luck, the owner of the saloon or the manager of the theater where they performed would pay their bail, or if not he would leave them to languish in their jail cells, but the *Tribune*'s reporter wasn't at all interested in that part of Janes and Smith's story and never mentioned what happened to them after the police nabbed them.

The reporter also never bothered to divulge their real names.

What did catch his interest, and what he spent most of the brief article describing, was the box the men used to hide the loot they had lifted. The reporter called it "one of the cleverest methods of shoplifting that have come to the notice of the police for some time." Assigned to cases booked at Chicago's Central Station for quite some time now, the reporter knew what he was talking about. He never showed the least bit of surprise that the shoplifters were men who dressed as women. He had seen his share of female impersonators paraded in and out of Central Station on a variety of charges, and shoplifting was probably the most mundane of them all.

Mundane or not, the story was interesting enough that it was reported across the country. Details about the female impersonators and their contrivance appeared as far away as Texas in the *Galveston Daily News* and, in the opposite direction, in New York's *Evening World*. On November 23, Janes and Smith were tried, convicted, and fined seventy-five dollars each. Thereafter, the two disappeared from history, although the description of the contraption that wasn't what it appeared to be remains a memorial to their cleverness offstage.

Female impersonators had already been a staple of Chicago theater entertainment for many decades before Janes and Smith's illegal spree in the Loop. Two years after John M. Wing arrived in Chicago, Richard M. "Uncle Dick" Hooley, an Irish immigrant and theater impresario, rented Bryan Hall on North Clark Street between Washington and Randolph Streets and began staging minstrel shows, the latest entertainment fad, to standing-room-only crowds. After the Great Chicago Fire of 1871 destroyed the theater—along with everything else in the area bounded in the west by the Chicago River and Halsted Street, on the south by Harrison Street, and on the north by Fullerton Avenue—Hooley constructed another theater on Randolph Street, between Clark and LaSalle, a stone's throw from the original site. The new Hooley's Opera House became an important attraction, not just to Chicago's ever-burgeoning population but also to its thousands of visitors, and is considered to have been the "most successful theater in 19th-century Chicago."

The key to Hooley's renewed success was the fact that he didn't change the entertainment lineup after the fire but continued to capitalize on the popularity of the minstrel show. Minstrel troupes presented plays or skits that included singers and dancers and even comedians, as well as at least one female impersonator—all in blackface. Historian Nan Alamilla Boyd has revealed that as minstrel troupes became popular, "a variety of different types of female impersonator roles evolved," allowing "white men to experiment with race, ethnicity, gender—and sexuality." The cross-dressing performers' regular fare included "songs, jokes, and comic narratives" that often "alluded to sexual relations between men."

Despite the fact that the theatergoing public usually accepted female impersonators onstage, typical Chicagoans began to question, at least occasionally, something they had never paid attention to before: the cross-dressing performer's sexual practices. Their suspicions were fueled by sporadic reports about biological men who cross-dressed for no apparent legitimate reason. They were not members of minstrel troupes but ordinary men whom the police caught in peculiar circumstances, detained, and hauled off to jail or who had lived as women for quite some time, their masquerade a well-kept secret. When their secret was exposed, it left their neighbors, and others who learned about it, shocked and wondering what prompted them—*and* the stage masqueraders—to cross-dress in the first place.

On November 9, 1878, for example, the story of a man who had lived for at least ten years, and perhaps longer, as a woman surfaced in an article titled "A Frontier Mystery," the first of three articles about "Mrs. Noonan," as she was called, that were published in the *Inter Ocean*. During her life at Fort Abraham Lincoln, headquarters of George Armstrong Custer and his Seventh Calvary, the first report began, Mrs. Noonan had "earned the reputation of being a most estimable woman . . . an exemplary laundress and a most efficient nurse" to those who were ill. She had married three men who had been stationed at the fort. The first, in 1869, was Private John Clifford, but they soon separated. Two years later she married James Nash, but they too went their separate ways. She married John Noonan, either a sergeant or a corporal (reports vary), in 1873 and lived with him until her death. She "never had a maiden name," the *Inter Ocean*'s article continued, "in the popular acceptation of that term"—a not-too-subtle hint about the "mystery" surrounding Mrs. Noonan.

John Noonan was away, assigned to the field with his regiment, when Mrs. Noonan died on October 31, 1878. She had been very ill for nearly two weeks, and although she had often told friends that when she took her last breath, she wanted to be buried immediately in the dress she happened to be wearing at the time, the women at the fort ignored her wishes and prepared her body for burial. That was when her secret was discovered—that she was a biological man—and it wasn't long before everyone at the fort, soldiers and civilians alike, found out. They were "surprised and shocked," "curious," and perhaps most of all, "baffled." They weren't just confused by her cross-dressing, which no one seems to have ever suspected, but also because she had been married to three different men at the fort, none of whom had revealed her secret to a soul. Had Clifford and Nash discovered her masquerade and left her because of it? No one knew.

Word of Mrs. Noonan's secret spread like wildfire across the Dakota Territory. Her masquerade became such a hot topic that a reporter interviewed her husband John Noonan a month after her death. From the beginning to the end of his conversation with the reporter, Noonan swore over and over again that he had no idea that his wife was a biological male. "There is some terrible mystery about this thing that I can't understand," he told the reporter. A few moments later, he repeated, "There is something dark and something terrible about this thing," and added this time, "I am doomed to the infamy and can find no relief." With Mrs. Noonan's secret common knowledge, he had become the butt of jokes and other comments from the soldiers at the fort, and "the shame that fell on him . . . undermined his desire for existence." Two days after the interview, he went into the fort's stables and shot himself in "the heart."

The *Inter Ocean*'s reporter didn't even try to address the husbands' tight lips. Instead he "thoughtfully pointed to the many understandable reasons a woman might switch her clothing and live as a man" and wondered why the cross-dresser Mrs. Noonan abandoned "the wide field of action vouchsafed to man" to "take upon himself the drudgery incident to a poor woman's life on the frontier?" He never once entertained the thought that perhaps Mrs. Noonan may have had a man's body but what was then considered only a woman's desires nor that she might have adopted female clothing and a female role in life as camouflage that would allow her to live openly in a relationship with another man.

With the mysterious case of Mrs. Noonan firmly entrenched in the public's mind, it's perhaps no wonder, then, that a few theatergoers began to question the motives of the female impersonators who were performing on Chicago's stages. Although, unlike Mrs. Noonan, they cross-dressed because of their profession, their choice of profession was as much their prerogative as Mrs. Noonan's choice of wardrobe, and that led to speculation that at least some of the cross-dressing performers sought same-sex sexual relationships, as Mrs. Noonan had.

Seven months after "A Frontier Mystery" appeared, a columnist for the *Chicago Daily Tribune* reviewed a performance by the Megatherian Minstrels, a group of fifty white men who performed in blackface. The reviewer focused his attention on one of the fifty performers, the troupe's only crossed-dressed actor: "Burt Shepherd, a female impersonator," he said, "opens the second part" of the show. "We never liked his species," he admitted, "and we cannot say that we tackle kindly to Mr. Shepherd. Unless it be in broad burlesque, there is something nauseating in seeing a man in petticoats." The reviewer's negative criticism had nothing to do with Shepherd's abilities and everything to do with his "species."

Certainly, reviewers had axed other cross-dressers' acts in the past. In fact, Shepherd received a thumbs down in another review of his performance published seven months before Mrs. Noonan's secret became public knowledge. But that reviewer said nothing about Shepherd's "species" and only criticized the performer's lack of talent. Shepherd, the reviewer said, was "so decidedly bad that no one" in the audience applauded his performance except for the "clacquers." The difference between the two reviewers' comments—the one, which was published before Mrs. Noonan's story broke, that criticized the performer's talent, and the other, which was published after the Noonan revelation, that disparaged the type of person Shepherd was—may have been coincidental, but at the same time, several other troupes that included female impersonator acts in their fare found themselves under fire.

A reviewer for the *Inter Ocean* applauded the manager of the Georgia's Minstrels because, the reviewer claimed, he was the "first . . . to get rid of the female impersonator" in his troupe and deserved "great credit for it." The reviewer never disclosed what the performer had done to be fired. Two days later another reviewer praised Hooley because he had begun regulating the material that the female impersonators could and couldn't use in their acts when performing in his theater, although he had been hiring troupes with cross-dressing entertainers without interfering in their acts for over a dozen years. "He deserves," the reviewer wrote, "the highest praise for the wisdom and regard for the sensibilities of his patrons, which prompted him to abolish that bane of minstrelsy, the female impersonator. In time past attention has been called to the reprehensible features of this kind of performances, and we are glad to find a manager like Mr. Hooley indorsing [*sic*] the objections." Whether the theatergoers' "sensibilities" had anything to do with the focus of the performers' presumed sexual desires or their lewd material is unclear, as are "the reprehensible features" of their performances. What is clear is that as time progressed other, similar comments began to appear more and more in reviews, although those remarks focused unambiguously and exclusively on the performer's talent—or lack thereof—and not on his private life. The comments ranged from complaining about the inexperience of a performer—a "callow youth" who performed in women's clothing "had better be stopped short"—to carping about the performer's material or actions (or both), calling him "objectionable" and "vulgar." *Lewd* and *obscene* also joined some reviewers' vocabularies.

In the same year that police arrested Janes and Smith, Chicago hosted a celebration of Christopher Columbus's arrival in the Western Hemisphere four hundred years earlier. The World's Columbian Exposition, popularly known as the World's Fair, was held from the fall of 1892 to the spring of 1893 and introduced scores of new inventions—including electricity, the Ferris wheel, the zipper, and Cracker Jack—to the over twenty million Chicagoans and tourists who attended. Among the many forms of entertainment available to the fairgoers, one of the most popular acts was the performance of a belly dancer called Fatima. A hit of the Midway Plaisance, which "featured over a score of exotic dances," Fatima's was "the wildest of them all." She danced with such "wild abandon" and her movements were so lewd that the police felt obliged to step in and stop her act almost daily. As Fatima's act grew in popularity, a rumor began to circulate. *She* was really a *he*, the gossipers claimed, a rumor that has been since verified by historian Joe McKennon.

However, it wasn't just Fatima's "abandon" that got her in trouble with the Chicago police. Anti-vice crusades had become concerned that her act employed strong "erotic imagery calculated to arouse male members of the audience." They believed that her act's overt and unbridled sexuality might titillate young and naive men and adolescents so much that it would leave them defenseless against the sexual advances of queer men in the audience or out on the street. To counter the explicit sexual nature of her dance, police began raiding her act and hauling her off to jail. When Fatima returned to the stage after a few hours of detention at police headquarters, she always resumed her lewdness, to the delight of her nearly all-male audiences.

Interestingly, Fatima wasn't the only female impersonator on the World's Fair stages. A Chinese female impersonator "played the part of a woman in the 'God of Heaven' performance at the Chinese temple" also "on the Midway Plaisance." However, unlike Fatima, her act was not the least bit erotic, and because not a soul thought she was a threat to any young man or teenager, she didn't have a single run-in with the law.

4 | A Fine Piece of Nude

Sieveking likes to see Sandow's muscles work. Both enjoy themselves and neither loses any time.

WHILE FATIMA WAS BEING HAULED into police headquarters on a regular basis for enthralling audiences with her nearly naked dance at the World Columbian Exposition, Eugen Sandow, who would become a renowned body-builder and idol to thousands, landed a role, although a bit part, in the smash-hit play *Adonis*, which was then being presented at one of New York City's premiere theaters, the Casino. The play starred matinee idol Henry E. Dixey.

The plot of *Adonis* parodied the myth of Pygmalion and Galatea:

A sculptress has created in her statue of Adonis a "perfect figure." Indeed, he is so beautiful and alluring that she cannot bear to sell him as promised to a wealthy duchess. Seeing Adonis, the duchess, together with her four daughters, is instantly and passionately smitten as well. The daughters try to conceal their ardor [but fail]. To resolve the question of ownership, an obliging goddess brings the statue to life. . . . The pursuit of Adonis [by the women] rapidly [ensues]. . . . Ultimately, Adonis is cornered by all his female pursuers, who demand that he choose among them. Instead, he beseeches the goddess who gave him life, "Oh take me away and petrify me— place me on my old familiar pedestal—and hang a placard round my neck:—HANDS OFF." Thus, exhausted by his stint as a flesh-and-blood object of desire, Dixey as Adonis reassumed the pose of a perfect work of art as the curtain fell.

34

When the curtain fell on the night of Sandow's debut, the audience applauded then waited for the curtain to rise and for Dixey and other cast members to return front and center for ovations. Instead, when the curtain rose, Sandow stood in the same pose that Dixey had been in when, as Adonis, Dixey was returned to stone and a "perfect work of art." The audience was stunned, it gasped, then it went wild. Sandow was an immediate sensation.

While performing at the Casino, Sandow was also living in "happy domesticity" with another man, Martinus Sieveking. The two had met when they were nineteen, and when Sandow moved from Europe to New York for his role in *Adonis*, he brought Sieveking with him. Sieveking wasn't just the muscleman's lover; he was a concert pianist and composer in his own right.

Sandow was able to live openly with his "great and inseparable friend" without compromising his heterosexual facade or his career. A reporter for the *New York World* mentioned in an article that the two lived in the same apartment, that Sieveking thought that "Sandow is a truly original Hercules," and that Sandow believed Sieveking was "the greatest pianist in the world." The reporter called them "bosom friends," one of the phrases that queer men of the nineteenth century often used to indicate erotic intimacy between themselves and other men. (Other phrases included "great and inseparable friend," "special friend," and similar expressions.) While most readers would have thought the phrases suggested only a very close friendship between the two, queer men would have immediately understood just how close Sandow and Sieveking's friendship was. Then to underscore their relationship, the reporter noted that Sieveking "practices" at his piano "stripped to the waist," with Sandow "beside him . . . working his muscles. He is fond of the music and Sieveking likes to see Sandow's muscles work. Both enjoy themselves and neither loses any time."

Sieveking wasn't the first of Sandow's "bosom friends." Born Friedrich Wilhelm Müller in 1867, Sandow left his home in Prussia when he was eighteen to escape military service and toured the Continent with circuses, taking part in wrestling matches and giving exhibits of strength to earn a living. In early 1887 the nineteen-year-old Sandow was stranded jobless in Brussels. To make ends meet, he modeled nude for artists, some of whom paid for more than his ability to stand without moving a muscle for long intervals. Befriended by Professor Attila (Louis Durlacher), a famous local strongman and founder of his own bodybuilding school, Sandow became Attila's star pupil, and for the next year, Sandow diligently chiseled his body into a piece of art, one rivaling the classical statues he admired.

Fig. 3. Eugen Sandow (1867–1925) began posing when nineteen years old (left). On the right, he wears one of the costumes he typically wore in his weight-lifting act before he performed virtually nude in Chicago. *Collection of Jim Elledge*

Sandow left Brussels for Venice the following year and met English painter E. Aubrey Hunt on the Lido, a well-known spot where men picked up other men for sex. Sandow claimed that he had been swimming in the ocean and, while walking across the beach in his bathing suit, which would have clung to his body because it was still wet, he caught "the particular attraction" of "a gentleman" who happened to be "sauntering by." Sandow "apologized" for "passing him." As he did, the man congratulated Sandow on his "perfect physique and beauty of form," and afterward they developed what Sandow called a "close friendship," culminating with him "posing" as "a Roman gladiator" for the artist.

Here too, queer men would have easily read between the lines. Hunt was cruising the beach. Sandow was drumming up trade and knew he had caught Hunt's eye. By speaking first Sandow indicated that he was available, allowing Hunt to respond (if he was attracted) or not (if he wasn't). By complimenting the Adonis on his body instead of offering a simple hello, the thirty-three-year-old gentleman declared his desire for a "close friendship" with the twenty-two-year-old.

The Gladiator, Hunt's painting of Sandow, has nothing to do with anything gladiatorial but everything to do with the hunk. Sandow stands in the middle of a blur of colors that certainly represents an arena full of Romans but is, nevertheless, a blur. What *is* in focus is Sandow's highly chiseled flesh, his beauty, and his youth. He's there to be to be envied, to be adored, to be ogled. *The Gladiator* is nineteenth-century soft porn, and it gave Sandow an idea.

For the next six years, Sandow merchandised his body by posing for photographs and garnered profit and publicity in the process. In the photographs he is often nude, and in frontal shots a well-positioned fig leaf hides his genitals. The photos were distributed publicly as studies, or models, for men engaged in "physical culture," the nineteenth century's phrase for bodybuilding.

While his form may have inspired bodybuilders, Sandow's photographs were also highly erotic images, the sort that one of his contemporaries called "a fine piece of nude." The shape of the fig leaf, how the photographer (or Sandow) positioned it, how the photographer arranged the studio light to strike it, and even its size would have fueled queer men's fantasies. How the studio light struck a fig leaf could suggest penis length and girth, and in at least one of Sandow's photos, the fig leaf was positioned to suggest an erection.

Edmund Gosse, a well-known English writer, discovered and bought Sandow's photographs in a London shop. He described them as "a beautiful set of poses showing the young strongman clad only in a fig leaf." Gosse was so enthralled with them that he not only snuck them into the funeral of poet Robert Browning at Westminster Abbey so that he could peek at them during

Fig. 4. Sandow often posed in the nude, imitating classical statues. Here he replicates, but puts a unique spin on, *The Dying Gaul* (a.k.a. *The Dying Gladiator*) by pushing away—or reaching for—his attacker. *Collection of Jim Elledge*

the service, he also shared them with John Addington Symonds, another queer author. In acknowledging the gift in a note to Gosse, Symonds was circumspect, although his prurient exuberance comes through loud and clear. "The Sandow photographs arrived," Symonds wrote. "They are very interesting, & the full length studies quite confirm my anticipations." Gosse and Symonds were members of a group of queer men, which included Oscar Wilde's lover Alfred Douglas, who exchanged nude photos of young men with one another. Sandow's pictures were likely among them.

Sandow wasn't the only physical culturalist to be photographed during the late 1880s, but he was unique among them. Others had developed their bodies into machines that could lift incredible amounts of weight, and their stage performances were limited to that and nothing more. Sandow's performances included weight-lifting extravaganzas, as theirs did, but he also *posed* his sculpted body in an exhibition meant to titillate anyone who saw it. Audiences might be in awe of the hundreds of pounds that one of Sandow's rivals, world-champion Louis Cyr, could lift, but the barrel-shaped Cyr's sex appeal escaped most spectators. When the buff Sandow stepped on to the stage for one of his

Fig. 5. Strongman and Sandow rival, Luis Cyr (1863–1912) lifted a 534-pound weight with a single finger and beat Sandow in a weight-lifting contest, but unlike the Adonis, Cyr's sex appeal was limited. *Collection of Jim Elledge*

performances, a writer for the *Literary Digest* declared, audiences cared "little how much he could lift, or whether he could lift anything at all," because they, like Hunt, Gosse, Symonds, Douglas, and countless other queer men, "attended his exhibitions to look and be exalted by pure beauty."

At virtually the same time that Sandow was making a huge stir in *Adonis* at the Casino, the Chicago World's Fair opened, and thousands began to attend it daily. The father of Chicago-born Flo Ziegfeld, who would later become one of Broadway's most successful impresarios with his *Ziegfeld Follies*, had bought the Trocadero Music Hall near the corner of Monroe Street and Michigan Avenue and planned to make huge profit by drawing fairgoers to performances there. The Trocadero's board of directors sent Flo Ziegfeld to New York to hire Sandow, and on August 1, 1893, Sandow debuted at the Trocadero as the season's headliner for a three-month run. Martinus Sieveking wrote two pieces of music, "March of the Athletes" and "Sandowia," for his lover's performances and played the songs as the Adonis went through his routine onstage, giving the act a touch of class.

However, Ziegfeld realized immediately that Sandow's relationship with Sieveking presented a problem. To deflect gossip about them, Ziegfeld, now Sandow's manager, began to fabricate rumors about the bodybuilder's romantic conquests of a series of well-known women, among them Lillian Russell, the most alluring beauty of the time. Ziegfeld also beefed up Sandow's act to generate free, wildfire publicity, increase profits, and catapult the Adonis into international superstardom in a few simple steps.

First, Ziegfeld pasted the "nude portrait of the well-muscled Hercules, shielded with a discreet fig leaf" on the exterior walls of the Trocadero at sidewalk level. The display along busy Michigan Avenue certainly caught the attention of any and all passersby. Second, he revamped Sandow's costume. Before debuting in Chicago, the bodybuilder performed in a neck-to-toe pink leotard over which he wore a blue singlet; Ziegfeld stripped him to nothing but a pair of skintight "white silk trunks" for his stage performances in Chicago. The only men who had performed in such a scanty costume onstage were female impersonators in specialty acts like Fatima's, and certainly no he-man like Sandow ever had worn such a thing. Newspaper illustrations of Sandow wearing his new costume almost always showed him from behind, suggesting the briefs revealed so much that a frontal view would have been far too scandalous to publish. In the few frontal views that were printed, his trunks were blackened to obliterate any offending bulge.

Ziegfeld wasn't sure if those two strategies would be enough, so he had a third one up his sleeve. At the end of his debut performance in Chicago, as Sandow took his final bows in his clinging silk trunks to thunderous applause, Ziegfeld suddenly appeared onstage. He raised his hands to quiet the audience and announced that any women who donated $300 or more to charity could come to Sandow's dressing room to examine his muscles intimately. Mrs. Potter Palmer and Mrs. George Pullman, grand dames of Chicago society, were the first in line to caress the Adonis's flesh. Mrs. Palmer "stroked Sandow's massive chest" and later, when interviewed by a newspaper about her experience, declared that touching him had "thrilled" her "to the spine." Staff drama reviewer for the *Chicago Daily News* Amy Leslie also examined Sandow's body and later gushed that he was "a dangerously handsome young man."

Of course, Ziegfeld also allowed men to visit Sandow's dressing room, but they got in for free, and they, not women, crowded the Adonis's room to grope him, as illustrations from newspapers show. Despite their majority, their reactions to Sandow weren't quoted in the press.

The night of his Chicago debut at the Trocadero wasn't the first of Sandow's dressing-room performances. In Europe he had hosted private soirees after the last curtain fell, but they had been confidential and very sporadic. Ziegfeld made them public and regular, guaranteeing that they would be *the* topic of gossip among Chicago's theatergoing public as well as the queer subculture for months. In fact, the soirees were so successful that Sandow continued to hold them during his entire run at the Trocadero. "One thing seems certain," one writer declared, "while his admirers were fondling Sandow's muscles, they were satisfying feelings other than mere curiosity." It's just as obvious that Sandow's performances at the Trocadero—both onstage and in his dressing room—had catapulted him into national attention, and unlike Fatima he hadn't been hauled into jail by the police even once.

Two weeks after Sandow's risqué debut, a large group of physicians gathered a few steps away from the Trocadero Music Hall to listen to a paper that would affect queer life in Chicago, and across the nation, in terrible, previously unimaginable ways. The physicians were part of the exposition's program of presenting new, radical concepts and inventions to fairgoers, and the meeting was a joint affair of the World's Columbian Auxiliary

Congress and the International Medico-Legal Congress held on August 16, 1893. Among the many doctors who presented papers to the august body was F. E. Daniel, who read his "Should Insane Criminals or Sexual Perverts Be Permitted to Procreate?" In it Daniel recommended castration as a cure for a host of social problems: "Rape, sodomy, beastiality [*sic*], pederasty and habitual masturbation."

While a few physicians had already used castration in the hopes of curing masturbation and homosexuality, this was the first time that a physician made a concerted effort to talk a large number of his colleagues into approving the surgery in order to stop same-sex sexual desires. Daniel's theory was neither accepted nor rejected by the physicians who attended, but his paper was later published in three different medical journals and created a stir among physicians nationwide. With such a wide distribution, it influenced a number of state legislatures to establish laws that permitted doctors and directors of mental asylums to castrate their queer patients as a means to cure—and to punish—them. The specter of castration would haunt queer men for over half a century.

Once his run at the Trocadero ended, Sandow and Sieveking hurried back to New York City and set sail for England. But before leaving, Sandow visited Thomas Edison's studio and was filmed as he went through a series of bodybuilding poses. After arriving in England he visited Warwick Brookes, who had photographed him four years earlier, and met Warwick's daughter, Blanche, with whom he began corresponding. A reporter described her in terms that evoke Sieveking: "tall, slender, exquisitely beautiful," "eyes . . . large and soft, black as night, and very sensitive," and "hair . . . just as black." Within weeks Sandow and Sieveking returned to New York to begin their first coast-to-coast tour, which began in December and closed the following July. Wherever he performed, Sandow conquered the hearts—and libidos—of his audiences, those in the theaters as well as those at his post-performance soirees. Their tour was so successful that it lasted twice as long as their contract required.

As soon as it was over, Sandow and Sieveking sailed back to England, and on August 8, 1894, shortly after his twenty-seventh birthday, Sandow married Blanche Brookes. Regardless of whatever else it may have provided, Sandow's wedding camouflaged his and Sieveking's relationship. With a wife the Adonis could have his cupcake and eat him too. Yet the men called it quits within a year, and the newly married Sandows and Ziegfeld immediately began planning a second US tour—without Sieveking.

Sandow also changed his performance drastically, and Ziegfeld wasn't happy about it. With wife in tow, Sandow axed the private, flesh-caressing soirees. Whether he decided to make the change on his own or Blanche demanded it is unknown, but the second tour became a lackluster series of performances that lasted seven and a half grueling months. By its end, the two men were barley speaking, and Blanche, who left the tour early, was pregnant with the first of the couple's two daughters.

Following Sandow's lead, Sieveking also married, in 1899, and fathered a son. He moved to the United States, giving concerts to good-to-lukewarm reviews at Carnegie Hall and other venues, opened a piano school, and wrote and published scholarly essays about piano playing. He and his wife eventually separated, and he moved to Pasadena, California, where he died at eighty-three on November 26, 1950.

Eugen and Blanche remained married, raising their two daughters together. Sandow toured many countries throughout the world, created an empire of bodybuilding schools, published a bodybuilding journal titled *Physical Culture*, invented several physique-training devices, and endorsed dozens of products, all of which made him wealthy and a household name across the globe. He was only fifty-eight when he died on October 14, 1925. Authorities officially, and ironically, attributed his death to a strain he received when he righted his car after it flipped over during an accident.

Sandow's legacy had rooted itself in the queer subculture of the United States long before his death, but its influence would not be immediately recognized. Eventually it would give rise to what would be called *beefcake*, which is

a sub-culture of muscle admiration developed in photography which dated back to the Father of Bodybuilding himself, Eugen Sandow. Developing from this came physique magazines, making it possible for closeted men to see muscular bodies without going to the gym or to rarely-held bodybuilding contests. A niche market opened whereby magazines published specifically for gay men were promoted as ordinary physique magazines—the "beefcake" magazines. They catered for [sic] those who were attracted to a wide variety of muscular types, from massive bodybuilders to slimmer, toned athletes.

Two of the most influential forerunners of beefcake—Bernarr Macfadden and Charles Atlas—had strong ties to Sandow and owe a great deal to him for their successes in physical culture/bodybuilding.

Bernarr Macfadden, who spent much of his childhood in Chicago, was in the audience one evening during Sandow's 1893 run at the Trocadero. A year younger than the Adonis, Macfadden would follow in Sandow's footsteps, beginning with adhering to his own regimen of bodybuilding and "modeling himself after Sandow." In 1909 he founded a magazine, *Physical Culture*, stealing the title of Sandow's magazine for his own. That same year Macfadden opened the Macfadden Healthatorium at Forty-Second Street and Grand Boulevard in Chicago. A combination sanitarium and school for instruction in physical culture, it became "a great success." Perhaps Macfadden's greatest influence on beefcake would happen in 1903, when he sponsored the first bodybuilding competition in the United States. Again he was following in Sandow's footsteps: Sandow had held the world's first bodybuilding competition in London two years earlier.

But it was Macfadden who discovered a new star of bodybuilding. In 1909 Angelo Sciliano, a young Italian immigrant who lived in Brooklyn, taped a photo of Eugen Sandow to his bedroom mirror and, with Sandow as his inspiration, set out on his own course of physical training. His body developed rapidly, and like Sandow he began to pose for artists and photographers. The photographs "of him in classic poses, nude or shockingly close to it and with more than a whiff of eroticism, suggest how much he liked the camera and the camera liked him." His body also became the centerpiece of sculptures across the United States, including *Patriotism* at the Elks' national headquarters in Chicago. In 1921 he entered one of Macfadden's bodybuilding competitions for the title of "the Most Beautiful Man of the World" and won the $1,000 purse hands down. The following year Sciliano won Macfadden's second competition, "the World's Most Perfectly Developed Man," and soon after changed his name to Charles Atlas. Like Sandow before him, Atlas combined "the qualities of Adonis and Hercules"—male beauty *and* strength—and became the quintessential bodybuilding model for the twentieth century, as Sandow had been for the nineteenth.

Chicagoan Chuck Renslow and his Kris Studios became a leader in the beefcake industry, initially distributing photographs of good-looking, physically fit young men wearing very little or nothing at all. He soon began publishing

Mars magazine, which included scores of beefcake photographs. While beefcake models abandoned the fig leaf for the posing strap, many continued to pose, whether they knew it or not, in the positions that Sandow had assumed in his photographs years earlier.

After Sandow's death, his body, which had given him fame and fortune, which had been *oooh*ed and *ahhh*ed over by millions, which had been caressed by hundreds of trembling hands, and which had been photographed naked in every pose imaginable, was buried without a tombstone, then ignored. In fact, Blanche vehemently denied fans the opportunity to raise a headstone to their hero no matter how many times they asked for her permission.

She may have been retaliating. Immediately after Sandow's death in 1925, reports began to surface that threw suspicion on the official explanation of his death. Friends claimed he had been obviously ill for at least a year and linked the strongman's death to syphilis, which was then difficult to cure and could be lethal. Perhaps Blanche had been a victim of his carousing. At the very least, she had probably heard the rumors about his liaisons with men long after he and Sieveking broke up. She likely also knew that certain vaudeville acts hired Sandow lookalikes to poke fun at the muscleman. In one such revue, *L'Amour*, an "actor representing . . . Sandow impersonating a statue," as Sandow had done decades earlier in *Adonis*, is "standing on a pedestal in a park. A bevy of young beauties cross in front. No reaction. Finally a sailor passes, and the fig leaf begins to rise and rise, until it stands straight out supported, obviously, by an erection."

5 | My Vileness Is Uncontrollable

Last summer Clifford and I began a friendship which developed into love.

SNOW HAD RECENTLY BLANKETED CHICAGO, and mail carrier William L. Clifford had just picked up the letters and packages he was to deliver to homes and businesses that afternoon. He was strolling north on Clark Street, being careful not to slip on the ice, with fellow postal employees. Some of his companions were also on their way to make deliveries, others to have lunch. It was noon on Wednesday, March 28, 1894. As Clifford neared Madison Avenue, shots rang out, and he fell into a pile of snow. He had been shot from behind, once in his "loins" and three times in the back of his head and shoulders.

The lunch-hour crowd burst from local restaurants and swarmed the gunman, thirty-year-old Guy T. Olmstead, Clifford's former lover and now, perhaps, his murderer. According to news reports, a crowd of men yelled, "Lynch him!" as they surrounded Olmstead. He waved his pistol at them, swearing, "I'll never be taken alive!" As they got within reach of him, he yelled, "Don't take my gun; let me finish what I have to do," at the top of his voice. Because they had corralled him, he couldn't run away. The crowd grabbed him and then dragged him to a nearby lamppost, where they planned to string him up. They would have, too, had it not been for "the arrival of a dozen" policemen led by an officer named Fitzgerald. Fitzgerald got Olmstead away from the vengeful crowd, arrested him, and ushered him into a paddy wagon, which took him safely to jail.

Olmstead wasn't the first queer man in Chicago to have been threatened with lynching by a crowd. Magnus Hirschfeld planned to publish a journal that he tentatively titled *Uranus*, and among the topics he scheduled for covering in either the February or March 1870 issue was a report on an "attempted lynching of an Urning" in Chicago in 1845. Unfortunately he never printed a single issue of the magazine, and no report about the incident exists.

The details of Olmstead's early life are sketchy. Born in Catlin, Illinois, near the Indiana border, Olmstead had been sexually involved with a man who boarded with the family when he was twelve years old. Eventually he moved to Connecticut, earned his living as a teacher, and married a young woman who was the daughter of a rich farmer, but shortly thereafter, according to sexologist Havelock Ellis, he "fell in love" with one of her cousins, a "very handsome young man." What, if anything, became of his attraction to his wife's cousin was never recorded, but he and his wife separated, and he moved back to Illinois.

From October 1886 to May 1889, Olmstead was confined to the Illinois Eastern Hospital for the Insane in Kankakee, Illinois, a few miles southwest of Chicago, because he had been diagnosed as paranoid. According to medical records from the asylum, Olmstead had a full head of sand-colored hair and deep-set, small gray eyes. At five feet, eight inches tall, he weighed 159 pounds, and he was so wrinkled that he looked "at least ten years older than his actual age." His nose, ears, hands, and feet were large, his penis "abnormally small." Once he was released, he went to Chicago, found work as a wagon driver for a bakery, and then, in October 1892, became a mail carrier. He met Clifford on the job. Like Olmstead, Clifford had once been a schoolteacher. Olmstead boarded at 357 Ohio Street in Towertown, and Clifford rented a place at 635 West Adams Street, at the threshold of the West Madison Street vice district, where queer men cruised day and night for other men and adolescents.

Chicago's vice areas became particularly important to many of the city's queer population. Although usually identified as virtually unpoliced neighborhoods where non-queer men could "indulge in . . . tabooed activities" without being caught, vice districts afforded the same smokescreen to queer men. Non-queer men who visited the vice districts were hiding their activities from wives, children, employers, neighbors, the law, and the church, and many "sex perverts" were too. In fact, queer men of all sorts felt safe from detection in vice areas. Because there was no visible difference between these "normal" men and their non-queer counterparts, if they were seen there, they would be mistaken for a non-queer man, and on the dimly lit streets of any of Chicago's three major vice areas—the South Side Levee, West Madison Street, and the Rialto of North Clark Street—female impersonators easily passed as biological women.

Taking its name from its chief thoroughfare, the West Madison Street vice district extended from Halsted Street westward for a mile. Whorehouses, burlesque theaters, cheap saloons, and even cheaper flophouses lined both sides of the street. Years later a man who grew up along West Madison Street called the area "a rather dark section of the city" and a playground for "a lot of homosexuals." To emphasize the fact, he revealed that during his childhood, "as I'd walk along Madison Street there'd always be some man to stop me and coax me into having sex relations with him." It wasn't always the adult man who propositioned the boy for sex, as men working for the Juvenile Protective Association discovered. A "young boy" offered himself for "acts of perversion" to the inspectors who were making their rounds through Chicago's West Side investigating pool halls.

Although their relationship had begun platonically enough, Olmstead had "developed a passion" for Clifford by June 1893. Clifford reciprocated, and the two became lovers. A few months later Clifford broke off the relationship and tried to convince his ex-lover "to undergo medical treatment" to cure him of his "passion," and he even told Olmstead that he was willing to pay for the treatment.

Olmstead refused Clifford's offer, and instead he began to stalk Clifford, making his previous lover's life "miserable." In November Olmstead contacted Clifford's family and told them that he and Clifford had been married, although they hadn't, and Clifford was "so frightened, hurt, and angry" by what Olmstead had done that he talked Olmstead into a suicide pact. Olmstead quickly agreed to it, but shortly thereafter Clifford changed his mind.

Sometime between the end of November and the beginning of December, Clifford gave the Chicago postmaster a group of "passionate" letters that Olmstead had written to him because he was tired of Olmstead's unwanted attentions and hoped the postmaster would put an end to them. The postmaster fired Olmstead on December 5, 1893. Although Olmstead appealed his firing, his petition was bluntly denied. On the advice of his friends who knew about his love for Clifford, Olmstead checked himself into Chicago's Polyclinic Hospital on January 7, 1894, where Dr. W. T. Belfield castrated him at his request. He hoped the operation would cure him of his homosexuality, and this may have been the treatment Clifford had offered to pay for earlier. Olmstead left the hospital nearly a month later, on February 5.

Understandably Olmstead now suffered from "hysterical melancholia" and checked himself into Chicago's Mercy Hospital for treatment, although he realized all too quickly that there was no cure for homosexuality. While hospitalized he wrote the first of several letters to Dr. E. S. Talbot, another of Chicago's well-known authorities on human sexuality. "I might as well go to Hades," he complained to Talbot, "as far as any hope of my getting well is concerned."

Having undergone a horrific surgical procedure to transform himself into a "decent creature," Olmstead had to face the fact that the operation was unsuccessful, and he wondered in his letter to Talbot if "doctors knew that after emasculation" a man could still have "erections, commit masturbation, and have the same passion as before." He came to the conclusion that "this disease"—his homosexuality—"was born in me, and will leave me only when my breath leaves me." Then Olmstead sank into despair: "I am utterly incorrigible, utterly incurable, and utterly impossible. . . . Heaven only knows how hard I have tried to make a decent creature out of myself, but my vileness is uncontrollable, and I might as well give up and die."

Although he considered his homosexuality an illness, and even a "monster," Olmstead also believed that it was natural—that it was "born in me." That comment would appear in Talbot and Ellis's essay "A Case of Developmental Degenerative Insanity, with Sexual Inversion, Melancholia Following Removal of Testicles, Attempted Murder and Suicide" two years after Talbot's arrest, but unfortunately Olmstead's important assertion about his homosexuality being natural went unnoticed by the medical profession. When Ellis reprinted the essay in his book *Sexual Inversion*, he omitted any reference to Olmstead's belief that men were born queer.

Nine days later, having written Talbot again and frustrated beyond endurance, Olmstead made a last-ditch effort to rid himself of the "monster." He shot Clifford in the back, in broad daylight, in view of scores of witnesses. When Officer Fitzgerald searched Olmstead, he found a suicide note that Olmstead had written the day before in which he briefly described his relationship with Clifford:

> Fearing that my motives in killing Clifford and myself may be misun-
> derstood, I write this to explain the cause of this homicide and suicide.
> Last summer Clifford and I began a friendship which developed into
> love. . . . Clifford's love has, alas! turned to deadly hatred. For some
> reason Clifford suddenly ended our relations and friendship.

While in jail awaiting trial for attempted murder, Olmstead made several suicide attempts, which included "butting his head against the bars of the cell" and the walls and "swallowing . . . a mixture of rat poison and arsenic, which he had sewn in the waistband of his trousers" several days before shooting Clifford. Immediately after taking the mixture, he called for his jailor, who rushed him to Presbyterian Hospital, where physicians pumped his stomach and saved his life.

In the meantime doctors at that same hospital, where Clifford was taken after being shot, reported that they had removed the bullets from his body and predicted that he would survive if blood poisoning didn't develop. It didn't. The *Chicago Tribune* later reported that Clifford's condition had improved greatly and physicians believed he would recover.

While still in jail the following summer, Olmstead wrote a third letter to Talbot, discussing his body, his thoughts about Clifford, and the fact that he'd kept what he believed to be an "improvement" in his "passion for other men" a secret from everyone. Instead of feeling sexual urges, he now only felt "sharp, shooting pains down the abdomen to the scrotum" that became "worse at the base of the penis." He kept his condition a secret because he was convinced that, first, if the authorities learned that he no longer felt "passion for other men," they would send him to a prison and, second, that to live in an asylum would be far easier than in a prison. He ended his letter by asking Talbot if he really did "consider sexual perversion an insanity."

Once Olmstead was tried, he was convicted, and the judge sentenced him to the Asylum for Insane Criminals downstate in Chester. After several years Olmstead was pronounced sane and released. He immediately returned to Chicago, where he accused the same postmaster who had fired him years earlier of being the leader of a conspiracy against him, and he demanded that the postmaster return his testicles. He was quickly taken into custody and subsequently confined at the Cook County Hospital for the Insane in Chicago. Later he would be relocated to the Illinois Eastern Hospital for the Insane, his second stay there.

In late 1899 or early 1900, the superintendent of the Hospital for the Insane wrote to the state attorney general, E. C. Akin, asking him to transfer Olmstead back to the Asylum for Insane Criminals in Chester, where he had been incarcerated right after his trial. What Olmstead had done that made the superintendent want to transfer him was never recorded. Nevertheless, Akin refused the superintendent's request. Olmstead had been confined to the Hospital for the Insane because he was insane, Akin wrote to the superintendent, and not because he was an "insane criminal." The subject was dropped, and Olmstead continued to live at the Hospital for the Insane for the next twenty-seven years. He was put on its staff, and to earn his keep he worked there, first as a teacher and then as a laborer, a common situation in asylums at the time. He died behind its walls on January 15, 1927.

Clifford fared far better than his former lover. By 1896 he had moved to 2208 West Congress Parkway. Four and a half years after Olmstead shot him, Clifford married Alice B. Snow, and their daughter was born in 1905. He continued working at the US post office in Chicago until he retired, after which he became a shop owner. He died on February 15, 1941.

Olmstead's crime was reported in newspapers across the United States. Reporters who covered the attempted murder didn't know how to deal with Olmstead's love for Clifford. Had their relationship simply been a sexual escapade, the reporters would have known how to respond to it, but the mention of *love* left them dumbfounded. Often they simply hinted at something shameful but unidentified between the two men, as New York's *Utica Daily* did when it declared, "A scandal is said to be back of the shooting." Occasionally the reporter judged Olmstead without the benefit of consulting a medical expert, as happened in Indiana's *Elkhart Daily Review*, which stated, "He is probably insane."

However, an editor at the *Chicago Daily Tribune* didn't ignore the reason for Olmstead's crime, nor did he dismiss it with a sneer. Instead he dealt openly and even sympathetically with it. Printed the day after Olmstead shot Clifford in the back, the editorial first urged the Chicago court to take pains to ensure that Olmstead would receive a substantial defense despite his being queer. The writer insisted that Olmstead should be afforded the same justice that was due any of Chicago's citizens. "It is evident," he wrote, "that Olmstead has few friends and no money. He will probably be quickly tried and hanged, without benefit of clergy, unless the bench, acting together, shall intervene in his behalf at the earliest possible moment."

Then the editorial's writer showed an unprecedented amount of empathy and even a real understanding of the intricacies of human—even queer human—emotion when he asserted, "Olmstead shot a man because he loved him."

For someone to write an editorial in a national publication meant for a mainstream audience associating love with same-sex sexuality was an amazing response in the nineteenth century. Although at least some Chicagoans understood that some men engaged in sexual acts with other men, as disturbing as the thought may have been to them, few ever imagined that a man could actually fall in love with another man. That was beyond comprehension for most. Nevertheless, on March 29, 1894, one man believed that same-sex relationships could be based on something other than perversity or sin or the exchange of money for sexual favors, and on that day "the love that dare not speak its name" actually spoke it in the *Chicago Daily Tribune*.

6 | The Hottest Show on Earth!

Chicago ain't no sissy town.

IN THE SUMMER OF 1909, Chicago was abuzz over a striptease act at the Riverview Exposition, later known as the Riverview Amusement Park, not only because the performers flouted the era's taboo against showing naked flesh in public but, even more scandalous, because the strippers weren't women at all but female impersonators: twenty-one-year-old Quincy de Lang and twenty-year-old George Quinn. The two were members of Duncan Clark's Female Minstrels, a traveling troupe popular throughout the Midwest—and especially in Chicago, where they performed in a variety of venues, including several in the Loop. Queer men were titillating their audiences overtly and unapologetically, and newspaper editorials demanded that something had to be done to stop them from luring men, especially the young and naive, into perverted sexual practices.

On Sunday, July 11, after watching what they considered to be an especially besotted performance, several detectives swung into action. They followed de Lang and Quinn offstage, burst into their dressing room, handcuffed the duo, and hauled them off to the Harrison Street police station. The police also confiscated their costumes as evidence against them because the prosecution planned to charge them with "impersonating a female." Neither Duncan Clark nor the amusement park's manager could have paid for better publicity than what the newspapers would provide over the next few weeks.

Beginning a few months earlier, several citizens' groups had decided to dedicate themselves to cleaning up what they considered to be moral filth that, in their minds, littered Chicago's neighborhoods by investigating various resorts in the city. Leaders of the citizens' groups assigned investigators to specific establishments, and these investigators then wrote reports that noted any performances or activities they deemed objectionable. Three resorts—White City, San Souci, and Riverview Exposition, all amusement parks—became the reformers' targets that summer. By the beginning of July, one citizens' group in particular, the Chicago Law and Order League, was ready to move against the resorts, and its recently elected president, A. B. Farwell, was perched to lead his minions to victory. "The indecent show at the amusement parks," one newspaper report predicted with bravado, "is doomed."

Chicago's burlesque aficionados were well aware of the presence of female impersonators in Duncan Clark's troupe long before de Lang and Quinn made headline news. A brief article about Clark's "female minstrels" that was published in *Billboard* the year before de Lang and Quinn's arrest declared loud and clear that "all female characters" in Clark's productions were "taken by the very best impersonators only" and not by biological females. It's very likely, then, that neither the authorities nor audiences were at all shocked that men were performing as women. It's just as likely that de Lang and Quinn must have been very accomplished at stripping and titillating the men in the audience, given the uproar their act created among the anti-vice groups, but that should have been expected. After all, the troupe's slogan was "The Hottest Show on Earth!" as newspaper advertisements for the troupe reveal. In fact, titillation, and not art, was undoubtedly the troupe's goal. An early reviewer of Duncan Clark's Female Minstrels even declared, "This co. is one of the poorest combs. on the road. It does not possess a single redeeming feature."

The investigators agreed wholeheartedly with the reviewer. Not only were de Lang and Quinn "artfully dressed in women's clothing" during that Sunday evening's performance, but the detectives, who had been keeping an eye on the pair for at least a month, reported that "the dancing of the team was to them of a vulgar character," an "immoral and lewd exhibition," and "a menace to the morals of young men." Too young to have seen Fatima onstage during the Chicago World's Fair of 1893, de Lang and Quinn were, nevertheless, carrying on in the tradition she had established nearly twenty years earlier, a tradition that would remain vibrant in Chicago for decades to come.

Key to the prosecution's strategy for convicting de Lang and Quinn was the word *artfully*: "artfully dressed in women's clothing." The authorities must have believed that de Lang and Quinn were excellent impersonators and able to pass as women if they chose to do so. How easy it would be, the authorities feared, for de Lang and Quinn to hoodwink one or two unsuspecting men (or, worse yet, boys), sneak off after a performance with them in tow, and engage them in God knows what vile acts before the men (or boys) realized they'd been turned into perverts, no better than those who had duped then seduced them in the first place. The authorities' fear was somewhat justified. During the fin-de-siècle, "the most reprehensible phase of burlesque developed," as historian David Dressler has noted, in which "the girls, or female impersonators, left the stage" after their performance "to go to the saloon in back of the theater to drum up trade in drinks, or to pick up a customer for sexual relations."

The prosecuting attorney was ready to try the two men for dressing as women, and he had the ammunition he needed to convict de Lang and Quinn too. In 1851, fourteen years before John Wing arrived in Chicago, the city legislature had adopted a law that the prosecuting attorney would be using against de Lang and Quinn. It prohibited not only public nudity but crossdressing as well:

> If any person shall appear in a public place in a state of nudity, or in a dress not belonging to his or her sex, or in an indecent or lewd dress, or shall make any indecent exposure of his or her person, or be guilty of any lewd or indecent act or behavior, he shall be subject to a fine of not less than twenty dollars, nor exceeding one hundred dollars.

But three days after de Lang and Quinn's arrest, on Wednesday, July 14, a reporter for the *Chicago Daily Tribune* announced that de Lang and Quinn would be tried "on the charge of conducting an objectionable performance" instead of "impersonating a female." The authorities were wavering in their resolve and confidence, and they were trying to shore up their case. Assistant Chief of Police Herman Schuettler publicly explained the difficulties he faced in trying to get rid of such acts. "We arrest men who impersonate females and perform dances" that were objectionable because of their sexual content, he said, but risqué performances like de Lang and Quinn's were so profitable that the acts' managers had plenty of money on hand for hiring the savviest lawyers, who were always able to get the charges dropped.

Fig. 6. In 1904, Julius Duc was arrested for impersonating a woman, a crime in Chicago since 1851. Why Duc cross-dressed or whether he was convicted or not is unknown. *DN-0004110,* Chicago Daily News *negatives collection, Chicago History Museum*

Burlesque had already begun to replace the minstrel show as the chief theatrical entertainment for most Chicagoans. In its early days, burlesque had nothing to do with striptease but was, more or less, simply a variety show during which troupes presented plays that were satirical in nature, just as minstrel shows had often done. Although their fare was decidedly burlesque, many troupes acknowledged their minstrel origins by including *minstrel* in their names, just as Duncan Clark had done. Among the song-and-dance acts, the jugglers and weight-lifters, the comedy duos, and the harmonica players and bird-whistlers who often appeared on burlesque stages, more risqué forms of entertainment were the most popular. Some troupes were even dedicated to it.

At the same time that de Lang and Quinn were awaiting trial, another public scandal was brewing: the "case against Bertha Faulk, nicknamed the 'bare bronze beauty,' who was appearing at White City." The biologically female Faulk had been taken into custody for her "vulgar" performance, and although de Lang and Quinn had been his initial target, Farwell now pursued Faulk with a vengeance and ignored the female impersonators. Newspapers followed suit. They stopped reporting about de Lang and Quinn's case and began publishing articles about Faulk. One reporter revealed that moments after Faulk's trial began, men who had heard a rumor that she would "dance for the benefit of the court" flooded the courtroom. When they learned that she wouldn't, they left in a huff.

At her trial the prosecuting attorney asked her how she dressed during her performances, and Faulk didn't seem the least bit embarrassed to describe "her 'scant' costume." It was just "a waistband, one or two yards of veiling, and a small string of beads," she testified. After being sent out of the courtroom to deliberate, the jury took only nineteen minutes to return its verdict. Faulk's act, it concluded, "was nothing if not morally elevating and decent in every sense of the word." She was, the jury asserted, an "'art' dancer and poser," with nothing at all indecent in her act. The fact that the jury was composed solely of men didn't hurt her defense in the least.

De Lang and Quinn, who had been arrested before Faulk in the citywide crackdown on vice, were second to be tried. Their trial resulted in an acquittal too, but by the time their verdict was announced, interest in them was negligible. Faulk had stolen the public's attention. The only mention of the female impersonators' victory in the news was an offhand comment made weeks after the fact. On August 5 the *Chicago Record-Herald* declared, "Twice beaten in jury trials [police] officers have apparently become discouraged" by the setbacks, and the "degeneracy" of the Riverview acts, which had never stopped despite de Lang and Quinn's run-in with the law, had gotten worse. Performances like de Lang and Quinn's were being loudly hawked carnival-barker style to the guffaws of the crowds:

> Ladies and gentlemen, before I start . . . I want to say a few words regarding this show. This is an oriental dancing show to the limit. This is not a bible class. We don't have them here. The management of the park does not pay for the privilege of holding bible classes and Sunday school. I have never heard of a bible class being held in Riverview.
>
> If you are looking for such things you are in the wrong place. You ought to be at a Salvation army hall or at a church. An amusement park is no place for you.

Farwell and his Law and Order League weren't the first social reformers to attack social evil—like *vice*, a catch-all phrase for prostitution, gambling, drugs and alcohol—and "illicit sexuality" in its many varieties. In fact, such reform movements have a long history in Chicago. One of the first of the social reformers to reveal the city's "rampant vice" was William Stead, an English journalist who gave public lectures in Chicago from 1893 to 1894 and published a book outlining his views, *If Christ Came to Chicago*, in 1894. In the book, he revealed Chicago's sinful ways, especially in the South Side Levee. Although he doesn't seem to have been aware of the existence of queer men—or thought them too unimportant or too few to mention—he set a precedent of sorts. Other exposés of vice in Chicago would quickly follow and with them their antithesis, guidebooks for tourists and locals not already in the know that pinpointed exactly where vice could be found for anyone who cared to look.

Four distinct groups were active in the anti-vice movement in Chicago during the first years of the 1900s. The Chicago Society for Social Hygiene set out to control venereal diseases and to promote "sex education." The Committee of Fifteen, composed of "an elite group of businessmen," sought to do away with prostitution. The Christian-based Illinois Vigilance Association focused on destroying white slavery—a common term for the practice of kidnapping women and girls and forcing them into prostitution—as well as censoring books, films, and theater performances. Last was the Juvenile Protective Association, composed primarily of women with connections to Hull House, the social reform center established on the Near West Side in 1889 by Jane Addams and Ellen Gates Starr. The JPA worked "to protect children and young women from the ravages of urban vice." Members of the organizations patrolled the streets of Chicago's vice districts as well as the exhibitions of its three amusement parks looking to weed out vice wherever they might find it.

Following de Lang and Quinn's trial, another situation that had been vexing Farwell and similar social reformers since at least 1903 resurfaced. Held annually since 1896, the Grand Reception of the First Ward Democratic Club—or the First Ward ball, as it was popularly called—was nothing more than a campaign fundraiser through which the aldermen of Chicago's First Ward, Mike "Hinky Dink" Kenna and John "Bathhouse John" Coughlin, elicited protection money. Initially the aldermen held the masquerade balls at the Seventh Regiment Armory but soon had to move them to the Coliseum because the crowds at the balls had grown too large for the Armory. Early Chicago sociologist Walter Reckless believed that Hinky Dink and Bathhouse John earned "about $50,000" ($1,179,777 in today's money) annually from the festivities, which they took turns pocketing, and one of the balls was so wildly attended that it knotted up traffic around the Coliseum for blocks.

The First Ward included the Loop, "the old Custom House Place vice district," and "the infamous 22nd and Dearborn 'Levee,'" also called the South Side Levee, where bordellos, saloons, opium dens, gambling houses, and similar resorts lined the streets for blocks. The ward's nefarious businesses made it the wealthiest district in all of Chicago and attracted so-called respectable people who enjoyed sordid pastimes, as well as those already knee-deep in crime. "If a great disaster had befallen the Coliseum last night," one reporter quipped after the 1907 masquerade, "there would not have been a second story worker, a dip or plug ugly, porch climber, dope fiend or scarlet woman remaining in Chicago."

Kenna's and Coughlin's criminal activities, including their masquerade balls, were legendary, even during their lifetime. If the First Ward's bordello madams, street-corner pimps, saloonkeepers, opium-den owners, and gambling-ring leaders didn't want police to harass their establishments, their employees, or their clients, and if they didn't want their operations shut down, they had to buy tickets to the event—and not just a handful or even dozens but hundreds of them. They would then distribute the tickets to their employees and clients to ensure a healthy turnout at the balls. At the same time, others who had no business interests in the vice districts were also strong-armed into buying tickets and perhaps even attending if they wanted to keep their jobs. Policemen stationed within the First Ward, for example, had to pay ten dollars per ticket ($250 in today's money) to avoid being fired. On the other hand, those female impersonators who could afford a ticket readily bought one, because it would guarantee them a night out on the town in full drag—their chosen masquerade costume—without the threat of arrest and with the added possibility of catching the attention of a "normal" man. The "normal" man would have been just as willing to buy a ticket because for him it would open the door to a bevy of female impersonators—or other "normal" men.

The aldermen's wildly successful racket was an open secret in Chicago. An editorial cartoon by John T. McCutcheon titled "The Grand March at Bathhouse John's Ball" depicts the chaotic merriment at one of the balls and includes a beer barrow in the foreground on which one of the aldermen's minions has posted a threat that makes Kenna's and Coughlin's power all too obvious. "Guests not contributing voluntarily," the sign reads, "will REGRET IT!"

While both aldermen were acutely aware of the backlash against the First Ward balls, they were so confident in their positions that they could thumb their noses at the opposition. Bathhouse John bragged to a reporter who was interviewing him during one of the revelries, "'These reform guys are after me, but look at that,' pointing proudly to the multitude. 'Nothin' to it, absolutely nothin'.'" Some experts even described the festivities in a positive light. Famed sociologist Jacob Riis, who attended one of the masquerade balls, reported, "It was surprising in a dozen ways. There has not been and probably could not be anything like it in the East. Certainly not in New York. It was so surprisingly frank. When they give a French ball in New York . . . there is a veneering over it. This one was natural and frank."

Besides, the aldermen knew that Farwell and the other reformers had little support among typical Chicagoans, who were far more fascinated by what happened at the aldermen's balls—drunken brawls, prostitutes and their cadets (pimps) trolling for clients, and the orchestra playing current hits—than by high-minded morality. For the average person, being at one of the First Ward balls and watching the "female impersonators," some of whom "performed impromptu acts" as lascivious as the ones de Lang and Quinn performed at

Riverview, was far more thrilling than sitting in an auditorium or church, listening to a reformer's or minister's diatribe.

So sure of their ability to withstand any onslaught by the reformers, a certainty that bordered on hubris, Hinky Dink and Bathhouse John invited Wallen T. Sumner, dean of Saints Peter and Paul Cathedral, to attend the December 1907 festivities. He was appalled by what he saw taking place in the Coliseum and called the female impersonators who arrived in full drag "unbelievably appalling and nauseating." The following October a group of Methodist ministers demanded that Mayor Fred A. Busse and Chief of Police George M. Shippy close the First Ward balls down once and for all. Calling them a "debauch, which reminds one of pagan Rome in her most degenerate days," the reformers joined forces with the *Chicago Daily Tribune*'s leadership, and in September 1908 the newspaper reported that it would assign men "with batteries of cameras to 'snap' business and other respectable men who lend encouragement" to the goings-on at the masquerade balls "by their presence." The *Tribune* promised to include the men's names alongside their photos in its pages.

Then at 8:20 PM on December 13, 1908, the night before the First Ward ball was to be held, an unidentified person threw a bomb into a building adjacent to the Coliseum. The explosion broke windows in nearby buildings and was heard for several blocks. A reporter interviewed Police Inspector Wheeler at the scene of the crime. He believed that one of the "reformers of a certain type" who "have turned Heaven and earth in their efforts to prevent the ball being held" had resorted to violence to stop it. He was pointing his finger at the anti-vice groups. Bathhouse John agreed. He declared, "It would be better for the preachers . . . to get men into the church in the same proportion as women. They would be in better business than attacking our dance." The police never caught the bomber, but Hinky Dink and Bathhouse John weren't deterred. They held their masquerade ball the next night as planned.

The following spring, Farwell's investigators discovered de Lang and Quinn's act, and he decided to focus on the female impersonators, who, he believed, would be a much easier target than the powerful aldermen had been. Farwell and his minions were still smarting over their defeat in the de Lang–Quinn case when police received two letters whose writers promised to ignite bombs at the next masquerade ball if it wasn't cancelled. Kenna was quick to try to deflect the extortion by asserting that "Chicago ain't no sissy town" and couldn't be bullied by intimidation, but he and Coughlin took the warning seriously. In order to safeguard the revelers, which had nothing to do with the aldermen's altruism and everything to do with their hope for large profits, they consented to a heavy policing of attendees, to allow police to arrest any known criminal who appeared, and to place restrictions on drinking, which included where the bars would be located and a strict closing time for them, but under no circumstances would the aldermen cancel the ball.

Also important is that Hinky Dink and Bathhouse John agreed to ban certain categories of people who had traditionally been welcomed at the ball. Prostitutes and playboys were among those who were barred, and the "female impersonator" also "received the critical ax." In fact, the police warned that "the first male who appears in dresses will occupy a patrol wagon all to himself for a swift ride to Harrison street," the nearest police headquarters. Female impersonators had been the highlight of past balls, but they kept clear of the 1909 festivities—or at least remained in men's clothes all night. Of course "normal" men had nothing to be concerned about.

Although a *Tribune* headline promised COUGHLIN YIELDS; ORGY CALLED OFF, nothing of the sort happened. The ban against female impersonators and others was a slight victory for reformers, but the First Ward masquerade balls resumed their typical format the following year without compromise or incident. Female impersonators and other queer men returned to the festivities in full force along with the other denizens of Chicago's underworld.

In 1911 the "superintendent of the Chicago department of the Anti-Saloon League of Illinois" attended the masquerade ball and sent a report about the goings-on that he witnessed there to the "clergymen of Chicago" and to the *Chicago Daily Tribune*. The *Tribune* ran an article on the ball in which it quoted this ambiguous sentence from the superintendent's report: "Two women and their male companions embraced each other and interchanged kisses." While the clergyman was probably appalled by the thought of two non-queer couples kissing in public, a taboo in the early days of the twentieth century, he may have actually witnessed two female impersonators kissing one another—and two "normal" men escorts—or pickups—doing the same thing.

7

A Sodomist Is One Who Enlarges the Circles of His Friends

> Though one might be teased for being a sissy, no one
> could believe that any person actually engaged in the
> "abominable sin." We lived under the shadow and
> cover of such naiveté.

NO DOUBT ABOUT IT, Edward Clasby was campy as hell. He "wore extravagant clothes and spoke in a high lisping voice" and loved to make lewd, risqué comments about sex—queer sex, non-queer sex, he didn't care which as long as he shocked whoever happened to be within earshot. That's what made him such a prominent fixture in Towertown. That's also what made his Seven Arts Club one of Chicago's most talked-about scenes. Clasby wasn't just a queer man. He was an obvious one—and he promoted his sexuality.

Clasby began the Seven Arts Club, a "roving lecture forum that took up temporary residence in a variety of 'alley garages and hotels'" throughout Towertown, in 1916. One of the more popular places where Clasby held court every Saturday and Sunday night was "the second floor of an old stable at the rear of a garden." The club's lectures often focused on literary topics. One investigated "Theodore Dreiser." Another argued, "Is Lewis' Elmer Gantry a Fair Picture of the American Preacher?" A third outlined "The Philosophy of James Joyce and His Ulysses." The club's highbrow events camouflaged its other, more popular activities, especially the drag shows that were held almost nightly and MCed by Clasby himself. Typical for him, he once loudly announced to the audience that Oscar Wilde "was a sodomist" and then, in case no one there knew what one was, defined it for them—"A sodomist is one who enlarges the circles of his friends"—to the loud guffaws of some and the beet-red faces of others.

Eventually Clasby decided to charge admission to anyone attending the lectures or drag shows and to serve food, "mostly sandwiches, salads, and coffee or tea." John Drury, one of Chicago's most highly respected restaurant reviewers, wrote about the Seven Arts Club in his book of restaurant reviews, *Dining in Chicago*. He claimed it had "a truly bohemian atmosphere," and true to the liberal ambiance of Towertown, the Seven Arts Club welcomed all comers, regardless of their sexual orientation. Nevertheless, because its speakers, performers, and audience members often acted and spoke outrageously, "only the most daring and knowledgeable heterosexuals frequented" it. Jack Ryan established a slightly less outré lecture series at his Phalanstery, a seafood restaurant at 915 Rush Street, also in Towertown, where he and his wife served sandwiches and coffee. Every weekend night, rain or shine, the bohemians showed up for intellectual pursuits, but as with the Seven Arts Club, intellectual concerns often gave way to sexual ones.

The Phalanstery and the Seven Arts Club quickly began to serve as "a point of entry to the homosexual underground" for many men. By attending their lectures or drag shows, a closeted or otherwise out-of-the-loop queer man could make contacts through whom he could learn which cafés, saloons, rooming houses, hotels, and other establishments would welcome him and which would not. In fact, plenty of the "owners of . . . rooming houses . . . on the Near North Side . . . rented almost exclusively to young gay men who worked as 'counter jumpers,'" a derogatory term for male salespeople, who because they held jobs usually associated with women were automatically considered sexual deviants whether they were queer or not. Occasionally, queer attendees might also find solace at the lectures, anything from a one-night stand to a boyfriend or lover, as well as friends.

Towertown, also called "the Quarter" and "the Village," extended from the Water Tower at Michigan Avenue, which had survived the Great Chicago Fire of 1871 without a scratch, westward for almost a mile, according to some, and was bounded by the wealthy Gold Coast to the east and what was called Little Italy to the west. Its main drags included Wabash Avenue and Ohio, Erie, Huron, Superior, Pearson, Chestnut and State Streets. Some of the bohemians lived as far west as LaSalle Street, or in fringy areas outside Towertown proper.

Historians often mark 1879 as the year in which Towertown began to attract Chicago's young politics-, arts-, and literature-focused bohemians. That year was the one in which "reading tournaments" began to be staged at McCormick Hall on North Clark Street. While the tournaments often highlighted Chicago poets, some of the most popular actors and elocutionists of the day, such as George Vanderhoff and James E. Murdock, were also invited to its stage. The next year Francis Fisher Browne revived the transcendental literary review the *Dial* at 815 Wabash Avenue, and in 1912 Harriet Monroe founded *Poetry* at 543 Wabash. Towertown became "the geographical center of what was perhaps the most vital literary and artistic upsurge in the history of the country"—the Chicago Renaissance—as well as a haven for queer men.

The editorial staffs of both journals, and some of their contributors, were closely allied with many of Chicago's other creative individuals who had offices and studios in other parts of the city but especially those headquartered in the Fine Arts Building at Michigan Avenue and Van Buren Street. These included artists Lorado Taft and J. C. Leyendecker and the cartoonist John McCutcheon, who had lampooned the First Ward balls in an editorial cartoon in 1908.

McCutcheon also sketched two men sitting on a streetcar, one with his arm around the other's shoulders, in a portrait of sorts titled *Laying Bare Their Private Lives*, the first time two masculine queer men were depicted being intimate—their arms around one another—in public. McCutcheon was George Ade's friend and had been mentored by William Herman Schmedtgen. He and Ade had not only roomed together for a number of years, but they collaborated on a series of newspaper articles that McCutcheon illustrated.

At the same time that both Taft and McCutcheon were making a name for themselves, Leyendecker quickly rose to become one of the most prominent—and popular—commercial artists in the country. Born in Germany in 1874, Joseph Christian "J. C." Leyendecker and his family immigrated to the United States and settled in Chicago in 1882. At fifteen he became an apprentice to the owner of an engraving and printing house in the Loop, where he designed posters and ads,

Fig. 7. *Chicago Tribune* cartoonist John T. McCutcheon (1870–1949) depicted an intimate moment between two men on a trolley in his drawing *Laying Bare Their Private Lives*. *Chicago History Museum, ICHi-062275, John T. McCutcheon, illustrator*

and enrolled in evening classes at the Art Institute. Leyendecker came to national attention in 1896 when he won first place in *Century Magazine*'s cover competition. That fall he and his brother Frank, also an artist, studied in Paris. They returned to Chicago two years later and opened a studio. Almost immediately, J. C. began working for major, national magazines, and in 1900 the brothers closed their Chicago business and moved to New York, where they opened a new studio.

Shortly after opening their atelier in Manhattan, Frank Leyendecker hired seventeen-year-old Charles O. Beach to model for the studio. Though both brothers were queer, it was J. C. who quickly became Beach's lover—and Beach became his favorite model. During their fifty-year relationship, Leyendecker designed and painted the magazine covers of most of the United States' most popular magazines, advertisements for the most influential companies that sold men's clothing, and war propaganda. More often than not, he used Beach as his model, often depicting him as a "near-naked male on a pedestal." Through Leyendecker's genius, Beach quickly became "the icon of American masculinity." Interestingly, Leyendecker often portrayed Beach multiple times in one design and occasionally as a woman or as a child, as in the poster he designed to advertise war bonds. On it Beach appears as both a Boy Scout *and* as Lady Liberty.

Fig. 8. J. C. Leyendecker (1874–1951), a very successful magazine illustrator, created covers for the most popular magazines, including the *Saturday Evening Post*, and designed ads for the most notable menswear companies. *Collection of Jim Elledge*

Sensible, quality clothes that fit and have real style —
commonsense smartness. Clothes for American men, whether they live in town or in the country.
The HOUSE *of* KUPPENHEIMER

Fig. 9. Charles Beach (1886–1952) modeled for menswear ads and magazine covers designed by his lover, J. C. Leyendecker. Here, as in many others, Leyendecker depicted Beach more than once. *Collection of Jim Elledge*

There were many reasons why Leyendecker, Taft, and other artists preferred having studios in the Fine Arts Building rather than in Towertown, not the least of which was the fact that many of the buildings of the North Side neighborhood were, in a word, dilapidated. Towertown's apartments, mostly studios, were so small and lacked so many of the basic accommodations that residents shared "kitchens and baths." Not only were the living quarters substandard, the "nearby teashops were similarly decrepit. In these establishments," as well as in cafés and restaurants in the neighborhood, "tablecloths were lacking, windowpanes were cracked, and 'candle wax dripped in lumps on the bare and dirty floors.'" Given its shoddiness, rent in Towertown was initially very cheap, which attracted bohemians, artists, and queer men alike.

Chicago sociologists Harvey Warren Zorbaugh and Walter Reckless became authorities on Towertown and its queer community. Zorbaugh observed that "distorted forms of sex behavior . . . find a harbor in the 'village.' Many homosexuals are among the frequenters of 'village' tearooms and studios." Reckless added that "the apartment area," with its "anonymous living conditions," allowed queer men a "secret habitat for vice." In short, many queer men were drawn to Towertown not only because of the inexpensive rent but also because they could develop whatever sort of life they wanted without anyone noticing or interfering with them. The large number of people crammed together there made it possible for individuals to be completely ignored by their neighbors and to live in virtual anonymity—unlike the small towns many had left behind, where one's personal business easily became everyone else's. In Towertown not a soul would notice anything a queer man happened to say or do, and those who did notice wouldn't bother to respond or interfere. Or they just might join in.

Queer novelist and tattoo artist Samuel Steward mentioned another aspect of the invisibility that society in general afforded queer men, understanding the complexity of the phenomenon:

> Midwest American views on homosexuality . . . were very quaint, and were based on the assumption that all people raised in civilized Christian countries knew better than to fall in love with, or bed, persons of the same sex. Knowing better, then, the [typical Chicagoan's] mind made two breathtaking leaps of illogic: people did not do such things,

and therefore such things must be nonexistent. This kind of thinking protected us all. . . . Though one might be teased for being a sissy, no one could believe that any person actually engaged in the "abominable sin." We lived under the shadow and cover of such naiveté.

As important was the fact that because of their free-love ideals, non-queer "bohemians willingly 'accepted'" queer men into the neighborhood whether they had artistic inclinations or not. In fact, as Ben Reitman observed,

> The homosexual group . . . flocked to bohemia, [to] go [to] the forums, the street meetings, the tearooms, and the hangouts. And whenever one goes to any kind of bohemian and radical meeting he is sure to find a number of homos. They are accepted in full fellowship. No one insults them by calling them queer or kids them for being sissies.

Reitman was also one of the first non-queer men to record that queer men had developed their own slang and a transgressive disregard for gender cues in language. He observed:

> In bohemia the homos can speak their own language. Two male homos will meet a radical and say, "You know this is my wife Ell," or "I brought Kitty along. She is looking for trade." I have said to a casual visitor to the Dill Pickle when introducing a group of male homos, "I want you to meet these boys, they are a couple of the best known Michigan Avenue 'bitches' in town," and everybody smiled.

By the end of the first decade of the twentieth century, female impersonators had become well enough known to the general newspaper reader that they appeared in several stories printed in Chicago's *Day Book*, a news-culture magazine aimed at the working class. These included "Joe the Bigamist" by George Munson in 1915 and Harold Carter's "The Impersonator" two years later. Newspapers even printed jokes about them. In "Such Is Life in Chicago," a Windy City

> female impersonator, who is at times a cut-up, sauntered into the small town general store.
> "Give me a pound of your best mixed candy," he said to the clerk.

As the clerk turned to execute the order, he added, in a falsetto
voice, "And a sack of flour."

"Well, don't be in a hurry," snapped the clerk, "I can't wait on
both of you at once."

Jack Jones established what many considered to be the single most important site for both queer and non-queer people in Towertown in 1915, the
Dill (sometimes Dil) Pickle Club. Attracting more politicos and poets than
the Seven Arts Club and the Phalanstery put together, the Dill Pickle Club's
dances, lectures, masquerades, debates, and plays were held in a barn at 18
Tooker Alley just off Dearborn Avenue. "On any night of the week, a mixed
crowd listened to the famous, infamous, or unknown debate the merits of current popular topics" in a "carnival atmosphere." Many of the Pickle's patrons
knew Havelock Ellis's *Sexual Inversion,* and one of its habitués mentioned the
book's popularity among its customers: "On galactic Summer nights, pale girls
with daring bobbed heads . . . and tortoise-shelled glasses discuss . . . Nietzsche
and Prudhomme [*sic*] and Havelock Ellis with boys whose eyes dreamed and
visioned."

At least one other book was instrumental in helping Chicagoans understand the queer men among them. Tennessee Mitchell, a young woman from
a small town in Michigan, moved to Chicago in the early 1890s. After several
short-lived and tumultuous romantic relationships with men she met not long
after she arrived, she befriended a group of young men in Towertown who,
she was later to learn, committed the "crime of Oscar Wilde" daily. Decades
later when she wrote her autobiography, she recalled them in a rather brief
but revealing passage:

> I soon found myself with a group of young men who were inter-
> ested in and intelligent about the arts, with whom I felt free to be
> friends with a sense of sureness that the element of sex would not
> be disrupting.
>
> It was a calm sea after a short but rough voyage [i.e., after the
> breakups] and I settled myself to quiet enjoyment. It was of short
> duration. I was told that my new friends were homosexuals. I had
> vaguely heard of the crime of Oscar Wilde and in my ignorance was
> only horrified and repelled and made no attempt to be intelligent.

She rejected her new friends, became a respected sculptor, and married Sherwood Anderson in 1916, three days after he divorced his first wife. Their marriage lasted two years.

In the last sentence of her autobiography, Mitchell revealed her regret over distancing herself from her young male friends: "Later I happened onto Edward Carpenter's *The Intermediate Sex*, which was of great assistance in helping me to sympathetically comprehend—understand and re-evaluate the experience." *Intermediate sex* was another term synonymous with *homosexual*. Years later Ben Reitman would validate Anderson's assertion that Carpenter's book was "largely responsible for the sympathetic attitude toward the homo" that many non-queer people were beginning to feel.

One evening in August 1920, Jack Ryan lay down his apron, told his wife to look after the Phalanstery's customers, and hurried off to the Dill Pickle to take part in a debate with lawyer William Seed on "the third sex," a label often used for queer men in the early decades of the twentieth century. The place was so packed that many in the audience had to stand. A few years later, Ben Reitman took part in a good natured, humorous debate also held at the Pickle. On one side of the question "Do Perverts Menace Society?" Frank Midney and R. H. Mencken argued that queer men were a threat, and on the other side, Reitman and John Loughman argued that they weren't. Reitman had already earned an "unconventional reputation as an anarchist, Emma Goldman's lover," and an advocate "of causes both illegal and unpopular," so the audience wasn't at all surprised about which side of the issue Reitman stood on. At the end of the debate, Bert Weber, the debate's MC, asked the audience to vote on whether the *yay*s or the *nay*s had won the argument, and Midney and Mencken "lost hands down." Not surprisingly, the Dill Pickle's customers had rallied behind homosexuality.

Towertown's resorts—its clubs, cabarets, saloons, lecture circuits, and cafés—that welcomed, and often catered to, queer men were following a long-established Chicago tradition, albeit one that had survived underground. As sexologist Havelock Ellis reported in his *Sexual Inversion*, Chicago's community of inverts had gathered for decades at a variety of establishments without being harassed, including "certain churches where inverts congregate; certain cafes well known for the inverted character of their patrons; certain streets where at night every fifth man is an invert."

By April 1917, when Uncle Sam threw his hat into the ring and joined his European allies in the Great War, the vice district known as the South Side Levee had been virtually shut down by the Chicago city government or by the Committee of Fifteen in yet another anti-vice campaign. Several military bases were within a few hours' train ride to Chicago, and the campaign left the doughboys, a nickname for World War I infantrymen, with few places where they could blow off steam. Their circumstances, such as their finances, social standing, and so on, usually kept them out of the specialty resorts, which had high cover charges, or the Chicago Athletic Club with its by-invitation-only membership code. But Towertown's highly publicized "debates on free love and its reputation for promiscuity, coupled with its unconventionality and anonymity," drew them by the hundreds.

Specialty resorts offered services or practices that other establishments didn't. Ye Black Cat, for example, began as a "semi-private club for the more affluent elements" within the queer community. For a steep price, its owners would find "sexual partners" for their "regular clientele." Eventually its glamour faded, its exclusiveness waned, and it became known throughout Chicago for its lackluster drag shows and the scores of the poverty-stricken and homeless who crowded its audiences. With the same exclusiveness that Ye Black Cat offered, Vincenc Noga established his Cold Coast House of Corrections, a prison-themed saloon, and a man known simply as "Big John" established his Coal Scuttle with a coal-mining motif. Both resorts tried to attract "affluent Chicagoans, queer and not, into a world far removed from urbanity" as sexual vacations.

It wasn't just the doughboys who were attracted to Towertown because of its reputation, but all sorts of civilians, many of whom weren't nearly as sophisticated as they thought they were. They often ended up being shocked by its depth of sexual unconventionality. A resident of Towertown recalled that he took a friend of his to an afternoon soiree where "men were smoking and talking in one end of the room, the women in the other. There was a good deal of taking one another's arms, sitting on the arms of another's chairs, and of throwing an arm about one another's shoulders. But he thought it was merely that the group were old friends." They left after a few hours.

The resident invited his friend to another soiree a month or so later hosted by the same person, but they stayed until after dark this time. Suddenly the friend noticed "men . . . fondling one another." One even propositioned him.

Shocked by the come-on, he told his friend, the Towertown resident, that he couldn't stay, and the two left. The Towertown resident was surprised by his friend's reaction. "Why, I thought you knew," he said, "the best-known fairies . . . in Chicago were there."

Most queer men would have felt lucky to have been invited to such a party. Attending one where dozens of queer men let down their hair would have been an easy, relatively risk-free way of entering Towertown's queer community, but getting an invitation was all but impossible for newcomers. Instead they were left on their own to discover which cafés, tearooms, cabarets, and saloons—among them the Wind Blew Inn, the Green Lantern, and the Blue Fish—were the best for meeting kindred spirits.

The Green Mask Inn, for example, was by far one of Towertown's most notorious hot spots because its ambiance "combined literary and political modernism with sexual and gender liberalism." Behind its walls, many of the neighborhood's most infamous personalities found a home—if not a stage—including

> "a hermaphrodite violinist"; "[the] great female impersonators Bert Savoy, Julian Eltinge . . . [and] Carole Normand, 'The Creole Fashion Plate,' known to her friends as 'The Queer Old Chafing Dish'"; "[a] little Mexican fairy known as Theda Bara, and her knife-toting pal, who weighed about four hundred pounds, the Slim Princess";

as well as "a very light, freckled-faced Negro . . . who claimed to be the illegitimate son of a British admiral and a Haitian princess." This faux aristocrat "had dyed red hair, ultraconservative clothes in the height of fashion, and wore an egg-shaped eyeglass without ribbon or rim."

According to one of Towertown's queer residents, the easiest of all the options that queer men had for meeting one another was in a saloon. "At a bar it is simple," he claimed. "You have a few drinks, look over the crowd, see someone you like and then buy him a drink. The most frequent contact is through liquor. I don't care for it and I never get drunk. . . . I don't need alcohol to get amorous desires but I like to get others elated by drinking."

By the end of the 1910s, "a group of male homosexuals who frequented the 'village'" had become well known in Towertown. Called the Blue Birds after their leader's nickname, they could be seen on "warm summer evenings" walking south "along the benches and the esplanade" of Oak Street Beach, following their leader, who drifted "toward the Drake" Hotel as other queer men watched and waited, hoping to be selected by the leader for his special attention that night. "From bench to bench," the onlookers would whisper, "'here comes the blue bird!' They would flirt with him as he passed by until he selected a partner for the night. Then the rest of them" on the benches "would pair off" with members of his entourage.

Other outdoor sites for sexual rendezvous dotted Towertown, and in many cases they were also places where female prostitutes strolled, trolling for johns. "Broads on the make roam the streets of the near north side," one observer noted. "Cruising behind them," he continued, "are the lily bearers seeking trade." *Trade* was a male prostitute who presented himself as non-queer, whether he actually was or not. After all, it was the he-man label that attracted many queer clients to him. However, the spot with perhaps the heaviest traffic of queer men hunting for sex partners was Bughouse Square.

By the end of the 1920s, large numbers of homosexual men could be seen at any given time, day or night, walking along Towertown's streets, eating in its restaurants, sipping tea, coffee, or something stronger in its cafés and saloons, or relaxing, painting, or partying through the windows of the studios and apartments they rented. The change from a mere eight years earlier, when the response to the Chicago Vice Commission's discovery of "whole groups and colonies of . . . men who are sex perverts" was a jaw-dropping disbelief, was striking. The sudden and visible influx of queer men into Towertown was not lost on its non-queer residents, some of whom resented their new neighbors' presence. "Everywhere I go," one male resident complained, "everybody is homosexual. I sit and paint on the ground floor and men stop and try to make dates with me. At the hospital where they had me under observation two of the doctors were homosexual. Married couples and everybody are having homosexual relations. The world is going crazy."

Not all of the non-queer men who lived in Towertown reacted with as much exasperation to the come-ons they received from queer men. Three years after the World's Fair closed, Sherwood Anderson, best known for his collection of stories, the ground-breaking *Winesburg, Ohio*, moved to Chicago and found a job working "on an unloading platform at [a] warehouse door" in Towertown. Occasionally effeminate queer men who lived in a house on the same street as the warehouse would drop by to flirt with Anderson and his coworkers. "The men who were so much like women," Anderson wrote in his memoir, had "painted cheeks and lips" and "giggled at" him and the other men. For a lark, some of the workers flirted back, calling out, "Ah, you Mable" and "Why, if that isn't Sweet Little Sugar." One of the men on the platform wasn't amused by the men who would be labeled *pansies* and threatened them. "If one of them made a pass at me," he declared, "I'd knock his goddamn block off."

One fall evening, after the sun had set and Anderson was working by himself, "one of them stopped . . . and whispered" to him:

> "Don't you want to come and see me some night?"
> I didn't answer, was a little shocked and even frightened.
> "I have had my eyes on you. You do not shout insults at us as the others do. You know where I live. Do come some night. There is so much I could teach you."
> He went off along the street, turning to throw a kiss at me, and I stood dumbly staring at him.

Anderson had grown up in a small town and had only a vague awareness of "sissies," men and boys who "were no good at baseball, or at the football," who "walked with mincing steps," who "often outdid us all in the classes," and who "spoke with soft feminine voices." He was taken aback by the queer men's obvious adoption of female gender codes and overt, public come-ons, and in response he asked himself, "What did it all mean?" Eventually he answered his own question: "I felt a strange unhealth within myself. I was not angry and am quite sure that, when this happened, I felt even a kind of pity. There was a kind of door opened, as though I looked down through the door into a kind of dark pit, a place of monstrous shapes a world of strange unhealth." Anderson began to wonder, "What makes men like that?" He even "went further. Perhaps I expressed a kind of fear of something in life I couldn't understand and the fear in me was pounced upon."

Anderson's struggle to make sense of his reaction to the flirtatious man climaxed in a remarkable moment of self-analysis with his wondering whether or not he too might not be like Mable or Sweet Little Sugar: "Why, I was myself, unconsciously, one of them. The thing was in me too and the fear I had expressed was a sure sign of its presence." He could easily have become homophobic, ranting against them, threatening to bash the man who had flirted with him the next time they crossed paths, but he didn't. Instead, while living at 735 Cass Street in Towertown, he wrote "Hands," a tender portrayal of a queer man and one of the most important short stories of the early twentieth century, because he realized he "could sympathize with them in their plight."

In the meantime the Lawson YMCA, on the southern border of Towertown and one of the least expensive places to rent a room, became known citywide as a hotbed of queer sexual activity, and one of its non-queer residents, Edwin A. Teeter, grumbled loudly about its "prick lickers," as he called queer men. One evening Teeter answered a knock on his door and one of them was standing there. Teeter invited him into his room, and no sooner had Teeter closed the door than the visitor began complimenting him. "What a fine physique you have," he said. "What wide shoulders." The man began unbuttoning Teeter's shirt and caressing his chest as he slipped his hand from Teeter's neck to his waist. That was when Teeter became suspicious. "Hold off," he said. "What are you trying to do?" The visitor replied, "Pardon me for being personal," and began unbuttoning Teeter's fly. "You red-haired bastard," Teeter yelled. "You stop that or I will beat you up." This time Teeter's visitor stopped.

Another evening at the same YMCA, a queer man was visiting his friend, whom he identified as "the queen type," or an effeminate queer man, when two other men arrived at the friend's room. One of the two announced that he and his companion, Bob, "were in love." The radio was playing, the men sat down, and the four began discussing whatever popped into their heads. Then some "very snappy dance tunes" came on the radio, the four began to dance, and before the visitor knew it, the couple "began to hug and kiss each other just as if it were a fellow and girl." It wasn't long before the couple's "emotions were greatly intensified" and "to such a degree that it seemed . . . they would like to put on a party for each other." *Party* was early twentieth-century queer slang for "having sex."

A reporter for the *Brevities*, which was published in New York, claimed the atmosphere of lawlessness in Towertown was notorious for its "marihuana, acrobatic sex, paranoia, and rampant licentiousness" and underscored by "drags for the third sex and sex circuses for the inhibited," all of which, he concluded, made "reality fantastic" for its residents and visitors. In fact, Towertown had become identified citywide with a motto: "Gin, din, and sin for a fin." *Fin* was slang for a five-dollar bill.

The inviting environment that the north-side neighborhood held for queer men caused a substantial migration of them into Towertown between the beginning of World War I and the end of the decade. As the demand for housing rose, landlords realized they could charge more for the tiny rooms and studios they owned. Some of Towertown's earliest resident artists couldn't afford the increasing cost of living there, and so Lorado Taft, Sherwood Anderson, Carl Sandburg, and others migrated to an enclave of small buildings near Fifty-Seventh Street and Stony Island that had been used by the Columbian Exhibition of 1892–1893 but then had been abandoned when the fair closed. An art and bohemian colony similar to Towertown in its politics and focus on the arts, it nevertheless lacked Towertown's bright lights and buzz.

Few reports about queer life in this small but vibrant community remain. However, in one report Ralph Berton described a party hosted by a queer man that he and jazz impresario Bix Beiderbecke attended in the spring of 1923. Berton's brother Eugene was queer and the host's friend, and he invited Berton and Beiderbecke to go to the party with him. It was "quite a scene," crowded with "girlish boys, smoking, sipping wine, wooing, necking, or just chatting." Some were former habitués of the Dill Pickle and Towertown art galleries and either "taught at or attended various art, music, and dance studios" there, but

Fig. 10. Sculptor Lorado Taft (1860–1936) moved out of Towertown into a less expensive neighborhood near the University of Chicago, one of the first of many artists, writers, and bohemians to do so. *Collection of Jim Elledge*

others were "Plain Janes—boys" who worked as "stockroom help or shipping clerks at Marshall Field's." Their "only common bond with the other guests was their homosexuality—a rather firm bond," according to Ralph Berton.

Jazz played in darkened, exotically decorated rooms:

> Candles in bottles heavily fraught with dripped wax like stalagmites on the floor of a cave, Turkish screens and hanging lamps, the air warm and close with perfumes and incense, a huge low studio couch taking up half the livingroom, covered with tie-dyed monk's cloth and varicolored cushions, the floor also strewn with large Oriental-looking cushions and low hassock.

The men danced with one another, "perhaps half" wearing wigs and female clothing.

Eugene Berton had begun a career in opera as a child prodigy and had become quite well known nationally, but he had given it up to compose songs for the more popular, and more financially lucrative, musicals. Several

Fig. 11. Eugene Berton (1903–1969) had a career in opera before he abandoned it for one writing music for Broadway and Hollywood productions. *Collection of Jim Elledge*

partygoers tried to get him to sing, but he refused, because he was afraid the cigarette smoke in the apartment would ruin his voice. "He zings like an anchel!" a young German who belonged to a group of "ballet boys" said, hoping to talk Eugene Berton into singing for them but without success.

Another group of men were huddled together, gossiping. A man "somewhat made up but not in drag" led the group, which was dishing another queer man, Harlow James. James had decided to marry a woman. The queer man described the bride-to-be as "some WAN little debutante from Oak Park," a Chicago suburb, "who has No idea of Harlow's PAST. But her mother has nearly two million dollars SALTED away in TRUST for her pet, so Harlow has learned to care." The point of their conversation was the fact that Harlow was marrying her for her money, and in case anyone in the group didn't know who the woman was, the group's leader identified her: Tweeny Simmons.

Then the group turned on her. She "isn't exactly a virgin herself, my dear. Except possibly between the left armpit and the right pinky," one man said to loud laughter. Another came back with "Our Harlow a fish queen! I shall take SLOW poison!" and that caused a new round of hilarity. *Fish queen* was slang for queer men who had sex with women. A third man told them that the mother had hired an investigator to follow Harlow around and had "SHELVES full of details to regale her with," to which "a slight, girlish chap who had just come up" said, "Ssssounds like the perfect marriage to me." The music, flirtations, and the gossip lasted long into the night.

Unfortunately the colony lasted only a short time once its principle artistic voices, such as Anderson, Sandburg, and even the Berton brothers, moved to New York, seeking the fame and fortune that eluded them in Chicago.

And yet despite the live-and-let-live vibe of Towertown, Chicago's city fathers viewed the goings-on there askance and, early on, gave the police carte blanche in dealing with what they considered out-of-the-ordinary resorts and the sexually nonconforming men who often patronized them. One evening while poets Eunice Tietjens, Harriet Monroe, Edgar Lee Masters, and Carl Sandburg were giving a reading of their poetry in the south Loop, the Dill Pickle was hosting a costume ball at 820 North Clark Street in Towertown. A reporter who was covering the event for the *Chicago Tribune* noticed a large number of "men in girls' costumes" among the dancers and eavesdropped as two policewomen, who had been stationed there to keep the peace, were discussing them. "My Lord—ain't that terrible!" Theresa Johnson said to Agnes Walsh, pointing to the men. Walsh replied, "Yeah—I'm goin' to stop it." She stepped in and threatened them with arrest: "If you don't beat it quick I'll call the wagon and give you some police station blues." The men left.

A short time later, George Lexington, a local poet, was giving a reading of his own work at the Green Mask, a cabaret, when the police barged in and hauled the audience of twelve women and twenty-three men off to jail because Lexington had been reading aloud what the police considered "indecent poetry." They booked the café's owner, Agnes "Bunny" Weiner, for being the "keeper of a disorderly house," a term often reserved for whore-house madams.

That was the last time police targeted the Green Mask and for a very good reason, as poet Kenneth Rexroth, who worked there as a young man, explained. The Green Mask was in an "English basement. Upstairs was a row of limestone-front houses which had been knocked together to form one immense brothel run by the Greek syndicate." Although the Green Mask's owners had nothing to do with the brothel, and no one from the brothel, including clients, ever came downstairs for a drink, the Greek Syndicate, which was considerably smaller than the Italian Mafioso, had paid the police to turn a blind eye to the goings-on there. The payoff also covered the Green Mask simply because it happened to be in the same building.

As "the bark of the sub-machine-gun" occasionally echoed across Chicago, the Italian mob began buying up some of Towertown's more lucrative resorts while also demanding protection money from the owners of less profitable establishments. At the same time, they were lining the pockets of at least some of Chicago's finest, guaranteeing that the boys in blue would walk their Towertown beats softly, their eyes turned neither left nor right but kept straight ahead, and would mind their own business.

Variety reported in late 1929 that, by its estimate, "some 35" queer joints, which the article called "pansy parlors," had opened in Towertown during the previous July. Within three years the pansy had become so visible and so numerous in Chicago that the *Chicago Hush*, a tabloid, could announce in a front-page headline, PANSY BLACKMAILING PLAN FAILS TO FRIGHTEN PROF without explaining what a pansy was.

Pansy, also *fairy*, was a label for a type of queer man whose mannerisms were overtly effeminate. While not dressing completely in female clothing as inverts and female impersonators did, the pansy nevertheless wore makeup—powder, rouge, lipstick—and often wore his hair longish and bleached it blond. He stood out in a cabaret, on the street, or in a shop. He suddenly began appearing on stage and screen and in novels and became an acceptable part of the big-city landscape. Historians would call this period of queer visibility the Pansy Craze, a period that would last for about fifteen years.

Gangsters weren't only interested in making money from joints that may or may not have been queer focused or queer friendly, however. Some visited the pansy parlors for entertainment. One was David Petillo, who initially belonged to New York's Genovese family. It was rumored that he had been a "*finocchio*, which was . . . a male prostitute—often underage—who worked at brothels" with a queer clientele in New York's Little Italy until the boss of the Genovese family sent the eighteen-year-old to Al Capone in Chicago for straightening out. Whether or not Capone succeeded is unknown.

What is known about Petillo is that while he may have given up selling his body to other men, files from the FBI's investigations of him state several times that it was known throughout gangland that he dressed in women's clothing when he was sent out to murder one of the mob's targets. As one FBI informant disclosed, Petillo "and [Charles] Gagliodoto," Petillo's partner in crime, "were two of the most feared members of the Italian syndicate" in Chicago, and the informant also claimed that Petillo "often dressed as a woman and Gagliodoto accompanied him as an escort. In this manner, they aroused no suspicion in contacting the victim."

Proof of the mob's infiltration of Towertown was everywhere. Even as the police occasionally crashed a poetry reading, they ignored many other, vastly more lewd establishments. Begun by a Professor Lant, the Pit probably had the worst reputation of any of Towertown's many sordid venues:

> Professor Lant, so dignified in title . . . runs a . . . flamboyant club. . . . Were it not already known as The Pit I would suggest, as the more descriptive name, The Inferno. Here, night after night, huddle the sexually distorted and perverted, the uncouth forms, the pathological misfits: that mélange of middle sex which nature started but never finished. Prepare for consummate disgust for, in such vile and loathsome spots the "stripper" is omnipresent and there are everywhere evidences of grossly radical sex practices.

Initially, all of the professor's strippers were female impersonators, but after a few years he added a few women to his stage. Ignored by the police, the professor kept "his all-out-sexy night club" open for years, hoping against hope "to make enough money to keep himself alive until he could drink himself to death."

Other establishments also welcomed queer men, including virtually every resort up and down North Clark Street, which separated Towertown from Little Sicily on the west. There were plenty of joints to choose from because it boasted "57 saloons, 36 restaurants, and 20 cabarets." While working as an investigator for the Juvenile Protective Association, Nels Anderson went to the Erie Cabaret, on the corner of Clark and Erie streets, which was famous for the "singing and dancing" of its "entertainers"—including female impersonator Frances Carrick, who would become one of Towertown's most famous residents in a few years.

Anderson asked one of the waiters if "any pros"—prostitutes—worked there. He meant *female* prostitutes, but the waiter was more worldly than Anderson, and he replied, "You can always make up to any of these singers," who were both female and male, "but they can't leave the place until we close." The Derby, another very popular resort at 680 North Clark Street, staged "a man, garbed as a woman and singing in a high soprano voice." Other village hot spots included Bert Kelley's Stables, the Paradise Club, and Chez Pierre. Each offered "an atmosphere of abandonment and unconventional experiences," including drag shows, and the Stables and Chez Pierre quickly became hangouts for wealthy queer men. All were well known to the police. None was raided.

While the freethinkers of Towertown were ranting against anything that seemed, to them, to impede their liberties, racism could raise its ugly head among them, and Chicago's queer white men could be just as hypocritical in their political posturing as their non-queer counterparts. One observer noted how a group of queer men in an unidentified café at 19 West Pearson Street in Towertown ogled a white man who had come into the café but rankled over a man of color who was also in their midst:

A group of "homos" from the South Side . . . came in. They drank tea and talked loudly of labor. One was a beautiful boy with red hair and a dead white skin. He was a blousemaker. Another was named "Alonzo." He claims to be a Spaniard, but the village suspects him of being an octoroon, and will have nothing to do with him.

At about the same time, Nels Anderson noted the possible beginning of an interracial tryst at the Grey Cottage: "A white male prostitute trying to pick up 'a fine-looking Negro.'" Anderson never mentioned if the prostitute was successful or not. Even as a backlash against sexual contact between the races was occasionally reported in Towertown, one doctor noted just the opposite. He observed how "at 'certain cafes patronized by both negroes and whites,'" several "negro perverts" were actively "soliciting white men."

But Towertown wasn't the only center for queer life in Chicago. While it offered cheap rent and attracted the Windy City's radicals, writers, artists, and queer men, another center had sprung up on Chicago's Near West Side. While Towertown was cultural, exciting, and full of possibility, the West Madison Street vice district couldn't have been more different.

8 | They're Regular He-Whores

Unusually well developed genitalia.

BEFORE NELS ANDERSON WORKED for the Juvenile Protective Association, he was a graduate student in sociology at the University of Chicago. At the same time that Clasby was running the Seven Arts Club in Towertown and scandalizing Chicago with his sense of humor and drag shows, Anderson was engaged in interviewing the hobos who had made the neighborhood along West Madison Street their headquarters, gathering information for his master's thesis. One of the hobos who came to his attention, known only as "Mother Jones," was attractive and dressed immaculately, and although he was more than fifty years old, claimed that he made his living as a male prostitute. He "used to be a tramp," he told Anderson, "and while on the road," he "was initiated to the practice" of prostitution and "saw in it a means of livelihood." Having found himself a profession, "he left the tramp class" and adopted Chicago as his home. He was also a braggart. Jones told Anderson, "I never saw a boy I couldn't get next to," by which he meant seduce, and admitted that he took "either the female or the male role" during sex, an amazing declaration at a time in which queer men seemed to lock onto either the passive or the active role in sex and not stray from it.

From the late 1800s through the early twentieth century, hobos—also known as *vagabonds* and *tramps*—were an all-too-common sight in Chicago. Wanderlust, as it came to be known, dazzled a considerable number of teenagers and young men who were tired of the restrictions parents had placed on them while they were living at home. "Inspired by dime novels and also the work of Jack London," as one historian has noted, they set out in search of adventure, walking to the nearest railroad tracks, where they would catch a freight train headed anywhere away from home and toward what they thought would be freedom. Despite the romantic notions of wanderlust, many adolescents and young men took to the road for far more realistic reasons, such as "home trouble" or "avoiding the law." More than a few were queer and had either been thrown out of their homes or were forced to escape from them because of it.

The Windy City had become *the* hub for railroads in the nineteenth century and, subsequently, became the "headquarters for thousands of homeless, itinerant workers." The largest percentage of them ended up along West Madison Street on the Near West Side, while others crowded the area surrounding State Street south of the Loop, around Clark Street north of the Chicago River, and in Grant Park behind the Field Museum. These areas—often referred to as *hobohemias*—were considered Chicago's "backwash of flotsam and jetsam," an "underworld" of "men of almost every known description: drunkards, gamblers, dope fiends, grafters, derelicts, criminals, panhandlers, jack rollers, sex perverts, paupers, con men, beggars," and all the other "butt-ends of humanity."

Anderson, who had been a tramp when he was seventeen, wrote that homosexuality was rampant among the "butt-ends of humanity." He identified "two types of perverts" among them. The first included those who had "feminine traits and tastes." These, Anderson believed, were "predisposed to homosexuality," a faint echo of Olmstead's belief that his homosexuality was "inborn." The second group included men "who have temporarily substituted homosexual for heterosexual behavior" because "boys are accessible" to them "while women are not," what is now often referred to as "situational homosexuality."

Anderson also met a hobo nicknamed "Shorty," whose real name was Tom Gray. Forty-eight years old, he had lived in the West Madison Street district for thirty-nine years, since about 1880. True to his nickname, Shorty wasn't quite five feet tall. Although he occasionally worked in the stockyards, he typically only worked sweeping the floor at the Barber College, which was actually a barber shop and not a school, on West Madison Street and at Jim's, a lunch counter, next door to it. He had once been married, owned a house, and fathered a child.

Like Mother Jones, Shorty often bragged about his ability to attract teenage boys whom he would take under his wing. They would exchange sex with him for whatever he might be able to give them in return, and he often got into fights with other men over them. Once, Anderson ran into Shorty in front of the Workingmen's Palace at 623 West Madison Street and noticed cuts and bruises on Shorty's face. Anderson asked him what had happened, and Shorty told him that he had gotten into a fight with a man who had tried to steal his "kid" from him. In hobo lingo a *kid*, also called a *lamb* or a *punk*, was the younger, passive partner in a male-male sexual relationship, while the older, active partner was called a *wolf* or *jocker*. Police took Shorty into custody, but the other man had escaped.

Anderson ran into Shorty again a few days later, and Shorty showed him the nicks and bruises on his fists. He told Anderson he had gotten into a fight with a man who had tried to rape a boy. A few days passed, and on the evening of June 10, 1920, a Saturday, Anderson noticed Shorty and an eighteen-year-old working in the Barber College until around eleven o'clock. They left together, speaking softly to one another as they strolled aimlessly around Madison Street. Puzzled by them, Anderson followed the two when they slipped into an alley, then ducked into a condemned building to have sex. Anderson respected their desire for privacy and left.

The next evening, at about nine o'clock, Anderson noticed Shorty sitting outside of the Barber College, looking depressed. Anderson gave him the few coins he happened to have in his pocket, and Shorty began to talk to him, complaining about how he had helped numerous teenagers with what little money he had only to have them abandon him when he needed their help or when they were approached by a man with more money in his pocket than Shorty had. He never mentioned that the "kids" had paid him back with their sexual favors.

While Shorty was complaining to Anderson, another hobo, Harry Moore, walked by with a teenager in tow and stopped for a few seconds to chat with Shorty. Moore was drunk, and after they left Shorty gave Anderson the low-down: Moore was a jocker who had a number of boys begging on the street and giving him what they earned. As Shorty gossiped, men and boys walked by, and Shorty told Anderson which were wolves and which were their lambs, unable to keep the disdain from his voice. Anderson was surprised by Shorty's hypocrisy.

After talking with Shorty for an hour on the corner, Anderson said he needed to get some sleep and lied to Shorty, saying that he had been sleeping outside in Grant Park near the Field Museum. Shorty said he would tag along. On their way they picked up some newspapers, and once they got near the museum, they arranged the papers on the ground, their beds for the night.

Not wanting to fall asleep yet, Shorty began talking, and he soon turned the topic to sex. He admitted that he was married, but he and his wife had been separated for nearly a decade. When he left her, she told him he would be back with her in short order, but he told her that "as long as there were any 'punks' on Madison Street he would be satisfied." He also confessed to Anderson that he would "rather go fifty-fifty with a fellow than to stay with the best woman in town." *Fifty-fifty* was hobo slang, referring to men taking turns at being the active then the passive partner in sex with another man.

Anderson wanted Shorty to feel safe enough to speak his mind, so he told him that he didn't care what Shorty's sexual interests were. As Anderson hoped, Shorty then relayed more of his life story. He had been caught in flagrante delicto twice and arrested. The first time he was with a teenager in Sherman Park, west of the University of Chicago, and the second time with a man in an alley. He also revealed he had been in a relationship with another man for two months, and they went fifty-fifty in their relationship. Shorty even spilled the beans about the eighteen-year-old he had led through the alley to the dilapidated building the night before. A short time after their tryst, the eighteen-year-old had spotted another man who had more money than Shorty and had dumped him on the spot.

When Anderson asked him if men got as much pleasure from being the passive partner in anal intercourse as from being the active one, Shorty assured Anderson that they did. When Anderson said he doubted that there were many queers on West Madison Street, Shorty declared "there were hundreds" and many of those were the "big guys in the city," referring to Chicago's upper crust, who were "doing it too. There's more people doing it than you think," he told Anderson. Then, as Olmstead had decided years earlier, Shorty assured Anderson that sex between men was "natural." His statement may have opened Anderson's eyes and prompted Anderson to conclude in his later report that some men were born queer.

By now Shorty thought Anderson might be interested in something more than conversation, and he turned to the graduate student and asked if he had ever slept with any of the boys on the street. Anderson admitted that some had proposition him, but he wasn't interested.

It didn't take Anderson long to realized that all of the sex talk might lead to Shorty's trying to seduce him, so he told the older man that they needed to get some shut-eye, but within moments Shorty blurted out that if Anderson wouldn't tell anyone, he could "take a crack" at him. Anderson replied that he wouldn't tell anyone about what Shorty had told him, but again he didn't find other men sexually attractive. Not to be deterred, Shorty countered, saying he could change Anderson's mind if he would give him a chance, and exasperated by Shorty's unwillingness to take no for an answer, Anderson repeated that he wasn't interested.

Shorty rolled over and pretended to doze off, but Anderson noticed that Shorty moved in his "sleep," getting closer and closer to Anderson. When Shorty got so close that he could feel him, Anderson moved away, but that didn't deter Shorty. He continued the routine until Anderson was lying on the grass.

Then Shorty, still pretending to be asleep, threw his arm over Anderson, who pretended to wake and push it away. Then Shorty slung one of his legs over Anderson's, and Anderson sat up. It had gotten cold, and Shorty used the chill to rationalize yet another come-on: "We'll freeze here if we don't hug up and keep warm." Anderson told him in no uncertain terms that he was having no part in it, and finally accepting Anderson's rebuff, Shorty suggested they go back to West Madison Street and sleep in the backroom of Jim's, where it would be much warmer. By the time they left the park and got to the lunch counter, it was two o'clock in the morning.

They decided to have a "coffee and," hobo slang for a cup of coffee and a donut. While they were eating, Shorty pointed to two young men in the restaurant and told Anderson that they were prostitutes. Shorty offered to let Anderson sleep in the back with him, but Anderson had had enough of fighting off Shorty for one night. He said he would find other arrangements and left.

Two weeks later, on June 26, a Saturday, Anderson happened to be back in Grant Park when he noticed a group of "men and boys" across the street from the "Blackstone Hotel." Among them was an older man who called himself "Fatima" after the female impersonator who danced at the 1892 Chicago World's Fair. This new Fatima was the focus of the group's attention. His voice, Anderson noted, was decidedly feminine although he occasionally cussed "in a really mannish fashion."

At one point Anderson heard Fatima claim, "I'm getting a little old, but when I shave up I still look fresh and girlish." A man who called himself "Fat" was in the company of a teenage boy called "Kitty," and while Fatima and Fat were talking, Kitty flirted with some of the men at another bench, which made Fat jealous.

Fatima had been out of town for the past two years, had just returned the previous Thursday, and was happy to see two of the young men in the group. They had been "punks in knickerbockers" the last time Fatima was in Chicago, and he addressed one of the young men as "Miss Smith." Fatima then turned abruptly to address the group and said loudly, "Any of you want a nice, virtuous old lady for the night?" He didn't get any takers.

Fatima and Miss Smith began to reminisce about the past, and during their gabfest, Anderson became confused because the men were using female pronouns and names usually associated with women for one another. He was beginning to understand what the investigator for the Chicago Vice Commission had discovered a decade earlier and what Ben Reitman was discovering in Towertown, that queer men often adopted female pronouns as well as names when they congregated.

Besides Shorty, Anderson ended up interviewing four hundred tramps for his master's thesis and discovered that 139 of them (or 35 percent) had taken to the road by the time they were twenty years old. Some of the tramps were as young as twelve. Many sociologists put the number of boy tramps in Chicago as a fourth of the total tramp population, while others believed it was closer to a third. Regardless, not all of them were hoboes per se. A number were actually from Chicago and had drifted to its seamy hobohemias for a variety of reasons. Some were "runaways" who thought they had found refuge in the hobohemias, but others were actually from "the neighborhood," working as newsboys hawking newspapers or as bootblacks, and as Anderson discovered, "cheap burlesque shows and movies . . . attract many" from other parts of Chicago. West Madison Street had plenty of such resorts.

While platonic friendships between older and younger tramps were common, many other relationships were based solely on sex and often were "predatory" in nature. "Coercing, cajoling, or enticing punks into sex," the wolf "offered in exchange protection, money, or general instruction in the skills of begging, freight hopping, and securing food and shelter" and "commonly approached punks on the road, in the jungles, in parks, or even on the streets." A *jungle* was a makeshift camp where groups of hobos lived.

Some of the boys and young men escaped from the wolves' grasp through luck or brawn. One known only as "James F." was traveling from Aurora, Illinois, to Chicago when he was befriended in Aurora's jungle by a tramp who gave him food. Together they hitched a ride on a freight train bound for the city. After fashioning a bed out of the straw that happened to be in the car in which they were traveling, they fell asleep, but James awoke when the man tried to rape him. The man's earlier kindness to him had just been a tactic for getting him in a vulnerable situation. James picked up "a club" to protect himself and "lay down" at the other end of the car for the rest of the night.

Chicago poet Carl Sandburg, struck with wanderlust in 1897 when he was nineteen, set out to ride the rails from his home in Galesburg, Illinois, to the West Coast, working odd jobs whenever he could find them. By June 30 he had made it to Keokuk, Iowa, where he met a man who was also riding the rails. The man offered Sandburg a "lump," a handout of food. Sandburg took the gift and gobbled it down. An hour or so later, the man, who "had a slick tongue and a fast way of talking," put his "hand on [Sandburg] in a way [he]

Fig. 12. Ben L. Reitman (1879–1942) earned his MD from Chicago's College of Physicians and Surgeons and became caregiver to society's outcasts, including queer men.
Collection of Jim Elledge

didn't like." Sandburg later recalled, "I could see he wanted to take care of me in a way I didn't care for," and he left the man as quickly as possible. Not all boys were as lucky as James F. and Sandburg. Ben Reitman explained several similar experiences of his own.

Reitman "was hardly twelve years old" when he found himself "bumming around the battery in New York City" and met up with a "sailor" who "took me home to sleep with him." Then about a year later while riding the rails cross-country, he ended up sleeping in a barn during a layover in Parkersburg, West Virginia. As it so happened, a "mob of crooks" were also spending the evening there. "That night," Reitman added, "when the mob tried to pass me from one to another and I protested, they picked me up by the nap [sic] of the neck and the seat of the pants and threw me out of the hay loft." Later that same year, Reitman was kidnapped by a hobo called Ohio Skip and "fell prey to the sexual will" of the older man. When several "rival jockers" decided to steal Reitman and another lamb from Ohio Skip, a fight broke out, and Reitman was able to escape during the ruckus.

Around the same time, a man identified only as "C.J." who temporarily "worked on a boat plying between Michigan ports and Chicago" talked a runaway from Lansing into traveling "with him to Chicago. He promised to help the boy get a job, etc." After they landed he broke his promise to the teenager and instead locked him in "a room on South State Street where he held him for three days and had improper relations with him." After he tired of the runaway, he "turned the boy over to another man for the same purpose."

While some hobos manipulated boys into sex only for their own sexual benefit, others built a business of it. "Robert P.," who had traveled to Chicago as part of a circus in 1921, remained in the Windy City after the circus moved on. He set up headquarters in Grant Park and began to pimp his stable of "thirty-six boys." Several of them had been coerced into prostitution by Robert P.'s "other boys," sources reported, and they "became reconciled" to their situation. In March 1922 Robert P. was arrested and sent to the Illinois State Penitentiary in Joliet "for twenty years."

Despite those and similar accounts, many affairs blossomed between men and between men and teenagers that weren't based on one person strong-arming the other. Adolescents and young men on the road or in the hobohemias agreed to sex with a man for many reasons. Not only did the older man offer the younger one protection, he took care of the young man or teenager financially while also satisfying him sexually. Sometimes these relationships were based on genuine feeling that had grown up between them, and while many lasted for only a week or so, the relationships were nevertheless "very intense" while they lasted.

Anderson was also struck by how the older man might use "endearing terms" toward the younger and how considerate he could be of the younger's "comfort." Like the female impersonators the Chicago Vice Commission's investigator discovered, the hobos often used female names to address their younger partners, who borrowed familial markers, such as "'Auntie' and 'Mother,'" for their older paramours.

Because they rarely had any work skills and had no contacts that might develop into jobs, younger hobos who were unable or unwilling to enter into an actual relationship with another hobo had to rely on "stealing, begging, and selling sex" in order to get by. Both theft and panhandling required a certain talent for success, so instead large numbers decided to take the easiest of the choices before them, as had Mother Jones. They began to charge for their sexual favors.

One eighteen-year-old from Dayton, Ohio, known only as "Boy Tramp," a nickname that Anderson gave him to hide his identity, was in the dark about queer men until he took to the road in the summer of 1920, the year he turned sixteen. He met a man who shared his food with him and who eventually talked Boy Tramp into letting him "hug and kiss him" as well as "masturbate him each evening" for nearly a week. Eventually disgusted by his sexual activity with the man, Boy Tramp left him, but after a month of being on his own, he began a relationship with another man. That liaison lasted "two nights," until, again disgusted, the boy swore off sex with men. This time he was able to go it alone for "a week or two," but a third man made "advances," and Boy Tramp "yielded to them."

Boy Tramp left Chicago and went back home to Dayton for the winter, but as soon as the weather turned warm, he set out on the road again and again found himself involved with older men and, after a short time, began to enjoy his sexual experiences with them, freely offering himself to their pleasure. Finally, comfortable with what we would call his sexual orientation, he decided to put his sexuality to good use and became a prostitute. Boy Tramp was "an intelligent, handsome lad of good build," but he was so self-conscious about his poverty that he felt he had to ply his trade in the hobohemias rather than "solicit along the lake front," a probable reference to Towertown, where the more well-to-do men sought male prostitutes and where he could have demanded more money for this sexual favors. "He said that he would" have preferred to work there, but only "if he had the clothes to enable him to appear in such circles."

Another boy who was sixteen, and whom Anderson called simply "Tramp," grew up in Chicago and wasn't a hobo at all. He had a home but had a troublesome family life and said that he visited the West Madison Street vice district specifically to sell his sexual favors to men willing to pay for them. Because he was good looking, he was a hit.

One evening Anderson noticed an argument that Tramp was having with a drunken, older man who had tried to pick him up on the corner of Desplaines and Madison. Tramp wasn't interested in the man, and because Tramp had rejected him, he began calling Tramp a "punk." Tramp was insulted by the word, which to him suggested powerlessness and even femininity. He called the man a "wolf," suggesting the older man couldn't attract boys on his own but had to manipulate them into servicing him.

A few moments later, Tramp began talking to another man who had been watching the argument. It didn't take Tramp long to seal the deal, and he and the second man left the corner and remained in the man's room "for about half an hour."

Anderson approached the drunken man, who, angered by being rejected by Tramp, told Anderson that the teenager had gotten so uppity that he would have sex with anyone for as little as half a dollar. Later another man, who had also been watching Tramp and the drunk and whom Anderson identified as "S.", exchanged a few words with Anderson about Tramp:

> "Take it from me, I keep clear of that kind of a punk. They're regular he-whores."
> "You mean he is a flirt?" I asked.
> "Well, that may sound better, but the name does not change the nature of the beast."

Anderson wasn't the only person interested in documenting the queer side of Chicago's hobohemias. On an early spring day in 1933, Myles Vollmer, a graduate student in divinity at the University of Chicago who happened to take a graduate course in sociology and was conducting research on homosexuality, noticed nineteen-year-old Bill Kirkland on a corner of South State Street, assumed he was a prostitute, and approached him. Vollmer asked Kirkland for a cigarette as a way to begin a conversation with the teenager. Kirkland was "boyish looking, with sensual lips," "slim," "blonde," and "curly haired" with "large brown eyes." Vollmer also recorded in his field notes that Kirkland had "unusually well developed genitalia."

Almost immediately Kirkland told Vollmer that he wanted to have sex with him, and it was perhaps then that the nineteen-year-old showed Vollmer his penis, trying to tempt the graduate student into buying his sexual favors. Vollmer told Kirkland that he wasn't interested in sex with him and all he wanted was to interview the teenager. Because Vollmer hadn't jumped at the chance to bed Kirkland, the younger man was suddenly afraid that Vollmer was an undercover vice cop trying to entrap him. He became very "hesitant," not wanting to talk, much less have sex, with Vollmer. When Vollmer swore that he was on the up-and-up and promised not to snitch to the police, the teenager began to talk freely.

When Kirkland was sixteen, he told Vollmer, he moved from his small, Midwestern town to St. Louis to work with his uncles who lived there. One night while he was walking home, a young man in a car pulled over and asked Kirkland for directions. The young man told Kirkland that he had a date with a girl who had a friend and he needed another guy to accompany his date's friend. He invited Kirkland to join them. While waiting for the girls at the young man's apartment, the young man turned the conversation to sex. One thing led to another, and the two fell into bed together. The girls didn't exist; they had simply been a ruse for the young man to pick up Kirkland. Kirkland left, although not without making a date with the young man for a few days later.

After a number of similar meetings, Kirkland moved in with the young man, and their relationship lasted about three months. During that time, the young man taught Kirkland how to sell his body to queer men. He was to go to a public toilet and show his penis to whoever else came in. This would break the ice. The young man also explained to Kirkland all of the various ways queer men could engage in sex. Although he had gotten himself a job and didn't *need* extra money, Kirkland began picking up men in downtown St. Louis during the lunch hour, and occasionally he charged for his sexual favors.

After Kirkland moved out of his friend's place, he began hitchhiking across the western half of the country. He often panhandled or found a temporary job, but he also gave himself to queer men when "he needed money," and besides, he said that he "enjoyed it." Despite his many sexual encounters with other men, Kirkland claimed he wasn't "queer. I don't do anything . . . but let them fool with me," he said, but then he admitted, "I did jerk them off sometimes."

Unlike Kirkland, eighteen-year-old Edward Stevens had lived in Chicago all his life. As with Kirkland, Vollmer noticed Stevens on a corner of State Street on the evening of May 6, 1933, a Saturday, and he believed the teenager might be a prostitute. Vollmer decided to approach him. Stevens was "slim" but "muscular" with a "dark complexion, weighing about 133 pounds and . . . 5 feet 7 inches tall." He was a boxer. Like Boy Tramp, Stevens was too poor to dress well and was embarrassed by it. He worked as a newsboy on State Street.

After sizing Vollmer up, Stevens told him he would let Vollmer fellate him, if he wanted, and suggested that they go to the public toilet of the nearby elevated train station or to an alley. When Vollmer told Stevens he simply wanted to interview the teenager, Stevens "declined to talk" to him, but after a few minutes, he agreed "to meet" Vollmer later that night and began walking toward Michigan Avenue. He didn't show up that evening, but the following Saturday night, Vollmer saw him on the same corner again. This time Vollmer promised Stevens "cigarettes, a haircut," and "a meal" for his story, and he agreed.

Stevens first learned about queer men when he was fifteen. He was sitting in a movie theater at the corner of Madison and Halsted Streets, the threshold of the West Madison Street vice district, when the man who was in the seat beside him began to touch him. Stevens pushed the man's hands away, but the man wouldn't stop. Stevens moved. The man followed him and offered him money to let him masturbate Stevens. The boy told him he didn't want to and hurried out of the theater. Then another newsboy told him he could "make some easy money"—at least "a buck or two"—if he would let men fellate him. The boy introduced him to a man named George who gave him two dollars for his sexual favors. Stevens swore to Vollmer that he "didn't do anything" in return, but he admitted he "liked the feeling."

A week later, at about one o'clock in the morning, Stevens was on State Street when a man who was about thirty years old picked him up and took him home. They mutually masturbated one another, and the older man paid Stevens $1.50. Stevens visited the man in his home every Tuesday night for two months, getting paid the same amount each time for the same activity.

Finally, he stopped seeing the man and swore off prostitution. That lasted for six months, until one night a man picked him up on Madison Street and paid Stevens $2.50 to let him perform fellatio on him. Stevens claimed, "I didn't like it, but I wanted the money."

Stevens was adamant with Vollmer, swearing to him that despite his sexual activities with other men, he wasn't interested in them sexually, wasn't queer at all, and sold his body to them only because they would pay for it. He told Vollmer he liked intercourse with women and said he would give up prostitution if he could "get a job." And yet Stevens admitted that he had performed fellatio on men, that he would "kiss" the men with whom he was having sex if they asked him to, and that he liked some of the queer men with whom he had sex "very much"—admissions that not only conflicted with his claim of strict heterosexuality but were at odds with the code that non-queer male prostitutes, or trade, followed. They never engaged in any activity considered effeminate. They would never kiss or show any affection to the queer men who picked them up, and they always took the penetrative role in both oral and anal sex.

During their conversation Stevens told Vollmer that at first he thought Vollmer was queer and on the make because he happened to be wearing a red tie. Stevens warned him not to wear the tie on State Street or in Bughouse Square, because he would be mistaken for queer. Stevens was teaching Vollmer about a signal the investigator for the Chicago Vice Commission had discovered more than two decades earlier.

Although Stevens told Vollmer that he didn't look queer, Stevens couldn't stop himself from flirting with Vollmer before the two separated. "Ya' know, I like you," he began, then said he would enjoy it if he could "pal around" with Vollmer, but because his clothes were shabby, he felt he would look and feel out of place beside Vollmer. He asked the graduate student if Vollmer could either buy him some new clothes or help him find a way to make some money. Stevens's message wasn't at all subtle. He would engage in sex with Vollmer if Vollmer would give Stevens a present or give him money. When Vollmer didn't respond but ignored the hint, the situation became uncomfortable for both of them. To lighten the situation up a little, Stevens cracked a joke. He quipped about how much he hated being interviewed by Vollmer because, after all, he didn't get anything, neither a gift nor cash, from just talking.

9 A Man Will Do When There Is Nothing Else in the World

I would like to have that bitch for myself. I would like to fuck him.

CHICAGO'S NORTH SIDE had glittery Towertown, with its cafés and specialty saloons full of bohemians with a live-and-let-live attitude. West Madison Street was Towertown's opposite: a shadowy district where the hopeless drifted, its despair infesting those already down on their luck. But on the South Side, a neighborhood sprung up that would put Chicago smack-dab in the heart of the new music then in vogue—jazz—and would give queer African American men a place to live, to work, and to be themselves. That enclave was called Bronzeville.

Beginning around 1912, Chicago drew thousands of African Americans from the South during a decades-long period now called the Great Migration. Looking for equality and employment, they found a home in Chicago's South Side. The area's entertainment district became known as Bronzeville, and its main thoroughfare, which was South State Street, became known simply as "the Stroll." Bronzeville quickly became bigger than a single street, and in fact it rapidly grew into a "'bright light' district," a strip of several blocks on both sides of State Street, "where cabarets and pool halls, vaudeville theaters, dance palaces, and chop suey parlors were the backdrop for fast-paced nightlife."

From Bronzeville's earliest days, queer men had been part and parcel of the neighborhood and found acceptance among its vast array of entertainers. One of its better-known queer musicians was George Hannah, who had a "high-pitched, feminine voice." He began appearing on Bronzeville's stages in the 1910s to wild applause and recorded his own compositions for both Vocalion and Paramount Records. Among his many recorded songs, a majority of which dealt with queer life, his "Freakish Man Blues" was one of his best known and most popular. In the popular argot, *freak* and *freakish* had long referred to queer men, and in the hit song, Hannah not only confessed to being a "freakish man" but he observed that men like him were "so common now, you" run across "one every day in the week." Although he had earned a place in the hearts of Bronzeville's cabaret-going public, Hannah never came close to the iconic popularity—a very real superstardom—that Tony Jackson was to achieve.

Born in 1882 and raised in New Orleans, Jackson learned the piano inside and out as a youngster. By the time he was fifteen, he was tickling the ivories in the Crescent City's vibrant honky-tonk scene that was centered in the bordellos of Storyville and developing the unique style that would become his calling card. In no time at all, he became "the outstanding favorite of New Orleans." Recalling his friend's talent, Jelly Roll Morton, himself a giant of barrelhouse and ragtime, once told a musicologist, "When Tony Jackson walked" into a joint, whoever was playing the piano would stop whatever he was playing and "get up from the piano stool. If he didn't, somebody was liable to say, 'Get up from that piano. Your [sic] hurting its feelings. Let Tony play.'" Morton also had important insight into why Jackson left New Orleans even though he had become one of its most popular musicians: "Tony happened to be one of those gentlemens that a lot of people call them lady or sissy . . . and that was the cause of him going to Chicago about 1906. He liked the freedom there." In fact, Morton also claimed that Jackson didn't actually leave New Orleans on his own accord but was run out of town because of his sexuality.

Jackson arrived in Bronzeville around 1905 or 1906—some say as late as 1912 or so—with a white pianist friend, Bob Cabell, who had also abandoned New Orleans for Chicago, perhaps for the same reason. Jackson moved into 4111 Wabash Avenue, his sister's place. She had moved to Bronzeville a few years earlier. One of Jackson's contemporaries described him as "dark-skinned and of slender build, about five feet ten in height. A distinctive mark was a tuft" of white hair "in the middle of his head. His eyes were protruding and heavy-lidded; a receding chin made a prominent feature of his mouth. The mouth could open, though, in a most expressive grin, and the long-fingered hands that swung loosely were made for the piano."

Fig. 13. Tony Jackson (standing, 1882–1921), superstar of ragtime, wrote "Pretty Baby" about a man he loved. The identity of the young man with him is unknown. *The William Russell Jazz Collection at the Historic New Orleans Collection, acquisition made possible by the Clarisse Claiborne Grima Fund, 92-48-L.242*

Jackson had no problems getting jobs in Bronzeville cabarets and was a hit everywhere he played, which included "the Dago, Russell's, Little Savoy, Monogram, Old Elite #1, and the Pekin Inn." While the other piano players who heard him ended up trying to copy his musical style, they failed miserably, and so wanting at least something of his greatness to rub off on them, they copied how he dressed. He typically wore "a pearl gray derby, checkered vest, ascot tie with a diamond stickpin, and sleeve garters that held up his sleeves as he played." One musician quipped, "If you can't play like Tony Jackson, at least you can look like him."

Besides playing piano, Jackson wrote scores of songs. "Pretty Baby" is the most famous of the lot. He wrote it about a "tall skinny young man" he loved, but when lyricist Gus Kahn included it near the end of the first act of the Broadway hit *The Passing Show of 1916* (which initially appeared at the Casino, where Eugen Sandow had made his American debut), it was apparent that Kahn had heterosexualized Jackson's original lyrics. Adding insult to injury, the song's publishers also underpaid Jackson for his work. The *Kansas City Sun* reported that Jackson had "only received $45" for "Pretty Baby." Although the song was a hit in Kahn's show and had made him "thousands of dollars," Jackson was left "pounding the piano every night" in juke joints "for a few dollars." A heavy drinker from an early age, Jackson died in 1921, only thirty-eight years old, too late to be a part of the Pansy Craze that was then just beginning to emerge across the country.

The year before Jackson died, one of the first published reports about the sudden visibility of openly queer men in public spaces in Bronzeville appeared in the *Chicago Whip*. The anonymous writer of the Nosey Sees All Knows All column noted that on Halloween night a week earlier, "he saw grown up men parading the highways in unspeakable costumes." *Unspeakable* was always a code word for *queer*, as in the phrase "the unspeakable crime against nature." In the same year, the *Whip* asked in a headline on its front page, HAVE WE A NEW SEX PROBLEM HERE? pointing to the increase in third-sexers in Bronzeville. Then a year later, the same columnist was shocked when he noticed "a man attired in a woman's dressing gown" in an apartment house near the Stroll. Queer men were becoming more visible than ever before, and regardless of the reporter's obvious disdain, Bronzeville generally accepted queer men, especially as entertainers, and would continue to do so for the next two decades. Nevertheless, some residents accepted them for other reasons.

Men who didn't think of themselves as queer nevertheless sought out those who did, such as female impersonators or pansies, for sex because so long as the non-queer men "were insertive rather than receptive" during any sexual act with another man and as long as they acted male, not female, in public situations, their "status" as non-queer would never be compromised. Many pansies and female impersonators were eager to engage in sex with Bronzeville's "normal" men.

One young man from Bronzeville, who identified as strictly non-queer, met a female impersonator who called herself "Co.Co." at a party. Later she performed oral sex on the young man, who explained that it was easy for him to have sex with another man because he knew that he was not "a real bitch," a label for an effeminate queer men. He declared that "a man will do when there is nothing else in the world, *preferably a she-man, because he is more womanly*" and being with a "she-man" was "something like" engaging in sex with an actual woman.

While Co.Co.'s sex partner preferred effeminate, cross-dressing men, his use of *preferably* suggests that he might engage in sex with a masculine man if a "she-man" weren't available. At the same time that men like Co.Co.'s sex partner enjoyed the sexual company of queer men, they might deride female impersonators or pansies when they noticed them on the street, as the columnist for the *Chicago Whip* had, without a hint of guile.

Another young man who called himself "Leo" was the opposite of Co.Co.'s sex partner. A nineteen-year-old who lived in Bronzeville, Leo was aware from an early age that some non-queer-appearing and -acting men found effeminate men attractive. He recalled that when he was in his midteens, some of the men in his neighborhood made snide comments about his being a "girlish looking boy," and that upset him. He also recalled that "there were quite a few pimps around Garfield Blvd. and Michigan," near where he lived, and he would hear them say to one another as he passed by, "'I would like to have that bitch for myself. I would like to fuck him.' They," he said, "would point at me."

Aware that he was effeminate, Leo wouldn't even dance with another effeminate man, much less share his bed with one. His point of view was simple. If a man presented himself publicly as manly, he should also be manly in private, and if a man acted womanly in public, he should continue to act like a woman in private. This was especially important for Leo when it came to sex. Only masculine men should take the active role in sex, feminine men should only take the passive roles, and the boundaries between the two must never be crossed. In fact Leo was so inflexible about sexual *do*s and *don't*s that a man with whom he was having a relationship ended up crossing this boundary and causing them to break up.

Leo said that the man was completely and utterly masculine, which is what had attracted him to the man in the first place. One night the man fellated Leo, and Leo decided the man wasn't masculine after all but feminine because he had performed a sex act that only effeminate men were supposed to engage in for the satisfaction of their masculine partners. Leo felt "deceived" and stopped seeing the man.

Unlike most of the cafés and cabarets in Towertown, Bronzeville's clubs welcomed all comers, black or white, queer or not, and because the races had the opportunity to mix, these establishments came to be known as *black and tans*. In one of her numerous reports for the Juvenile Protective Association, Jessie Binford noted that the Plantation Café, which didn't cater specifically to queer men as other Bronzeville and Towertown establishments did, nevertheless allowed men to dance together. In many ways the Plantation Café was a typical cabaret for the time, and a description of some of the goings-on behind its walls appeared in *Variety* in the mid-1920s, at the height of the café's popularity.

Written for *slummers*, a word in vogue at the time for middle-class queer and non-queer whites who visited Bronzeville for the varied entertainment that its resorts offered, the article begins with a note not only about the mixing of the races but also the acceptance of queer men: "The black and tan . . . is . . . paradise. Here" female impersonators "may parade their clothes, mingle with the white element that doesn't seem to care, and rub elbows companionably with daring youngsters and portly commercial men who loudly explain that they are there slumming." *Slumming* disguised their real intent: to ferret out places where queer men congregated and to which they could return on their own later. The black and tans weren't the only venues available for the sex hunt either. Many men found sexual partners at the South Side's many masquerade balls.

The first masquerade balls held specifically for queer female impersonators appeared in Chicago in the late 1800s, perhaps even earlier, organized "by the 'fruits' and the 'cabmen.'" They were advertised by placards across the city. In 1899 L. O. Curon published his diatribe against various forms of social evil titled *Chicago, Satan's Sanctum*, and in it he described a typical masquerade ball: "At these disreputable gatherings, the pervert of the male persuasion displays his habits by aping everything feminine. In speech, walk, dress, and adornment they are to all appearances women." He was sure that the men in drag were so good at their masquerade that "the uninformed observer" would probably not realize "what a seething mass of human corruption he is witnessing."

Halloween had traditionally been a night for costumes across the United States, and female impersonators took advantage of the tradition, protecting themselves from the law forbidding them to appear dressed as women in public by adding their drag to the mix of ghost and witch costumes. Bathhouse John and Hinky Dink's masked balls offered them another venue. Since 1896 the First Ward balls, held on or near December 31, had welcomed anyone from the underground, including queer men, regardless of whether they arrived in or out of drag.

Queer men simply scheduled their balls two months earlier than the First Ward balls, and initially promoters of Bronzeville's first masquerades held them in small venues. As they grew in popularity, with Chicagoans from all over the city attending, organizers needed larger spaces. One favorite spot was the Coliseum Annex, a large auditorium adjacent to the Coliseum proper just south of the Loop. The Coliseum was also Hinky Dink and Bathhouse John's favorite venue.

The North Shore Men's Club, an organization that, despite its name, was headquartered in the South Side's Bronzeville, sponsored its first masked ball in 1911. The following year the group held a second ball, offering a prize of "a silver cigarette case" awarded to "the best female impersonator." Four years later, in 1916, the club scheduled another ball, again with a prize for the best drag. This time, however, its promoters invited whole families to the festivities: "Come, bring your children to see the funny sights." Because all of the attendees were expected to wear masks, which were being sold onsite for a dime each, "funny sights" may not have referred only to the female impersonators but to everyone in costume.

Neither the female impersonators who flocked to the masquerade balls in droves nor the pansies who crowded Bronzeville's cabarets went unnoticed by the newspapers. While on one level some Chicagoans balked at the growing number of visible queer men on the city's streets and in its resorts, other citizens enjoyed the spectacle of glamour and the evidence of a third sex, neither exactly male nor female but a witches' brew of both. Surveying the Chicago scene, *Variety* declared that the "world's toughest town, Chicago, is going pansy. And liking it."

10 | Hell, I Wish They'd Give Me a Safety Razor and a Shot of Gin

A lot of prominent guys right in this city will die when they hear about me being a man.

NO SOONER HAD THE JUDGE banged his gavel to signal the end of the trial than Frances Carrick knew what her next move would be. She would spin straw—and pretty dirty straw it had become too—into gold. Her trial for murder had gotten an extraordinary amount of coverage in Chicago's newspapers and even across the country, which, as far as she was concerned, was just free publicity and nothing to be ashamed of. She was riding high now, popular *and* acquitted. She had gotten an offer to appear at the Rialto Theater, and she was developing a new act. She would take her story to the stage, add some songs and dance steps from the old days, maybe a few off-color jokes, and become a legend in her own time—and a very rich woman to boot.

Frances Carrick hadn't always been known as Frances Carrick. Her identities were a tangle of male and female names, with clothing to match. In the days when she ran a whorehouse at 43 North Dearborn Street, she was also Nanny White, and when she ran another one at the corner of Erie and LaSalle Streets in Towertown, she answered to Fay Holmes. Before then she was Frances Williams, fiancée of Frank Carrick, and before that, May Belmont, vaudeville singer-dancer and the prettier member of the team of Belmont and Brennan, the toast of the town. Before her vaudeville career, she was Harry Thompson, and on the day he was born, Harry had been named Fred G. Thompson.

Frances Carrick could have been so many more names and identities, female *and* male. Which one she decided to use at any given time depended on which served her best at that moment.

She always obscured her beginnings and early life, so she typically told anyone who asked that she had been born in Columbus, Ohio, in 1888 and was immediately adopted by a farm family, the Thompsons, who lived near Youngstown. She claimed that the man and woman who adopted her loved their sons dearly but had always wanted a girl. To make their dream come true, they dressed their adopted boy in frills, and that's how Frances spent her entire childhood, decked out in ribbons and lace, answering to a girl's name, although she never told a soul what that was, and playing with dollies. Her adopted parents had gotten her so used to cross-dressing that it became natural for her and something she continued to do off and on.

She decided to run away from home in 1901, her tale would continue, although she never offered a reason why, and ended up in Columbus, where she called herself Harry Thompson and became a bellboy in a hotel. Within a year Harry had saved up enough money to move to Chicago. Asked what he had done to survive in the Windy City, he would reply, "I'd hate to tell you," and added that he would spend "a week . . . in a boy's suit alternated with months of living in girl's skirts" making a living as a prostitute. Harry quickly grew tired of getting arrested on morals charges and fled Chicago.

Frances would leave the next few years a blank, and suddenly she was living in Syracuse, New York. She had created another identity for herself, one that included a whole new career: vaudeville entertainer May Belmont. As Belmont she became a respected singer, received five-star reviews, and toured across the eastern half of the United States. And that's where Frances's story usually ended, with her admission that she was once May Belmont. "The rest," she might say if pressed, "is history." Then she would giggle and bat her eyes. What really happened to Frances Carrick, female impersonator par excellence, is a somewhat different story.

The census report for 1900 reveals that Frances Carrick was actually born Fredrick George Thompson in Columbus, Ohio, in 1890, the oldest child of Milton C. and Flora Thompson. Milton was a butcher, and much of the time when Fred and his sister (Nellie) and two brothers (Milton and Harry) were growing up, they lived at 307 Cherry Street and never outside of Columbus's city limits. Frederick went to school like other boys his age, and there's no hint that he ever dressed in girls' clothing, although perhaps he did in private. At some point, perhaps during his adolescence, he discovered he had a talent for singing. The 1910 census reveals that the twenty-year-old had an occupation: "singer." The following year Frederick and his parents moved to 720 Parson Avenue in Columbus, and in the city directories for both 1912 and 1913, he continued to claim "singer" as his occupation but changed his name ever so slightly to G. Fredrick Thompson. Using an initial as the beginning added a touch of class to an otherwise ho-hum name. Then for the next decade, Fredrick G. Thompson—or G. Fredrick Thompson—vanished from all public records.

At least a decade before Thompson began claiming to be a singer on various public documents, a performer named May Belmont had been popular on the minstrel stage, and she had been receiving good notices in the newspapers since 1895, when Thompson was only five years old. She sang, she danced, she told jokes, she acted in comedy sketches. She performed with "well built athletes" named Grant and LaVelle, who were called the "Herculean marvels" and were, like Eugen Sandow, "models in classical and muscular posing." Later she teamed up with George Brennan, becoming a song-and-dance duo. Nevertheless, her real success came as a solo performer, and by 1910 she was something of a star in her own right, performing with several different troupes, principally the Frolicsome Lambs and the Tiger Lilies.

A second performer named May Belmont appeared in the 1910 census for Syracuse, New York, living in a boardinghouse at 257 North Salina Street run by Thomas Abbott and his wife, Della. The census gives this second May Belmont's age as twenty-three and adds that she made her living acting in concert-hall productions. Considerably younger than the first May Belmont would have been in 1910, the second May Belmont and Fredrick Thompson were both born in Ohio. Then during the summer of 1913, at the height of her stardom and while performing in Syracuse at the Palace Theater, Syracuse newspapers chronicled a scandal involving the second May Belmont.

One newspaper reported that she had been detained by the police because a "theater patron" had discovered a secret about her. The man claimed that Belmont was really a man without giving any details about how he happened to unmask her, and because specifics were missing, the article suggested all sorts of unprintable goings-on between the two. Another newspaper offered a slightly more particularized story.

Belmont was staying in a rooming house attached to and run by the Palace for its performers, the second article maintained, and a "Peeping Tom" had watched her undressing and discovered her secret on the night of Saturday, June 7. He turned her in to the police the next morning. Although more detailed, the second explanation is fishy. Like cross-dressing in public, voyeurism was also a crime, and the man who turned her in could have been arrested and fined at the same time that he was pointing his finger at Belmont.

It's more likely that the man who turned her in was a pickup or even a client who had paid for her sexual services, and having paid for and anticipated a woman's affections only to discover Belmont could only offer a man's, he was angry over being fooled. He may have turned her in to the authorities to get revenge. Regardless of how it happened, the only thing that is certain about the incident is that Belmont came to the police's attention.

The officer on duty sent Detective John Donovan to her room around noon that Sunday. He woke her—she was still in bed—and led her to jail, where she spent the rest of the day and into the early part of the evening in the room reserved for the police matron. While interrogated, Belmont confessed she was actually Harry Thompson.

Of course, the person beneath the makeup was not Harry Thompson at all but Fredrick Thompson. He had abandoned his real name and had confiscated his younger brother's. When and how Fred Thompson stepped into May Belmont's shoes is a complete mystery, as is where the first May Belmont went when she disappeared. It's probable that Thompson used his parents' home as his permanent address from at least 1910 to 1913 while he toured, singing as "May Belmont." Whether or not they knew of his cross-dressing vaudeville occupation is unknown. Regardless, the Syracuse police put Harry Thompson under arrest for impersonating a woman.

Later, during the evening of her arrest, a journalist from the *Syracuse Herald* interviewed Belmont. The reporter was amused by the story he was covering and milked it for as much humor as he could get by playing with gender-specific names. Should he call her "May or Harry" he mused in his piece, or "how would Mary do for a compromise?"

Then he began asking questions that he hoped would be just as entertaining to his readers. One was especially pointed. Had she ever planned to marry, he asked, and if she did would it be to "a woman or a man?" Belmont was coy. Perhaps she would, perhaps not. She hadn't really "decided." Without skipping a beat, the reporter said, "Which?" Would she marry or not? Would she marry a man or a woman? She didn't bother responding, or if she did, he didn't bother to record her answer.

There was no reason for the interviewer to think that Belmont might already be married, and she didn't bother to volunteer any information about herself. Nevertheless, the year before, on May 23, 1912, she adopted the name Frances Williams and legally married Frank Carrick in Crown Point, Indiana, appearing at the ceremony in full drag. The justice of the peace who married them didn't have a clue that she was really a he, just as no one in Syracuse knew the truth. Not, that is, until the Peeping Tom snitched on her.

Coy and flirtatious, Belmont cooed and batted her eyes at the reporter. The only question he asked that she answered truthfully was about how she kept so clean-shaven. She had discovered an "eradicator," she said, that kept her face beardless for a full day before her five o'clock shadow began to appear. The hair-removal lotion was one of the reasons why she was so credible as a woman. Despite her confession that she was a man, the authorities were still befuddled over which sex Belmont belonged to because she was so convincing as a woman, and to set the record straight once and for all, they had her physically examined later the evening of her arrest.

Belmont resisted the examination "so strenuously that four or five large men were detailed to assist the matron," who was given the task of looking at Belmont's genitals. Afterward the matron stepped back from Belmont, letting the female impersonator's skirts fall back into place, and announced that "the caged songbird was indeed masculine." The police charged Belmont with "masquerading in public" and put her into a cell. Once behind bars Belmont confessed that this wasn't the first time she had been arrested for her masquerade. She had been detained at least five times by the authorities, and although she was "searched by police matrons" each time, not once was she suspected of being male.

The next day, a Monday, Belmont was scheduled to be arraigned before Judge Shove shortly after noon. Her story had drawn the attention of Syracuse's flappers and sheiks, and they crowded the courtroom. But there was a long string of other cases that Shove had to get through before coming to Belmont's, and by late afternoon, he called for a recess. Tired of waiting for Belmont to appear, the flappers and sheiks left the courtroom.

Later that day she appeared in court, accompanied by her attorney Frank L. Woods, and her presence drew "a murmur of attention" from the spectators, which "rippled" through "the great hall." Making fun of the situation, one reporter quipped, "They made a striking pair. Both have prominent under jaws. Mr. Woods's was clean shaven. May hid . . . her mustache under a lace-edged handkerchief."

The *Syracuse Herald* sent the editor of its women's page to court for no other reason than to report, woman to woman, Belmont's uncanny ability to imitate women to perfection. Belmont was dressed in the latest fashion, including a hat with "ostrich feathers and a . . . willow plume" and a huge "diamond ring." Taking a different approach, one male reporter, who responded to the female impersonator's sexual allure, marveled over how womanly she was. "Her architecture," he wrote, "is most imposing, especially the fo'c'sle."

Judge Shove released her on her own recognizance and adjourned the case until ten o'clock the following Wednesday morning. He fixed Belmont's bail at one hundred dollars, which she paid with the help of a bond company. Wednesday morning came and went without Belmont. By noon it was apparent to Judge Shove that she had skipped bail, and the loan brokers Cohn & Fallett, who had provided her bail, forfeited their money to the court. Belmont had disappeared without a trace, but she remained in the minds of those who had read her story in newspapers.

During the next few weeks, the post office at Syracuse was inundated with letters from "beauty doctors, and from individuals" across the country who wanted to know how to contact Miss Belmont. While almost everyone claimed to be interested in the story of the man who dressed as a woman, who was an acclaimed stage performer as one, and who had been crossing-dressing for years, what they really wanted to know about most was her secret for removing her beard. Her smooth, whiskerless face had captured their imagination. During her interrogation, all she ever admitted was that "she had discovered an acid which would permanently remove 'her' whiskers," but she had never identified which acid it was, how to prepare it, how to apply it, or how long to leave it on. When Belmont disappeared she took her secret with her.

After she left Syracuse, May Belmont's career was over, but Harry Thompson was not about to let that get in his way. Shortly after Belmont's arrest in Syracuse, Thompson emerged in Chicago under new identities. He was known to the police as Nanny White and as Fay Holmes, madams of small-league whorehouses. Whether masquerading as White or Holmes, she was perfectly willing to entertain her male clients if none of her girls were available—or if a particular client happened to catch her eye. But her grocer and her neighbors knew her as Frances Carrick—Frank Carrick's missus.

It's unclear if Frank Carrick was with Frances in Syracuse or not, and how they met is unknown, but several facts about Frank are known. Chicago was his hometown. According to public records, he had lived there for most, if not all, of his life. By 1913 he hadn't held a job for years and depended on Frances's businesses for their livelihood. Last, he was addicted to heroin.

Although making a substantial living as a whorehouse madam, Frances longed to return to the stage and the limelight of the successful entertainer. She began singing in Towertown cabarets—at the Erie Cabaret, where sociologist Nels Anderson had been told he could have his pick of the female or male entertainers, as well as at the Athenia Inn and McGovern's Saloon. McGovern's was a well-known mob hangout where North Side crime boss Dion O'Banion began working as a singing waiter when he was sixteen. Frances also performed at two amusement parks: Riverview, where Quincy de Lang and George Quinn had been arrested because of their striptease act, and Forest Park.

Although Frances never received the acclaim on Chicago stages that May Belmont had in Syracuse, she would have resigned herself to her very local, very low-key celebrity had wealthy insurance adjuster Richard Tesmer not been shot by a woman, one of a pair of robbers, as he and his wife were putting their Durant away at eleven o'clock the night of June 5, 1923. Their garage was behind their building at 5835 Winthrop Avenue, and Tesmer fell out of the car and onto the ground, dying from his wound in the ally's grime.

Mrs. Tesmer claimed to have seen the woman's face clearly in the nano-second of light given off by the pistol blast. She described a gun-wielding, twenty-something-year-old woman who had blue eyes and light hair and who was wearing a brown dress and a floppy hat. The murderer smiled "an evil, leering, satanic grin" at Mr. Tesmer as she pulled the trigger.

Mrs. Tesmer never noticed the face of the woman's male accomplice.

During the next two weeks, police rounded up eight women, most of whom already had police records or were somehow tied to the underworld, hopeful that Mrs. Tesmer would identify one as the murderer. She did better than that. She pointed her finger at each of the suspects, one after the other, and claimed that each had murdered her husband. The first four were Gertrude Getson, who was on parole for theft; Anna Senback; Marge Bennett; and the wife of gangster Earl Dear. All four had alibis, and each was immediately released.

Then police took Bertha Schillo; manicurist Peggy Le Beaux; an unnamed actress who was reputed to have been a drug addict; Corinne Gillispie Lafferty, wife of a man serving time in Joliet; and eighteen-year-old Margaret Ryan into custody one after another. They too were paraded in front of Mrs. Tesmer, who swore—four more times—that each had shot her husband dead. All four of the second set of suspects had airtight alibis too, and the police released them as well. On the night of June 14, authorities questioned a man "whose name police would not disclose" but who had "been masquerading as a woman the night Tesmer was killed," but the police didn't take him to Mrs. Tesmer's to have her identify him. They checked his alibi first, and when it panned out, they released him, as they had all the women.

Finally, nearly a week later, police received a tip over the telephone and raided Frances and Frank Carrick's apartment very early on the morning of June 19, waking everyone in the apartment. Frances put up a fight, "kicking, screaming oaths, and shouting boasts" until the police were able to order her out of the kimono she was wearing and "bundled" her "into a blue frock and green hat" for the ride to Mrs. Tesmer's home. The police were sure the widow would identify their new suspect as the murderer, just as she had all the other suspects they had paraded in front of her.

At the Tesmer residence, police posed Frances with a pistol in her hand and told her to smile at the widow. Frances thought they were crazy, but she did what she was told. The widow fell into a near swoon and shouted, "My God! That is the girl who murdered my husband. I can never forget those eyes and that smile. There is no doubt of it. I'll never forget the look on her face. Lock her up. She can't lie out of this." Frances was the last of the "women" the widow identified as the murderer—the tenth suspect. The police arrested not only her but also the other three persons who had been in the Carricks' apartment: Frances's husband, Frank; a woman named Marie who was their lodger; and Anthony Kushar, whose relationship to the others was unclear at the time.

When the police finally got their haul to the Hyde Park police station for processing, they found themselves in a quandary. Frances's five-o'clock shadow was beginning to peek through her makeup, exactly as May Belmont's had while detained by the Syracuse police station a decade earlier, and they couldn't decide whether to lock her up with the men or the women. They called in two doctors, Clara Seippel of the Morals Court and the city physician, David J. Jones, to examine their prisoner. Afterward the doctors told the police that they had no doubt about it. Frances was a man.

Since the night of his death, the press had followed Tesmer's murder closely because of his wealth and social standing. Now that the police had someone in custody whose peculiarities drew the readers' attention, reporters began dropping by Frances's cell as often as possible. Articles in which reporters described her outfits or quoted her thoughts on whatever popped into her head began to appear daily.

Frances had a tough time dealing with the boredom while she was behind bars, but she figured out a few ways to liven things up. For starters she became quite vocal, and she even "discussed the possibility of writing a book" with the reporters. They ate it up, especially when she hinted about the secret lives of some of Chicago's upper crust. "A lot of prominent guys right in this city will die when they hear about me being a man," she told them without bothering to hide her glee.

She loved to strike poses for the photographers too, and they tended to shift from the defiant, with cigarette in hand, jaw set, eyes intense, to the coy, with her eyelids lowered and the hint of a smile on her lips. One of the more interesting ones showed her standing in front of a stove holding a coffee pot with her jailer William P. Neesen standing beside her. It appears she had just brewed him a cup of coffee. Another was a close-up of her holding a safety razor against her cheek. The photo was captioned "The Shaving Grace." As a last-ditch attempt to ward off boredom, Frances even volunteered to help the authorities find Richard Tesmer's murderer by taking them through the city's opium dens, where she was sure the woman would be, but the police didn't take her up on the offer. Even in the courtroom while the lawyers selected the jury, Frances was so bored that she "winked coquettishly at the men" to give herself something to do, but she "ignored the women."

Reporters even tried to explain Frances's sexuality to their readers. They claimed she had a "duplex psychology," a phrase suggesting another one that was common in the medical literature of the time, "psychic hermaphrodites." Initially she was allowed to wear women's clothing in her cell and even during her first few hearings, but when she was transferred from the police lockup to the county jail to await trial, the warden demanded that she dress in male clothing.

From the beginning Frances was confident that the police wouldn't be able to pin the murder on her, and the first night she was under arrest, she promised reporters from her jail cell, "I'm gonna fight." Then she "smoothed 'her' henna bob, deepened the mascarole under 'her' gimlet eyes of blue-grey, and traced a crimson cupid's bow about 'her' wide-spread mouth." As the reporters quickly scribbled their impressions of her down in their notebooks, Frances "rubbed stubby fingers over a chin smeared with rouge and whiskers" and grumbled, "Hell, I wish they'd give me a safety razor and a shot of gin."

As the police continued their investigation over the next few weeks, they questioned Frances's husband and her neighbors.

Frank Carrick was born in Chicago in 1888 to Thomas and Marcella, the youngest of nine children. His first name wasn't Frank at all. That was a name he adopted. His real name was Francis, the male version of his wife's name. Shortly after he was taken into custody, police realized he was a junky. Although during the first week or two of their investigation, the police constantly quizzed him to find out what he might know about Frances's involvement in the murder, he didn't tell them anything that would have implicated her. He "squirmed" as they badgered him. Sometimes he might "cough dryly," and at other times "he trembled and started at imaginary sounds."

Frank claimed he worked as an automobile mechanic, but he couldn't remember the names of any of his employers for the past three years. He also swore that he hadn't known Frances was biologically male until some six months after their marriage, and then only because she told him about some health problems she was having that would have revealed her secret to him. It's highly unlikely that he didn't know that Frances was a man.

All of Frances's neighbors swore that she was a biological woman, although they also had occasionally noticed a hint of a beard on her cheeks. When questioned by the police, Mrs. Della Thiele had no doubt that Frances was female and was just as convinced of Frances's innocence in the Tesmer murder. She couldn't imagine Frances being involved with any criminal activity. "We'd 'a' known it if she was up to that kinda stuff," Mrs. Thiele said.

Although at times reporters humorously played with the question of which pronoun to use to refer to her, just as the reporter in Syracuse had done with May Belmont, they also resorted calling Frances a "man-girl" or a "third-sexer." The majority of Chicagoans didn't know how to respond to the female impersonators or effeminate queer men among them. Were they men? Were they women? They seemed to be neither but something else. The sudden notoriety of Frances brought the questions to the public's attention over and over again. Reporters, who had no more knowledge about men like Frances than the average Chicagoan did, never resorted to calling her anything derogatory—such as *pervert*, *degenerate*, and so on—during the time she was in jail or when she was on trial but made a concerted effort to find a term that communicated her "duplex psychology."

Due to the extensive news coverage, Frances quickly became a cause célèbre and a Towertown sensation. Chief among her admirers were women and hundreds of men who were of the "cake eating type," as one reporter from the *Chicago Daily News* called the queer men watching the proceedings in the courtroom.

Frances's fate would depend on whether or not the all-male jury believed her or Mrs. Tesmer. Anna Tesmer had testified that the killer was a twenty-year-old woman, a blue-eyed blonde who had been dressed in a brown dress and hat, but as one reporter reminded his readers, Frances "didn't have light hair, but a streaked henna bob," not a single "brown dress" nor a "poke bonnet" had been found in her clothes closet, and "'her' eyes are more gray than blue." Besides, Frances was thirty-five, not in her twenties—and a man, not a woman, even if he did cross-dress. Most damning of all, the widow had already identified eight different women as her husband's murderer before pointing her finger at Frances. Although never mentioned in any newspaper, it's obvious that the police had kept Frances behind bars simply because she was the perfect scapegoat. Failing to track down a viable suspect, the police hauled in someone who didn't even look like the description their only witness gave them and hoped that the jury would convict her because of her crossing-dressing and her sexuality, not because she was a murderer.

Once the trial began, Frances's lawyer, Frank McDonnell, called Frances's husband to the stand. After being sworn in, McDonnell asked Frank Carrick if he and Frances had been married. When he said they had, Judge John Caverly interrupted the trial, told Carrick not to say another word, and dismissed him. Carrick had been exempted from testifying because Judge Caverly "held that the fact that Thompson is a man did not affect his status as a wife, insofar as interpretation of the law is concerned." Amazingly, not only did the court legally acknowledge a same-sex marriage in 1923, but it gave the same-sex married couple the same rights as opposite-sex married couples would have had in the same situation. Through the judge's dismissal of Frank, the court sanctified the Carricks' wedding. One reporter even called the judge's decision "precedent-making."

Although Frances's marriage to Frank was strange to most Chicagoans, even to the more sophisticated who were becoming aware of Chicago's subculture of queer men, it wasn't the last of the bombshells that fell on the courtroom. As it turned out, the woman named Marie who had been arrested in Frances and Frank's apartment wasn't just a friend or even just a lodger. She was also Frances's wife. Their marriage certificate was reproduced in the *Chicago American*.

In 1920 another madam, Helen Williams, had introduced Frances to Marie Clark, one of her prostitutes. Marie took an immediate liking to Frances, who had already decided she was going to save Marie from a life of prostitution. The two looked so much alike they were often mistaken for sisters. Discovering Marie's attraction to Frances, Helen told Marie that Frances was really Fred Thompson, but Marie fell in love with him anyway. When they began dating, Frances donned fashionable dresses, and after a few months, they decided to tie the knot. Fred showed up to the wedding wearing a man's suit. He was ready to marry a woman this time.

G. C. Prince officiated at the marriage of Marie Kosakowska (a.k.a. Marie Clark) and Fred G. Thompson on January 27, 1921, at the archly conservative Moody Bible Institute. Price was a minister there. Nellie Jestor and Francis Corey served as their witnesses. "Nellie Jestor" doesn't appear in any public record, and her name suggests she may have been a female impersonator with a name meant to be humorous. In queer slang, a *nellie* is a very effeminate-acting man. *Jester* is someone who makes jokes. Nellie Jester was one of the two jokes that Fred and Marie played on Rev. Prince. The other was simply that Fred G. Thompson was not only queer, ran several whorehouses, was a part-time prostitute and a female impersonator, but on that day, he became a bigamist too.

Once they were married, the two left Frank Carrick and moved to Elmhurst, a small town west of Chicago, where they bought land and began to farm. Frances wore men's clothing and lived as Fred. After five months of tilling the soil, they changed their minds about living off the land. Besides, Fred decided that living in the boondocks was not as much fun as living in Chicago. The couple moved back to Towertown, and Fred became Frances again. When Frank heard Frances was back, he showed up on their doorstep. She let him move in with them, and Frances returned to prostitution. Marie disliked it when Frances left the apartment to meet a man, and becoming more and more jealous of Frances's many male admirers, Marie began taking it out on Frank, picking a fight with him every chance she got. Not to be outdone by a woman, Frank fought back. After months of it, Marie turned to heroin for solace, as Frank had years earlier, and then after getting hooked, she decided to quit cold turkey.

She went home to her family in Detroit who sent her to a local hospital. While there, Marie developed blood poisoning and was on the verge of death when the family contacted Frances and begged her to come to Detroit and nurse their child back to health. She did. When Marie recovered, Frances brought her back to Chicago to live with her and Frank again.

The day after the judge stopped Frank Carrick from testifying, McDonnell called Frances Carrick to the stand. Through a gale of crocodile tears, she told one of the versions of the story of her life, explaining how she had

Fig. 14. While on trial for murder, Frances Carrick (right, 1890–1953) couldn't keep her secrets to herself any longer. A female impersonator, she had legally married a man *and* a woman and lived with both in a turbulent ménage. *DN-0076283*, Chicago Daily News *negatives collection*, Chicago History Museum

been adopted, how she had been given a girl's name, and how she had been dressed as a girl. She admitted she had spent her early life in Chicago as a prostitute—one day a boy, the next a girl, then back to being a boy again. She testified she had married not once but twice—to her husband and her wife. Her sobs became so infectious that, according to reporters, her fans in the courtroom began to cry too.

Then the jury was led away to deliberate Frances's fate, and after only two hours, it returned with a not-guilty verdict. Pandemonium broke out. Women and men in the audience bolted toward Frances to congratulate her, while at the same time she ran to the "jury box and shook hands with the jurors." The "bailiffs rushed here and there through the densely packed crowd, shouting for order, and engaged in a few skirmishes with spectators."

A photo from the *Chicago American* shows her surrounded by her fans, who had flowed around her moments after hearing the jury's verdict of not guilty. Of the fourteen people encircling her, a dozen were men and only two were women. It's not difficult to imagine that the men were queer and saw in Frances a kindred spirit who had been thrown into a nationwide spotlight and had emerged victorious.

On the courthouse steps a few minutes later, Frances spoke to reporters. "Everybody's been swell to me," she gushed, "but, my goodness!—I'll be glad to get some hair pins!" She was sending a message to the queer men on the courthouse steps with her and to those who would read her farewell in the evening editions of the newspapers. At the time "dropping hair pins" was a phrase common in the queer subculture that meant to reveal one's sexual orientation to others, to "come out" as it were. It was a phrase similar to "letting one's hair down." During her arrest and subsequent trial, she had been forced to drop her hairpins, to let her hair down, and to reveal things about herself that had been private. Shoved into the limelight, all of Chicago and much of the United States now knew *she* was a *he*. It was time that he returned to his female masquerade, pin her hair back into its proper place, and get on with her life.

Interviewed by the press about her future, Frances assured a reporter that she "wanted to live a quiet life," that she "had no desire for a public life of any kind," but regardless of what she said, she had no intention of abandoning the spotlight now that she was basking in it. Not since she was May Belmont had she gotten so much attention.

The managers of the Rialto, a burlesque theater at 336 State Street, who had begun posting "nude photos" of its striptease "performers in the lobby and on its façade" outside the year of Frances's trial, had been following her case as it played out in the news. No sooner had the police released her than the managers contacted her. They offered her a spot performing on their stage for $500 a week (over $7,000 in today's money). She signed on the dotted line, and soon thereafter she began entertaining standing-room-only crowds to her and the management's delight. Her act was as risqué as she could make it, and it was a huge hit. Frances was thrilled to be back in the limelight again, but not everyone was as happy about the turn of events.

Although the courts had upheld Frances and Frank's rights as a married couple and acknowledged her innocence in the murder of Richard Tesmer, the chief of police and the mayor of Chicago decided to join forces to stop her from capitalizing on her notoriety and the free publicity that her trial had generated.

When asked by reporters why the city wanted to shut down Frances's act, Mayor Dever said that no one should want to be entertained by "such a person" and that no theater should want to "cater" to the "perverted minds" that wanted to be entertained by her. Police Chief Collins promised, "I shall halt this indecent spectacle," and he explained that as far as he was concerned, Frances had become an "outrage to public morals" and shouldn't be permitted to "capitalize" on "his perverted mentality. The police will keep him off the Chicago stage." Chief Collins was good to his word. Strong-armed by the boys in blue, the Rialto's management broke Frances's contract and fired her.

At some point after the trial, Frank and Frances called it quits, but Frances never bothered to divorce Frank or Marie, nor did they think to divorce her.

Frank Carrick remained in Chicago. By 1930 he was renting the house at 4132 Hermitage Avenue. His brother, Thomas, who was seven years older than Frank, lived with him as did two male lodgers, George Nukom and Hobert Clark. Nukom drove a milk truck and Clark was a chef in a restaurant. Neither Frank nor his brother were employed. Five years later Frank moved back to Towertown, into a room at 853 North Clark Street. He was employed as a laborer with the Works Progress Administration. By 1942 he had developed a close relationship with another lodger, Joe Butts, whom Frank identified on his World War II draft card as the person who would always know his whereabouts. Twenty-five years earlier, he had put Frances on that line of his World War I draft card. On the census for 1940, Frank claimed he was a widower. He was still living in what had once been Towertown, at 730 N. Dearborn Street, when he died on June 22, 1948. He was buried at Mt. Olivet Cemetery in Chicago.

Marie disappeared after the trial, and what she did or where she went is unknown. Perhaps she had learned a lesson from Frances, took on a new identity, and moved to another city. What is certain is that somehow Marie Clark slipped out of the spotlight and escaped the notoriety that had been thrust on her by Frances's arrest and trial.

Frances Carrick, murder suspect, bigamist, legally married male spouse to another man, and female impersonator par excellence, disappeared from history as quickly and completely as May Belmont had done years earlier.

However, Fred G. Thompson left a trail behind him all the way back to Ohio.

According to the Akron, Ohio, city directory, the year after Frances's trial and her short-lived return to the stage, a man named Fred Thompson—who may or may not have once been Frances Carrick—found work at the Goodrich tire company there. He rented a room at 563 East Exchange Street, but then he disappeared from all public records for another sixteen years. He reemerged in the 1940 census, living at 1804 East Twentieth Street in Cleveland, where he took in lodgers. The census reveals he had lived there at least since 1935, and it also states he had income from another, undisclosed source. Perhaps he had created another identity and was singing his heart out in one of Cleveland's resorts.

In 1942 the US government required all men from forty-five to sixty-four years of age to register at their local draft boards in what was called the Old Man's Draft. Fred George Thompson registered on April 26 of that year. His draft card revealed that, now fifty-two years old, he stood five feet, four inches tall. His eyes were blue, and by then his hair had turned gray. He weighed 130 pounds and was partially blind. He was living at 1732 East Eighteenth Street, out of which he now ran a business. He was a peddler, but his draft card doesn't mention what he sold. However, a man named Tommy Baker is listed as the one person who would always know Thompson's address. Thompson could have listed either one of his two brothers or his sister, all of whom were still living at the time, but he chose Baker, who was then living at the same address. What their relationship was is unclear, but men typically listed the name of someone close to them in that blank on their draft card.

By 1952 Thompson had moved to Apartment 5 at 2082 West Sixty-Fifth Street in Cleveland, where he would live until the following year. He was hospitalized at Cleveland City Hospital on February 17, 1953, and on April 3, when he was sixty-three years old, Fredrick Thompson died of a variety of causes: "Shock and hemorrhage of upper G-I tract. Ruptured esophageal varices. Laennec's cirrhosis. Pneumonia, rt. Middle lobe, atelectasis tabes dorsais; charcot's joint & cord bladder. Pulmonary emphysema; generalized arteriosclerosis." He was buried in Calvary Cemetery in Cleveland under the name he was given at birth without a mention of either Frances Carrick or May Belmont.

11 | Used as a Pimp for Others to Get Their Meat

To hell with the do-gooders and filthy hypocrites trying to tell us how to fuck. Fuck 'em!

BEFORE IMMIGRATING TO THE UNITED STATES, twenty-one-year-
old Josef Heinrich Dittmar never thought of himself as queer despite the fact
that when he was eight years old, he had a male friend his age with whom he
"practiced 'friction,'" rubbing their clothed bodies against one another. That,
he thought, was something else, but he changed his mind thirteen years later
when he was hitchhiking across the western half of the United States. Another
twenty or so years would pass before, fully aware of his homosexuality and of
the plight that he and others like him faced daily, he decided that he had to
do something about it.

Dittmar, who was born on June 19, 1892, arrived at Ellis Island from
Bremen, Germany, on October 27, 1913, sailing across the Atlantic on the SS
George Washington with his younger sister, Anna. The ship's manifest reveals
that in Germany he had been an office clerk and she a cook. They each had
fifty dollars in their pockets, and after they landed, they planned to join a friend
of the family, F. Bauer, in Chicago. Shortly after disembarking, Dittmar began
calling himself Henry Gerber.

No sooner had he arrived in the Windy City than Gerber was struck with
the same wanderlust that hundreds of other young men had felt in the late
nineteenth and early twentieth centuries. He was eager to see as much of his

new homeland as possible before getting a job and putting down roots. On the train from New York to Illinois, he had seen a considerable amount of the eastern half of the United States, and now he decided to hitchhike to the West Coast. A young man in a car spotted him on the side of the highway in Kansas with his thumb in the air. The man pulled over, and Gerber hopped in. During the course of their conversation, the driver offered him a job stacking wheat on his father's large farm, adding that Gerber would sleep in the bunkhouse with the other farm hands, which included the driver. If Gerber had been clueless about his sexuality before, he would recognize it that night. When Gerber turned in, the driver and his boyfriend, the other field hand, invited him into their bed. Gerber later bragged in a letter to gay rights activist Manuel boyFrank that he and the other two performed sexual acts that would have turned sexologist "Krafft-Ebing . . . purple" with embarrassment.

When he returned from his trip to Chicago, Gerber couldn't find a job, and on January 26, 1914, he enlisted in the US Army and served for a year and a half. During her brother's stint in the military, Anna married George J. Meixner on June 12, 1915, and they lived at 3452 Oakley Avenue with Meixner's mother, Theresa, and his younger brother, Leo. Meixner delivered ice to homes for a living.

After receiving his discharge, Gerber moved in with his sister and her husband's family and found a job in the mail order department of Montgomery Ward, a large department store in the Loop, which he referred to as a "slave pen." While working there Gerber made friends with some of his queer coworkers, who told him about the "boy prostitutes" headquartered in Bughouse Square. It didn't take him long to acquaint himself with a few of them, who, for a price, would visit him on specific days of the week for sex. He preferred to take the penetrative role during sex.

Gerber also met another German immigrant, thirty-two-year-old Frank Spirk, who made his living as a bank clerk. Like Gerber, Spirk preferred younger bedmates. With a little disdain, Gerber called Spirk the "romantic type." Sociologist Harvey Warren Zorbaugh once observed a "romantic type" who lived in Towertown: "B— L— keeps a vermilion kitchenette apartment, with a four-poster bed hung with blue curtains and an electric moon over it. When he has his loves he gets violently domestic, tailors, mends, and cooks."

By the time he was introduced to the allure of Bughouse Square, Gerber had become fully aware of his sexuality, and he sharply defined how he would—or wouldn't—satisfy his sexual needs. First, he wasn't interested in pornographic photographs, claiming he was no more excited by them than a "squirrel" by an "advertisement of Planter's (pea)Nuts." Second, he wanted to know his bed partner before they had sex. Gerber maintained that he was uninterested in being "intimate with a perfect stranger," and so he "was never in a Turkish bath." Similarly, he did not go in for sex in public toilets. He knew of too many cases in which queer men were blackmailed by restroom pickups and of "quite a lot of knocked out queers" who were found unconscious "in urinals." Despite such declarations, Gerber would proposition male prostitutes on sidewalks, parks, and other places for most of the rest of his life.

On April 6, 1917, the United States joined the Allied forces to fight Germany in what would come to be called World War I, and two months later, on June 5, Gerber and George Meixner registered for the draft together. The twenty-four-year-old Gerber's registration card reveals that he was five feet, eight inches tall, slender, and had blue eyes and blond hair, and on it he identified himself as a conscientious objector. Meixner's card shows that he requested a deferment because he was the sole supporter of his wife and mother—not that it would end up mattering. Neither man was drafted.

At some point in 1917, Gerber entered into his first and only long-term relationship. He had met a younger man and they became lovers. Gerber moved out of his sister and brother-in-law's home and set up house with the young man, whom Gerber nicknamed the "young tenor." While Gerber worked, the "young tenor" took care of the "cooking and the usual duties of a wife," as Zorbaugh's B— L— had. It's likely that while Gerber was living with the young man, his sister and brother-in-law became suspicious about Gerber's relationship, and later that year, they decided to confine him to an insane asylum.

Locking boys and men up in mental institutions for being queer was not uncommon. From the mid-nineteenth to the first decades of the twentieth century, society blamed masturbation for causing boys and young men to become queer. In 1904, for example, the father of twelve-year-old Henry Darger banished him from Chicago to the Illinois Asylum for Feeble-Minded Children in downstate Lincoln because the boy had engaged in *self-abuse*, a euphemism for *masturbation* and, at the time, a code word for *homosexuality*. Within a few weeks of the first day of Darger's confinement, four other children, ranging in age from thirteen to nineteen, were also dumped at the same asylum by their families for self-abuse—that is, for being queer. Five years later Darger ran away from the asylum, walked more than 160 miles back to Chicago, and grew up to become one of the most innovative artists of the twentieth century. No one knows what happened to the other four.

As early as 1879, Allen W. Hagenbach, who was assistant physician at the Cook County Hospital for the Insane, reported that he had studied eight hundred male patients and that his investigation proved a "direct relationship between males who masturbated and the onset of several types of insanity, one of which he labeled 'corrupted sexual feelings' as a consequence of a continued indulgence in the bad habit." In the same report, he also recorded the case of "a 21-year-old male patient" who had engaged in self-abuse since he was fourteen years old and, consequently, had developed "a specific type" of insanity "marked by effeminacy and 'morbid attachments for persons of his sex.'" Just in case his findings were untenable, he validated them by mentioning a Professor Maudsley, who earlier had discovered "a characteristic variety of insanity, caused by self-abuse, which makes the patient very like a eunuch in character."

Other physicians across the country explored the association between masturbation and insanity. They developed a very complicated theory to explain the connection between the two, but, simply put, they believed that self-abuse sapped men's and boys' "vigor," their manliness, their sexual potency. Each time a boy or man masturbated to orgasm (or, for that matter, achieved orgasm through intercourse), he reduced his store of sperm, where his "vigor" resided, and his body had to work overtime to replenish it. The more often he achieved orgasm, the more intensely his body was forced to work to replace it. Too much, too often and his body and mind would be irreversibly damaged. Consequently, he would at least become insane—or something even more disastrous.

Stepping into the discussion, John Harvey Kellogg, who was the most celebrated of the time's health gurus and whose name is now synonymous with the breakfast cereal he invented, echoed the sentiments of the medical establishment but also declared that only a man with no self-restraint—and certainly only an insane man—would engage in such a debilitating activity as masturbation, and furthermore, a man who had no self-restraint was no *real* man. Such an individual had, in effect, insanely abandoned his manhood and the privilege it represented, had thoroughly feminized himself, and was on the same sociopolitical, cultural, and psychological rung as a woman. In Kellogg's view, a masturbator's body may have remained male, but every other aspect of his being was female. In other words, as physician George Beard noted, men who masturbated became "women . . . in their tastes, conduct, character, feelings and behavior," just as sexual inverts were considered to be. By 1900 *masturbator* and *sexual invert* had become interchangeable in many medico-legal texts, as well as in the popular imagination.

Institutionalizing boys and men wasn't the only way that the United States had begun trying to curtail homosexuality. Castration, as championed by Dr. F. E. Daniel during the 1893 World's Fair, was another but a far less popular treatment. Between those two extremes lay a third option: using one of the many devices invented to keep boys and young men from masturbating, which, in turn, would keep them from becoming queer. A large variety of contraptions were available to families at their wit's end over their degenerate sons or to men who were unwilling to face a life of perversion and shame.

One such device was a metal ring with spikes on the inside that was slipped onto the penis and held in place by ribbons or leather straps. If a child or young man developed an erection, the spikes would deflate it. Another was a metal pouch that was placed over the penis and held in place by a ribbon or strap. It kept a boy or man from touching himself. However, the masturbator could easily remove both the ring and the metal pouch, and so his hands had to be tied down. Consequently, neither device was as well received as the one sold by Sears, Roebuck. Founded and headquartered in Chicago, Sears, Roebuck marketed the best-seller of all the devices and, in the process, became the answer to thousands of Americans' prayers.

Besides selling everyday items such as plows and skillets, bedding and rifles through its catalog, Sears, Roebuck also sold the Heidelberg Belt. For "only $18.00" and with a "10 Days' Free Trial," customers could purchase relief from the "debilitated condition of the sexual organs, from any cause whatever," a carefully worded promise that was meant to be read as a cure for masturbation and, thus, homosexuality. The ad for the belt ironically highlighted a figure who modeled the device and was obviously meant to remind shoppers of queer physical culturalist Eugen Sandow.

The Heidelberg Belt buckled around the waist and had a battery pack from which a wire extended to encircle the penis and testicles. The steady current from the battery would invigorate the body, restore and then prevent further loss of vigor, and preserve the boy's or man's heterosexuality. The ad described the results in enthusiastic terms: "$18.00 will enable you to face the world anew. $18.00 will bring to you health and strength, vigor, manliness and happiness, a bigger measure for your money, a greater bargain than you could ever possibly secure in any other purchase." While Sears, Roebuck liked to brag that "only three customers ever returned a Heidelberg Belt," it's likely that the hundreds of others who bought the belt were too embarrassed to admit, even in a letter requesting a refund, that its "80-gauge current" hadn't altered their—or their sons'—desire for sexual contact with members of their own sex at all.

World War I continued while Gerber was institutionalized, and in the fall of 1919, nearly a year after the armistice, he was given the choice of being transferred from the asylum to a prison for being an "enemy alien," a term used to designate immigrants born in an enemy country, or to work on behalf of the Allied cause. Like Olmstead decades earlier, he preferred to be anywhere but in a prison, so he chose the military and reenlisted on October 2, 1919. He was stationed in Coblenz, Germany, with the US occupation forces there. He became a staff writer, and sometimes editor, for the army's daily paper, the *AMAROC News*, its title an acronym for AMerican ARmy of OCcupation. Published from 1919 to 1923 for the troops stationed in Germany, its staff of thirty-nine included "officers and enlisted personnel," who published its first issue on April 21, 1919, several months before Gerber arrived.

Gerber spent the next few years in Coblenz, and on his furloughs, he visited Berlin, where he became aware of Germany's various movements to secure rights for queer men and the vast difference between how queer Americans and their German counterparts dealt with their plight. Queer Americans, he decided, cowered before the government and its laws, but queer Germans organized to overturn laws that had been established against them. The most important organization in the German movement, and the longest lasting, was Magnus Hirschfeld's Wissenschaftlich-humanitäres Komitee (Scientific-Humanitarian Committee), which he organized in 1897, and another was Bund für Menschenrecht (Society for Human Rights). Gerber visited the headquarters of both. He was also surprised by the many magazines available at sidewalk newsstands to queer men in Germany. They could choose from "as many as twenty-five gay . . . magazines," he recalled, which even included "a satirical magazine" and "an S/M specialty mag."

Fig. 15. Henry Gerber (1892–1972) founded the Society for Human Rights in Chicago, the first American "homophile" organization. He was arrested during a police raid on his apartment.
Chicago History Museum, ICHi-024893

Once Gerber was discharged, he returned to Chicago. On July 10, 1923, he was hired for a part-time position at the Lakeview branch of the post office and was quickly promoted to full time, which included delivering the mail. Interestingly, Gerber lied on his job application, claiming to have been born in the United States. His lie was likely prompted by the anti-German sentiment at the time. Eight months later Gerber fell ill with "tonsillitis and syphilis." On April 1 he applied for an eleven-day leave of absence because, he claimed, he had to have his tonsils removed and needed enough time to recuperate. He didn't mention his venereal disease. The next day, his supervisor, Daniel T. Hickey, approved the request, but there was a complication. Hickey could only give him a five-day leave, which would begin on March 31, and Gerber would have to use his accrued vacation time for the remaining six days.

In responding to a nationwide epidemic of syphilis that began during World War I, Chicago's public health laws became very strict and required physicians whose patients had contracted a venereal disease to report the cases to the authorities and their place of employment. On April 19, pressured by the law to divulge his secret to his employer, Gerber filed his physician's official "diagnosis of 'secondary syphilis'" form with Hickey and asked for an additional, indeterminate leave. As it turned out, he didn't need it. He went to the Illinois Social Hygiene League, a clinic, for "nine successive treatments," and eight days later a league physician sent Hickey a letter stating that Gerber was cured; that his venereal disease had been "acquired accidentally," which suggests that Gerber hadn't mentioned his forays into Bughouse Square to the physician (or that the doctor was sympathetic to Gerber's situation); and that he could return to work. The following October, Hickey evaluated Gerber's job performance at 98 percent, and in April he ranked it at 99 percent.

Since returning from Coblenz, Gerber had been mulling over how in Germany queer men had organized to demand their rights, but in the United States no one had bothered. The more he thought about it, the more incensed he became over the injustice of US laws that called intimacy between men "immoral," and he railed against the hypocrisy of a "society which allowed the majority, frequently corrupt itself, to persecute those who deviated from the established norms in sexual matters." He also complained about effeminate queer men who refused to be discrete. He was convinced that the dominate society condemned of all queer men because of them. He decided he had to do something "to ameliorate the plight of homosexuals."

Gerber rented a room at 1719 Crilly Court, a few blocks northwest of Towertown. Now called Old Town, the neighborhood was populated by a large number of German immigrants and a small percentage of African Americans. Like Towertown, it was a district of boardinghouses, but it was substantially grittier. It didn't offer cultural events like those held at the Dill Pickle or by the Seven Arts Club, nor did it boast any popular cafés or cabarets such as the Green Mask Inn or the Erie Cabaret. Instead, bordellos stood sentry at both ends of Gerber's block of Crilly Court.

He had made a few queer friends, and he began discussing what he had learned in Germany with them, especially his desire to found an organization that would work for their rights. To his dismay, most of the men he knew told him not to do "anything so rash and futile" as trying to organize queer men, but he was not to be dissuaded. He believed that if he could consolidate them into a politically powerful group, they could change society's views of them and that he would be "known to history as deliverer of the downtrodden, even as Lincoln" was.

Gerber envisioned his organization to be a politically active group, not a loosely run club for men who simply wanted to socialize and make sexual contacts. To signal his seriousness, Gerber decided to have the organization legally incorporated. His supervisor at the post office, Hickey, helped him create the objectives for what he would call the Society for Human Rights, after the German group Bund für Menschenrecht: (1) It would invite queer men to join and swell the membership as large as they could. (2) It would sponsor programs to educate queer men about their situation and promote a hands-off policy when it came to sexual involvement with teenagers. (3) It would publish a magazine, *Friendship and Freedom*, named after a German magazine, *Freundschaft und Freiheit*, to which Gerber had subscribed while he was stationed in Germany. The magazine would offer newsworthy articles fit for public discussion and never include anything that could be construed as pornography. Gerber was perhaps thinking of magazines such as *Der Eigne*, another German magazine to which he subscribed, which published "nude sepia photographs" of young men in its pages. (4) The organization would work to educate the legal authorities about queer men and emphasize the fact that imprisoning them for long periods of time did nothing to weaken or change their sexual desire.

Gerber quickly discovered that Chicago's queer subculture wasn't as ready as he was to put everything they had—family ties and friends, social acceptance, and their jobs—on the line, and so the very first goal of the society was impossible for him to achieve. "The average homosexual," Gerber learned, "was ignorant concerning himself. Others were fearful. Still others were frantic or depraved. Some were blasé." Even those who agreed with Gerber believed "that as long as some homosexual sex acts are against the law, they should not let their names be on any homosexual organization's mailing list any more than notorious bandits would join a thieves' union."

Gerber even went so far as to contact non-queer "men of good reputation," particularly "noted medical authorities," to buttress his cause, but they "refused to endanger their reputations" by associating themselves with queers. Other "prominent persons" he spoke to simply "failed to understand our purpose. The big, fatal, fearful obstacle seemed always to be the almost willful misunderstanding and ignorance on the part of the general public concerning the nature of homosexuality. What people generally thought about when I mentioned the word had nothing to do with reality." It's likely that when Gerber tried to discuss queer men with them, most of the men he approached thought he was referring to the makeup-wearing, flamboyant pansy when, in fact, his concern was focused on the masculine-acting and -appearing man. Extremely frustrated by his experience, Gerber complained, "Against human stupidity even the gods fight in vain."

Despite such problems, Gerber persisted and persuaded half a dozen men he knew to join his organization, and they became its first members. The Reverend John T. Graves and Al Meininger served as president and vice president, respectively. Ellsworth Booher agreed to be its treasurer, Gerber took over the role of secretary, and Fred Panngburn, John Sather, and Henry Teacutter became trustees.

Teacutter rented a room in the same boardinghouse on Crilly Court in which Gerber lived, while Graves and Booher had rooms at 1151 Milton (now Cleveland) Avenue. Although Gerber mentioned in his memoir some forty years later that Graves was the minister of an African American congregation, he didn't mention that Graves was African American.

When Gerber first met him, Graves lived at 4105 S. Dearborn Street with a much younger man, John L. Sullivan, who worked as a "plumper" in a shop. Abraham Sutton, also a member of the society and biracial, lived in the same house with Graves and Sullivan. Sutton worked as a waiter in a railroad club car, but according to Gerber, Sutton's "job with the railroad was in jeopardy when his nature became known" to his bosses. Gerber was proud of the fact that he had no "racial prejudices," unlike many Americans he had met, and he described Graves's place on Dearborn Street as "a sort of hang-out" for queer men where Gerber "met many colored boys." Given his penchant for younger men, he may have been hinting that sexual relationships had developed between at least some of them and himself.

With a board of trustees selected and a set of objectives created, Gerber submitted the incorporation paperwork and a ten-dollar fee to the Illinois secretary of state, which sent him a charter for the Society for Human Rights within a few weeks. Dated December 10, 1924, the charter represents the first time in US history that an organization dedicated to the rights of queer men was not only established but also legally recognized by the government. In addition it has the distinction of being one of the very few organizations in the United States in the 1920s that not only included both white and African American members on its rolls but also had an African American as its president. Gerber's dream of changing the country and being hailed as another Abraham Lincoln had begun.

Gerber's *Friendship and Freedom* debuted in April 1925, and although no copies have survived, a French magazine, *L'Amitié*, published a review of it later that year. According to the review, it included "an article on 'self-control,' a poem by Walt Whitman, and an essay titled 'Green Carnations' about Oscar Wilde." In a note to his readers, Gerber promised that the Society for Human Rights "intended to use subscription fees" to the magazine "to establish a general assistance fund for homosexuals." *Friendship and Freedom* was the first queer magazine to be published in the United States, and it was quickly followed by at least two others.

The year after *Friendship and Freedom* debuted, Nels Anderson reported that a "paper" written and published by and for queer men was headquartered in Grant Park and that its writers used queer slang—"a vocabulary which no one outside the group could easily understand"—throughout its issues. He never mentioned its title or anything else about it. A few years later, Ben Reitman described a third paper published in the early 1930s by and for Chicago's queer community. In a manuscript that was meant to be a section of a book he was writing, Reitman included interesting excerpts from it.

Called the *Carpet Sweeper*, its motto assured its readers that it "picks up all the Dirt!" Like the magazine that Anderson discovered, it also used queer slang to hide what its writers were actually discussing in their articles from non-queer readers and, in the process, to make humorous double entendres throughout. The issue that Reitman excerpted included a phony "program" for the fabricated Spotlight Theatre's pretend production of a musical, a "brilliant extravaganza of Sex, Passion and Degeneracy entitled *The Masturbations of 1969*." The faux program included the titles of several songs from the musical: "When My Eyes of Blue Look into Your Brown," "It's Hard When I Kiss You Goodbye," and "Kiss It Again (in French)." The term *brown*, in this context, referred to the anus, and when used as a verb, it meant to have anal intercourse. *Hard*, of course, refers to an erection, and *French* means fellatio, which identifies the "it" to be kissed.

The *Carpet Sweeper* also included a series of jokes. One began "Maxine . . . and Rose," nicknames for two pansies, "say they never get sunburned when they go to the beach. They just brown!" It even included poems, one of which was titled "Rivals." Its anonymous author considered the antagonism that arose between female prostitutes who were "sauntering / Along the Avenue on an Afternoon" and the "Lithe, slim Youths," young queer men, who followed in their wake. The two groups found themselves competing with one another for men to bed. It's the only serious item that Reitman included in the excerpts.

From the very beginning, the founding members of the Society for Human Rights had agreed to "exclude the much larger circle of bisexuals" that they knew existed in Chicago, at least "for the time being." As Gerber's group used it, *bisexual* didn't refer to those who were attracted to both sexes per se but rather to queer men who married women and fathered children to camouflage their homosexuality. As it turned out, the group's concern over having "bisexuals" in their membership was prescient, as events that developed seven months later would prove.

On Sunday, July 12, 1925, Gerber had just gotten home from what he called "a visit downtown," by which he may have meant a trip to Bughouse Square, and was about to climb into bed when he heard loud pounding on his door. It was two o'clock in the morning, and he assumed it was his landlady. To his surprise, several men barged in when he opened the door. One, a detective, demanded, "Where's the boy?" Gerber was taken aback by the question. He didn't understand what the detective was talking about. A reporter from the *Chicago American* followed the detective in, as did a couple of uniformed policemen. The detective ordered one of the policemen to arrest Gerber and the other to search the room, although no one had shown Gerber a search warrant. The policeman discovered Gerber's files for the Society for Human Rights, his diary, and his typewriter, and the officers hauled Gerber and all of the items to police headquarters on Chicago Avenue at LaSalle.

The next day the *Chicago American* ran its reporter's article about the arrest, titled "Girl Reveals Strange Cult Run by Dad." It pointed out that Gerber, Meininger, and Graves had been arrested because Meininger's daughter had complained to the police a few days earlier about the men who visited her father during the afternoons and evenings and the "strange rites" the men "performed." The report claimed that police had corralled Meininger, Graves, and Gerber at Meininger's apartment at 532 N. Dearborn Street in Towertown and that they had found a copy of *Friendship and Freedom* there. However, the reporter was far from accurate, and Gerber clarified a great deal about the incident in his memoir about the Society for Human Rights, which was published in the early 1960s.

Of course, Meininger, Graves, and Gerber weren't arrested together at Meininger's home, but each at his own place. Gerber had believed that Meininger was simply "an indigent laundry queen," but in fact he was married and the father of four children, one of the "bisexuals" Gerber and the others had hoped to prohibit from the society in the first place. In retaliation for his sexual activities with other men, Meininger's wife, not his daughter, had complained to a social worker, and it was the social worker who tipped off the police. When the police arrived at Meininger's apartment, they found him with a young man named George and, deciding to search the place, came across a copy of *Friendship and Freedom*. Police took Meininger and George into custody, and during his interrogation Meininger confessed to being queer and explained the Society for Human Rights, which lead to Gerber's and Graves's arrests.

Besides running across his diary and the files of the Society for Human Rights, the detective also claimed to have found a "powder puff" in Gerber's room, proof enough, or so the detective believed, of Gerber's "deviance." "It was admitted as evidence," Gerber wrote, but he denied that he ever owned one and that he had ever "used rough [*sic*] or powder." Powder puffs and other makeup and accessories had already become associated, in the public's mind, with the pansy, and in 1926 Rudolph Valentino would be branded one in the *Chicago Tribune* because of a powder dispenser.

The quintessential matinee idol, considered by many to be the most handsome man in Hollywood, Valentino faced a backlash beginning in 1924 because of his role as *Monsieur Beaucaire*, a costume drama set in Louis XV's court. The role called for him to wear "heavy makeup and ruffled costumes," and many who saw the film felt it had "overtly feminized" him. Two years later an editorial writer for the *Chicago Tribune* would link Valentino with a "face-powder dispenser" and cause an uproar.

The dispenser had been installed in the men's room of an unidentified ball room on Chicago's North Side, probably the Aragon, which had opened four days earlier. The *Chicago Tribune*'s writer happened to be in the men's room when he noticed "two 'men' step up" to the dispenser, "insert coin, hold kerchief beneath the spout, pull the lever, then take the pretty pink stuff and put it on their cheeks in front of the mirror." He was infuriated by the "overtly feminized" public display of the two pansies and wrote a scathing editorial. "Homo Americanus!" he declared in it, "Why didn't someone quietly drown Rudolph Guglielmo, alias Valentino, years ago?" Men using powder were, the writer claimed, evidence of the "degeneration" of society "into effeminacy," and he blamed this "effeminacy" on Valentino. Although published without a byline, the editorial's author has since been identified as John Herrick.

Valentino heard about the editorial and sent a letter to the *Chicago Record-Herald*, which appeared in its pages the next day. In it Valentino challenged Herrick "to meet me in the boxing or wrestling arena to prove, in typically American fashion . . . which of us is more a man." Valentino promised to give Herrick a "beating" and taunted the writer:

> I will meet you immediately or give you a reasonable time in which to prepare, for I assume your muscles must be flabby and weak, judging by your cowardly mentality, and that you will have to replace the vitriol in your veins for red blood—if there be a place in such a body as your's [sic] for red blood and manly muscle.

Herrick chose not to meet Valentino.

During Gerber's initial hearing, the social worker whom Meininger's wife had contacted, and whom Gerber described as "a hatchet-faced female," was asked to testify against him. She had at least skimmed Gerber's diary and found what she believed to be a single, damning sentence and read it aloud to the court: "I love Karl." Gerber claimed that she had taken it "out of context" and that he hadn't ever "put down in my diaries anything that could be used against me." Nevertheless, he knew that he and the others were doomed. "The detective and the judge shuddered over such depravity. To the already prejudiced court," Gerber wrote, "we were obviously guilty."

Gerber and the others were locked up in the Cook County jail. He and Meininger shared a cell, and although Meininger was overwhelmed with guilt over having gotten himself and his friends into trouble with the law and broke down in tears, Gerber ignored him. Instead he befriended one of the prisoners in the next cell, who recommended a "'shyster' lawyer" to him, one who specialized in "doubtful cases." According to Gerber, the lawyer "also handled the bail bond racket and probably made additional money each month from this shady practice." He phoned the lawyer, who arrived the next morning and assured Gerber that he could get him released on bail.

The following Monday Gerber had the first of three hearings before a judge, and three days later, at the second hearing, one of "two postal inspectors" told Gerber and the other men while they were waiting for the hearing to begin that the judge was going to hand out "heavy prison sentences" to them "for infecting God's own country." During the hearing, the judge announced that the "federal commissioner" would probably charge Gerber with "obscenity" for sending *Friendship and Freedom* through the mail. He set a $1,000 bond for each of the men, and they were released. At 8:44 that evening, the assistant US postmaster general, John Bartlett, sent a telegram to the Chicago postmaster and ordered him to put Gerber on "suspension without pay." Gerber didn't learn about it until he arrived at work the next morning.

A few days later, Gerber stormed into the *Chicago American*'s editorial offices and demanded that the managing editor retract the article that had reported Gerber's arrest. The editor promised to look into Gerber's complaint, but once Gerber left his office, he forgot all about it. Gerber also considered suing the paper, but lawyers' fees had all but devoured his savings. His first two hearings had cost him $200 each in lawyer's fees, and he was facing at least one more court appearance. He couldn't afford to begin yet another court battle, "and that was the end of that," he said.

In the meantime Gerber decided to fire his "shyster lawyer" and hire the lawyer who had helped him with the charter for the Society for Human Rights. Gerber's new lawyer apparently had influence that his "shyster lawyer" didn't, and he told Gerber not to worry about his next court appearance because "everything had been 'arranged' satisfactorily." As it turned out, it had been. During Gerber's third hearing, the judge was suddenly far more respectful toward Gerber and far more knowledgeable about citizens' rights than he had been previously. Because the detective had searched Gerber's room without a warrant, the judge announced loudly to the courtroom that the detective's actions were "an outrage" and, with a bang of his gavel, dismissed the case against Gerber and the others. He also ordered the police to return Gerber's "property," but they had already turned his diaries and Society for Human Rights files over to the "postal inspectors" and had no way to retrieve them. They did, however, give him his typewriter. Unfortunately, Meininger had pleaded guilty to a charge of "disorderly conduct" on the night he was arrested, and he was fined ten dollars, which Gerber paid.

As Gerber was leaving the courtroom, the prosecuting attorney stopped him and admitted, "I had nothing on you, but the boy who had been rooming with the preacher had confessed to having sex with him." The "preacher" was undoubtedly Graves, but the detective may have been confusing Graves's arrest with Meininger's. Neither Gerber nor any other source mentions that Graves was with a teenager when he was arrested. Nevertheless, Gerber, who had been confounded when the detective who barged into his room demanded, "Where's the boy?" now understood what the detective had meant. He had assumed that, like Meininger, Gerber would be with a teenager when he banged on Gerber's door.

The prosecutor wasn't the only one to corner Gerber before he could leave the courtroom. The arresting detective demanded to know, "What was the idea of the Society for Human Rights anyway? Was it to give you birds the legal right to rape every boy on the street?" Gerber never recorded his reply.

After his release Gerber moved out of his room on Crilly Court and into one at 34 East Oak Street in Towertown, a few blocks from the beach. John Bartlett wrote to the Chicago postmaster again on August 10 and ordered him to fire Gerber "for conduct unbecoming a postal employee." Although Gerber's lawyer advised him to fight to get his job back, he was now broke *and* jobless, and he couldn't hire a lawyer to represent him in another court battle. Because he was the sole financial backer of the Society for Human Rights, his dismissal signaled the organization's demise only seven months after receiving its charter. Fed up with the "Unholy Inquisition" he had experienced, Gerber wrote to a friend in a fit of anger, "To hell with the do-gooders and filthy hypocrites trying to tell us how to fuck. Fuck 'em!" and abandoned Chicago for New York.

At first he lived on East Eleventh Street in Greenwich Village, even then considered a mecca for queer men just as Towertown was, but later that year he moved to 144 East Thirty-Fourth Street, where he lived for the next three years. A "punk" Gerber had propositioned on the street mugged him. Gerber tracked the robber down and "pressed charges" against him, but getting justice frustrated Gerber. Gerber was the only witness to the crime and had to appear in court, but the mugger's lawyer got the "trial postponed five times," hoping to wear Gerber down until he simply stopped coming to court. Instead, Gerber became more steadfast in his resolve to get justice with each delay because he "wanted to prove" that just because he was queer, he wasn't weak and that he deserved the same protection under the law as anyone else. Eventually a "jury

convicted" the young man of "assault in the third degree," and he was imprisoned in "Elmira," a reformatory in upstate New York, "for 'an indefinite term.'"

One of Gerber's New York friends, a man with whom he had worked
on the *AMAROC News* in Coblenz, told him about a "former Major General
of World War I" who needed a "good proofreader" for a publication being
issued from his office on Governors Island. Given Gerber's editing and writing
experience on *AMAROC News* years earlier, he was a shoo-in, but to accept
the job, Gerber had to reenlist in the army and move to Governors Island,
which he did in 1927. He would hold the position for the next seventeen years.

During off hours he busied himself writing articles for queer magazines
published in Germany, such as *Blätter für Menschenrecht* ("Journal of Human
Rights") and *Das Freundschaftsblatt* ("The Friendship Journal"), and the *Modern Thinker, American Mercury*, the *Freethinker*, and other politically liberal
magazines in the United States. He also managed a pen-pal organization
dubbed Contacts.

Contacts issued a newsletter, *Chanticleer*, which published personal ads
from anyone but especially from queer men. A synonym for *rooster*, which
is a synonym for *cock*, the newsletter's title signaled its welcome to queer
men. Gerber once claimed that publications like *Chanticleer* received ads from
"screwballs," "tramps expecting to marry a rich widow," "ugly old spinsters
dreaming" of "Prince Charming," and "the Don Juans, many married, who
like a little variety from cunt diet." One personal from *Chanticleer* is particularly notable: "NYC Male, 44. . . . Favored by nature with immunity to
female 'charms.' . . . Looking around in life, I can understand why monkeys
protested over Darwin's thesis." The profile belonged to Gerber. Few were as
witty as his, as is the case with this example of another personal ad from a
queer man: "Young college graduate desires male correspondence. Interested
in good music, psychology and walks in the country."

Gerber boasted that Contacts had nearly fifteen hundred members in its
heyday, but by September 1939, he realized that he was tempting fate by being
associated with it while also serving in the military. Besides, as he later claimed,
he'd grown weary of being "used as a pimp for others to get their meat," and
so he abandoned Contacts. With more free time on his hands, he was able to
go on vacation, visiting Miami with a brief side trip to Cuba. He had a good
time, he reported to friends, but there was one damper. He didn't know where
to go to meet young male prostitutes while he was in Havana.

Living on Governors Island was no picnic for Gerber. He was often blackmailed by his pickups and was beaten up several times. Military officials learned of the attacks, and in February 1942, a branch of the army's intelligence department, the G-2, searched Gerber's quarters. Although the investigators didn't discover anything illegal or even suggestive among his property, he was confined to the island's prison, Castle Williams, for several weeks. He was finally called before a "Section VIII board" that would decide whether or not he deserved a "Section 8," a dishonorable discharge that was given to soldiers considered undesirable for military service, often because they had been accused of being queer.

Surprisingly, the chief "investigator's limited understanding of Homosexuality" served Gerber in his defense. During the trial, Gerber admitted to sexual contact with other men, although he claimed that he "only practiced mutual masturbation with men over 21," but the chief didn't accept this as proof of Gerber's homosexuality. Even the board's psychiatrist insisted that Gerber was "not a homosexual." The board dismissed the charges against Gerber. "I nearly fell over the chair" in shock, Gerber recalled later, adding, "Imagine me fighting all my life for our cause and then be[ing] told I was not a homosexual."

Gerber resumed his duties, but by October 1942, he had moved off Governors Island and into his friend Frank McCourt's apartment at 516 West 140th Street. Gerber quickly decided the move was unsatisfactory. According to him, McCourt was more interested in "weekend orgies" and "erotic photographs" than supporting a queer political movement, and Gerber moved out.

In 1945 Gerber retired from the military at the rank of staff sergeant with a monthly pension as well as free health insurance and room and board. He moved into the US Soldiers' and Airmen's Home in Washington, DC, which he described as a "haven" as well as an "environment of old boozehounds" and the "semi-insane." He began working on a book, *Moral Delusions*, in which he explored current "sex laws" and tracked "them back through history to find their roots in primitive or Jewish taboos." He claimed to have finished it, but it was never published, and no copy has ever been found. He became acquainted with Washington's branch of the Mattachine Society, a queer rights organization, and published his translation of Magnus Hirschfeld's "Die Homosexualitat des Mannes und des Weibes" ("The Role of Homosexual Men and Women in Society") and a memoir of his work with the Society of Human Rights in the *ONE Institute Quarterly*, headquartered in Los Angeles. While he was willing to contribute to both the Mattachine Society and ONE, both early queer rights organizations, he wasn't convinced that either group would do anything to part "the lavender curtain of sex regimentation" in the United States. He also placed his own personal ads, and responded to others', in various magazines, including *Writer's Digest* and the *Saturday Review of Literature*, and spent time in the local X-rated movie theaters. They were full of attractive young men who were agreeable to his advances, although, he complained, his involvement with them in "nine out of ten cases" was "distinctly one-sided."

In the last years of his life, Gerber was understandably bitter toward the queer men he had spent so much time and effort trying to help only to have them reject his undertakings. His experiences in Chicago during 1924–1925 were paramount in his acrimony. "I once lost a good job in trying to bring them together," he wrote, but they were "too scared . . . to join any association trying to help them." Gerber also continued to attack the dominate culture, which sanctified "monogamy" and squelched "everything sexual" that did not promote it and "procreation." While Gerber held on to his belief that society could be changed, he had come to realize that it was such a huge undertaking that it could happen only a little bit at a time.

At once cynical about the past and yet, despite it all, somewhat optimistic for the future, Gerber couldn't help but dream up another organization, a "secret underground," that would "'protect homosexuals against persecution' through the legal process, the media, and networking." He christened it the Society Scouting Sex Superstition and planned to include the "better sort of homosexuals," not riffraff like Meininger, to provide a means by which members could "meet their kind safely" and to solicit—*and* receive—the kind of financial support it would need to fight "sex *fascism*." Gerber even planned on contributing his "$200 mustering out pay" to get the Society Scouting Sex Superstitions underway, but nothing ever came of his dream.

Except for a three-month trip to Germany in 1951, Gerber spent his days at the Soldiers' and Sailors' Home until New Year's Eve 1972, when he died of pneumonia and was buried in the cemetery associated with the home. He was eighty years old and had lived long enough to see the successful founding of several queer rights organizations across the United States, such as the Mattachine Society and ONE, and to witness the riot at the Stonewall Inn in 1969.

Although he often appears to have been curmudgeonly, cantankerous, and too serious for his own good in the letters, articles, and other documents he left behind, Gerber occasionally had his lighter moments. In a letter he sent to Manuel boyFrank in 1940, Gerber congratulated himself on being "practical" in love with a humorous metaphor. "I am like a Scotchman," he wrote, "only asking for love if it is free or not expensive. Like the Scotchman who gave his boyfriend an upright organ for Christmas!!!" At another time he joked, "If I were a fairy and glory in a big stiff prick, I would be like the queer" who, "when asked" by a naval recruiting officer "if he . . . had ever been in the navy," replied, "No, sir, quite . . . the contrary."

12

All Have Waitresses Who Are Lads in Gal's Clothing

Either put on pants or go to jail.

LORENZO BANYARD RECALLED THAT in the early 1930s, he would watch scores of female impersonators traipse down to "the street corner swishin'." It was a familiar scene in Bronzeville when he was an adolescent. Banyard had moved to Chicago the same year that Gerber founded the Society for Human Rights and was very aware of some of the queer men in the neighborhood. "I'd be standing at the corner," he continued, watching them, taking it all in, "'cause I *admired* them, you known, they had this long hair . . . and the makeup and every thing. . . . Plus they was making money, too, for dancing." A few years later, Banyard, who had realized he was queer when he was twelve, became a female impersonator himself and adopted the name Nancy Kelly. He appeared on the Cabin Inn's stage with Valda Gray, Petite Swanson, the Sepia Joan Crawford, and the Sepia Mae West, the queer, African American female impersonator superstars of Bronzeville. All of them performed at its hottest nightspots.

Whether appearing as solo artists or in chorus lines, Bronzeville's female impersonators appeared on the same stages as its musical giants, such as Jelly Roll Morton, Louis Armstrong, Fats Waller, and Cab Calloway. Their glimmering sequined gowns, expensive wigs, high heels, and ever-flawless makeup guaranteed fans would not simply lionize them but follow them puppy-dog-like from one cabaret to another, from theater to dance hall to cabaret. To be sure, there were other talented female impersonators around Bronzeville—Jean LaRue, Nina Mae McKinney, Peaches Browning, Doris White, Frances Dee, Dixie Lee—but they were only good, perhaps better than average, but had never quite earned superstar status. One of Chicago's entertainment reviewers claimed that there were countless female impersonators on the Windy City's stages but that didn't mean all were equally talented. He noted that "quite a few . . . can dress and look the part" and yet too many of those "have no stage ability." Some "can sing, but cannot dance; others handle their feet well on the floor but cannot sing." The reviewer concluded, "It really requires a combination of dance and song to win a place in one of these floor shows."

Queer men had become fixtures in Bronzeville almost as soon as its first cabaret opened its doors. Although the owners of the cafés and cabarets where the female impersonators performed were flaunting Chicago's ordinance against individuals wearing "a dress not belonging to his or her sex" in public, and although female impersonators might face a backlash from some of their family members, neighbors, and strangers because they cross-dressed and were queer, they also earned respect and even envy from many others. The cabarets in which they performed offered them better-than-average salaries. While Lorenzo Banyard made twelve dollars a week at his day job as dishwasher at a YMCA, his alter ego, Nancy Kelly, earned ten dollars a show, three shows a night, during the weekends. In short, he earned five times as much as a female impersonator during the weekend than he did at his day job the rest of the week.

Female impersonators sang—they didn't lip-synch to recordings—risqué renditions of popular songs, told off-color jokes, and hob-knobbed with the audience. They brought droves of fans into the cabarets and theaters where they performed, among them nationally known celebrities. It wasn't an easy job, either, as it may appear to have been. The Sepia Gloria Swanson (née Walter Winston), who was considered the best of the best, "literally entertained all night, entrancing patrons with a 'whiskey voice,' 'his every gesture and mannerism more feminine than those of any female, his corsets pushing his plumpness into a sweltering and well-modeled bosom.'"

The Sepia Gloria Swanson began her career at the Pleasure Inn at 505½ East Thirty-First Street in 1929, when she was twenty-two years old. Her version of Fats Waller's "Squeeze Me" became her theme song. She had rewritten Weller's original lyrics substantially, making his milder ones scandalous and a crowd-pleaser. She was also known far and wide for her version of Sophie

Tucker's "Some of These Days." Her dedication and hard work paid off. When she the appeared at the Annex Buffet, for example, she not only drew a standing-room-only crowd, but the composer William C. Handy and the country's premier boxer, Jack Johnson, were spotted in the audience enjoying her show. She became so famous, her act so lucrative that the Fisher Theater in Detroit hired her to perform in her very own revue, *Gloria's Follies.* Swanson could hold court—and mesmerize audiences—anywhere, at any time, and had such a good business sense that she opened her own place, aptly named Gloria's, in February 1930, across the street from another popular cabaret, the Sunset Café, at 315-17 East Thirty-Fifth Street.

Cabaret owners hired female impersonators to perform in their venues exclusively for a set period of time, so the performers moved constantly from café to dance hall to cabaret to theater and back again, hoping someday to land a permanent job. Gilda Gray, for example, appeared early in her career at the Club Piccadilly at 2652 Indiana Avenue, but as she developed as a performer in a variety of cafés and cabarets, she began drawing larger and larger crowds to her shows until, several years later, she couldn't pass up an offer to become the hostess at the much more popular Cabin Inn at 3119 Cottage Grove Avenue. She was a huge hit with her rendition of Sally Rand's fan dance, which Rand was performing—despite a great deal of trouble with morals crusaders and the police—at the Chicago World's Fair.

The 1933–1934 Century of Progress International Exposition, which like the World's Columbian Exposition of the 1890s was commonly called the Chicago World's Fair, was held just a stone's throw from Bronzeville. Meant to celebrate the Windy City's centennial, it staged a number of events that drew charges of obscenity and brought the police into action, just as Fatima's performance had done over forty years earlier at the Columbian Exposition.

Sally Rand's eyebrow-raising fan dance, a striptease with giant ostrich feathers, and her bubble dance, during which she used giant, translucent balls instead of feathers, received more press coverage than any other act at the fair. Police considered her dances so indecent that she was arrested four times in a single day—August 4, 1933. Besides constantly interrupting Rand's performances at the fair, police barged onto the stage of a female impersonator in the Slums of Cairo exhibit, dragged her off to jail, and closed the concession.

The charges of obscenity aimed at Rand and the female impersonator spread to nearby cabarets. For example, among the performers at the Picardy Club, which stood near the fairgrounds, were a number of female impersonators who danced and sang onstage while a "male 'hostess' with 'eyelids colored and lips rouged'" made the rounds though the audience, paying special attention to the men. The female impersonators were available for sex with any of the cabaret's male customers who might be interested and had a few extra dollars in their wallets. The Picardy wasn't the only such cabaret, however. According to an investigator for the Juvenile Protective Association, a number of resorts near the fair presented "spectacles of perversion" that, like the Picardy Club, included "floor shows" with female impersonators and "male hostesses," whose role was to entertain the customers at their tables and to make themselves available for sex.

The Chicago World's Fair also offered other, less obvious sites that men in search of sexual thrills with other men could visit. One was Lorado Taft's statue the *Fountain of Time*, which had been erected on the Midway Plaisance. Most of the people at the fair wouldn't have known that on the back of the statue, Taft had depicted himself holding hands with another man among a score of obviously non-queer couples. Rumor had it that Taft had had a relationship with the man, one of his assistants, and the word was out among queer men. The site became a rendezvous for male-male lovers and a cruising spot for those interested in a pickup.

With the fair bringing thousands to the Windy City each week, plenty of tourists were eager to visit the local hotspots in Bronzeville *and* in Towertown, and in fact a small but vibrant tourism industry developed in Towertown, with guided tours scheduled on a regular basis to introduce fairgoers and other out-of-towners to the "strange and little known sights" of Little Paris, as tour guides were marketing Towertown. To give visitors a warm welcome to Towertown, a group supporting tourism had hoisted a large banner above the intersection of Clark Street and Chicago Avenue bearing a message: "Welcome all to A Century of Progress, International Exposition, Chicago, 1933." As it turned out, the sights on the tour—the "McKinlock campus of Northwestern University, Tribune Tower, the Merchandise and Furniture marts, the Wrigley building, the Palmolive building, Lincoln Park and its museums, zoo, and conservatory, and a number of the city's radio stations"—were far tamer than advertisements for the excursions suggested. Visiting flappers and sheiks, bohemians and politicos, and other adventurous and liberal types had other ideas about what they wanted to see outside of the fair's boundaries, none of which included university campuses or furniture stores.

Fig. 16. Measuring 126' 10" long, 23' 6" wide, and 24' tall, Lorado Taft's sculpture the *Fountain of Time* includes over a hundred figures, one of which is Taft himself (right) on the back, holding his then lover's hand. *Courtesy of Jyoti Srivastava*

In the meantime, scores of new businesses opened, including queer and queer-friendly resorts. *Variety* announced that a large number of "pansy parlors" had opened across Chicago. Many dotted the North Side and were "operated by boys who won't throw open the doors" for business until they've spent "at least two hours . . . adjusting the drapes just so. . . . The southside . . . also has had an increase of these sort of joints." The article went on to claim that "all have waitresses who are lads in gal's clothing."

One such business was Towertown's K-9 Club. Opened in 1930 in the hope of being popular among fairgoers, the K-9 Club's reputation grew rapidly and peaked with the opening of the Chicago World's Fair three years later. For many out-of-towners, a trip to the fair wasn't complete without spending a few hours at the club. Occupying the "former quarters of a 'dog club,'" the K-9 Club became so popular, in fact, that restaurant reviewer John Drury mentioned it in his guidebook, *Dining in Chicago*. He hinted at its queer entertainers and clientele by calling it an "odd sort of place," and those savvy enough to read between the lines understood immediately what *odd* was meant to suggest. Similarly, the *Chicago Tribune* called it "an eccentric night life rendezvous," *eccentric* performing the same objective as *odd*.

Despite Drury's positive comments about the K-9 Club, it became popular among Chicagoans and tourists alike not because of its food or drinks but because of its "femme impersonators" and because it catered to queer men. One young woman from Chicago told a social worker that "she intended to go to a nightclub called the 'Canine Club.' She told me that she had heard that you couldn't go to a toilet there without some man or woman following you in." She planned to meet "a pervert and have a sexual experience with one of them. At this certain club many of the men wear women's clothes."

For the most part, Chicago's law enforcement ignored the resorts that had supported, and even endorsed, male prostitution on their premises during the fair because the Great Depression was still raging and the "impersonators" and "male hostesses" attracted customers who spent money to watch them, laugh at them, and perhaps even solicit them for sex—all while helping to boost the local economy. However, a reporter for *Variety* was prophetic, as it turned out, when he declared that Mayor Kelly would be working to establish a law that banned cross-dressing in public theaters or resorts, such as cabarets and amusement parks, as soon as the flow of tourist money into Chicago's businesses began to dry up. That's exactly what happened. No sooner had the fair closed its doors on Halloween 1934 than Mayor Edward J. Kelly began working to get "rid" of the "city's cabarets and theaters" that offered "striptease acts" and "female impersonators," and Chicago's "queer nightlife took the hardest hit."

Police began padlocking various resorts in or near Towertown, including Johnny McGovern's Liberty Inn, the Colonial Inn, the Roselle, and especially the K-9 Club. All, except perhaps the Colonial, either catered to queer customers or were queer friendly. According to Kelly, the K-9 Club was closed because it was "obnoxious" and its performances were "against law and public policy," and as the police's mantra, "Either put on pants or go to jail," was heard over and over again across Chicago's North Side, both the West and the East Coasts took note.

In Los Angeles, *Variety* described the situation succinctly: "After two years of fan dancers, Venuses on half-shell, World Fair strippers and general hotcha, Chicago" has "suddenly gone lily-white. Acts which formerly passed for cleanliness itself now find themselves before the courts on charges of bawdiness," and then *Variety* joked that the atmosphere in Chicago was so moralistically strict, that "fan dancers . . . are now doing their routines in red flannel underwear."

The Dill Pickle also fell on hard times, closing in 1934, three years after sexologist Magnus Hirschfeld delivered his standing-room-only lecture on homosexuality there. According to poet Kenneth Rexroth, the Pickle had grown "more and more vulgar," had been "taken over by the Organization," another name for the Italian mob that was headed by Al Capone, and had been "turned into a rough and fraudulent operation" and "a dangerous tourist trap."

Despite Mayor Kelly's focus on Towertown's cabarets and queer performers, they weren't his only targets. At the same time, he began to revoke the licenses of bathhouses. After receiving complaints about "immoral practices" taking place on the premises, Sgt. Frank O'Sullivan and his partner Thomas P. Lyons decided to investigate the Wacker Baths at 674½ North Clark Street. What exactly they witnessed was never reported in the newspapers, but they arrested the night manager, Arthur Heitz, and two of its customers, Horance Sudler and Louis Meyer. Public baths had long been places where men could pick up one another for sexual relations or where, after meeting at some other location, such as Bughouse Square, they could go and rent a private room for privacy.

As anti-vice groups eliminated one after another of the queer resorts from Towertown, it became a ghost of its former self. They hadn't turned their attention on Bronzeville yet, and its cabarets were still hopping. So North Side queers—and non-queers who were after musical thrills—flocked to the South Side in numbers larger than ever before and were rewarded for their effort.

Bronzeville's *first* Sepia Mae West (née Sam Fouche) had left Chicago in 1934 for what she believed would be greener pastures in New York's Harlem. As it turned out, the pastures there were even greener than she ever imagined. A review of the twenty-five-year-old's act shortly after her arrival called her a "rare quality." Nevertheless, by 1935 she had moved to Detroit, where she was an "entertainer" at a "night club" and lived with a lodger, Floyd William, who worked as kitchen help in a hotel and was a year younger than she.

Once the first Sepia Mae West left Chicago, a *second* Sepia Mae West (née Dick Barrow) took over where the first had left off—and with considerable acclaim. After performing at the Annex Buffet for some time, she moved to the Cabin Inn. Its slogan, "the South Side's Oddest Nite Club," suggested its queer performers and customers just as Drury's description of the K-9 Club as *odd* had. The Cabin Inn lived up to its catchphrase. The Sepia Mae

Fig. 17. The Cabin Inn was notorious throughout Chicago for its female impersonator performers, four of whom are shown here with jazz artist Jimmie Noone. *Courtesy of the Special Collections Research Center, University of Chicago Library*

West became so closely associated with the cabaret that she recorded a song about it—but under her birth name, Dick Barrow. The record was little more than an advertisement for the cabaret. Called "Down at the Cabin Inn," the recording opens with something like an invitation to listeners to visit the inn before Barrow mentions his alter ego, who was "producin' a show" there "that's grand," and that his sister cross-dressers, whom he never identifies by name, "do the rest."

While dozens of female impersonators became performers on Bronzeville's many stages, hundreds more dressed in drag at home or at private parties, or if in public, only on Halloween night or during New Year's Eve masquerades. To capitalize on the hundreds of such men who wanted a venue specifically for them, Johnny Ryan held what may have been Chicago's first drag ball at an unknown spot on New Year's Eve in 1932. Although attendance was disappointing at first, with only 100 or so men appearing by eleven o'clock that evening, some 250 more showed up during the hour before midnight and paid the $1.50 cover charge. An orchestra of black musicians and a female impersonator who sang popular songs entertained the crowd of mostly male-clad queer men. Only thirty or so of them had arrived in drag. They drank a considerable amount of booze, and around one o'clock in the morning, when one of the attendees was so drunk he made a nuisance of himself, pandemonium broke out. Police stormed the hall, everyone scattered, and the festivities broke up.

A very successful masquerade ball was held on October 30 that same year at the Coliseum Annex, with some one thousand men attending, of which a hundred or so arrived in drag. Frankie and Johnie, a queer man and lesbian duo, MCed the festivities. Although men of all ages filled the hall, many were around twenty-five years old, with a substantial number older than that. One of the oldest—an "elderly" man dressed in "women's clothing" and "glasses," whose wig was "a boyish bob," whose clothes were "out of date," and whose five o'clock shadow showed through his makeup—became the target of derision. While some of the men danced together, most didn't. The doors closed at around three o'clock in the morning.

Around the same time, another New Year's Eve masquerade ball was also held at the Coliseum Annex, and Myles Vollmer described the event. Outside, he wrote, "the sidewalks and entrance . . . were crowded with men hanging around, joking at the arrival of each newcomer in costume." Some of the men in the throng, he claimed, were there "just looking," amused by the spectacle unfolding before them, while others were after "a possible pick-up," and still others were eager to get in "to prey on the less experienced boys who were inside cavorting to the music."

Unlike the policewomen who had harassed the female impersonators at the Dill Pickle's masked ball on North Clark Street in 1920, the security guards hired for drag balls in the 1930s had a live-and-let-live attitude. Inside the Coliseum, security included "uniformed guards" who "were selected for their size and physique," which suggests they were not only able to protect the revelers but were also pleasing to the eye, as well as "numerous uniformed policemen, and several plain-clothesmen" provided by the city. Vollmer noted, "This was one occasion when official Chicago put its approval on the public appearance of its intermediate sex."

As at the other masquerades, not everyone appeared in drag. Vollmer recalled "two young men in street clothes dancing together, cheek to cheek holding one another in close embrace, as any girl and boy would at any dance, save, perhaps that the two youths were much more intense in their forbidden roles." Obviously, a desire to appear in public in women's clothing was not the only reason queer men attended the balls, but those who did attend in order to be seen and, perhaps, admired in their drag were "heavily powdered, with eye brows penciled and roughed [sic] lips and cheeks," "dressed in gorgeous evening gown . . . tiara . . . slim high French heeled satin slippers," and "heavily jeweled."

Then as now, cross-dressing posed problems for some queer men and sometimes developed into humorous situations for onlookers, as Vollmer reported. Fisticuffs ensued when two men dressed as women chose the "wrong" bathroom to use:

> There are shrill exclamations of glee and merriment as the men in women's clothing frequent the toilets marked plainly "Women." The men's toilets seem to be used only by those in masculine attire. It is not long before a real woman ventures into her proper restroom, and emerges to call a guard to dispossess the "girls" in there. A scuffle follows while a burly stadium guard attempts to expel the "girls" who shrilly protest that they belong in that particular restroom—the guard all the while trying to keep a serious face!

The men in gloves, gowns, high heels, and wigs were a sharp contrast to those "in street clothes, lacking courage to come in Drag" but who were "dancing with other men, occasionally kissing them in moments of abandon." In fact, attendees ran the full gamut of Chicago's queer community: "Young effeminate lads, older men of more masculinity and . . . old men, paunchy with bald heads and lustful expressions. These old men . . . are often businessmen with families, who have learned too late their true sexual natures." One of them was a "well known tradesman, a man of means, and a respectable member of a north side church," who was "dancing with a young pretty lad" in an especially "close embrace." Others stood along the periphery, unseen or ignored by most but watching everyone. They included men who were simply "curious" and those who didn't dare "dance for fear of recognition . . . others . . . waiting for their lovers; and finally those waiting for a pickup, to prey on the gullible homosexual." In short, "all types are there, pimps, panderers, blackmailers, 'trade,' the oversexed lower classes with no high moral code, ready for a fling, be it man or woman; prizefighters, the so-called 'meat' for homosexuals—and athletes . . . strangely susceptible to the advances of an effeminate youth, who will make love to them passionately."

Prizefighters weren't the only "meat" available. Decades after he attended one of the Halloween masquerade balls for the very first time, a man recalled that when he went to the washroom, he was confronted with "a man hanging over the washbasin and . . . a line-up of hard-ons waiting to penetrate him." The young attendee was shocked by the sight. "Oh, my God!" he said. "I didn't think I would recover."

Interestingly white men wrote reports about queer masquerade balls and wrote them for an all-white, all-non-queer male readership. Like Vollmer, they always commented on the "Negroes" who "mingle freely with whites" at the balls and came to the conclusion that "there seemingly is not race distinction between them." But African Americans weren't the only disenfranchised people these men noticed. Vollmer recalled "a preponderance of Jews and the Latin Nationalities" among the revelers, adding, "Many of the men are of Polish blood." With more than a tinge of disdain, he concluded from his observation that "homosexuality is no respecter of races."

The masquerade balls, whether held on the North Side or the South Side of Chicago, "enabled people who weren't able to risk a publicly queer life to look for lovers without having everyone else knowing their business." The balls were also important because they offered a sense of community for many queer men who, for whatever reason, didn't have access to it otherwise. As novelist and tattoo artist Samuel Steward recalled, the only sense of community among queer men that he noted in the 1930s happened on one, and only one, night of the year, "at the Halloween drag balls." It "was the only time," he said, "that everyone came out" and hob-knobbed with one another publicly. "The rest of the time it was still an individual matter. We all went our separate, very lonesome, very lonely ways to our neighborhood bars, seeing whom we could make."

Legend has it that a "double wedding"—both faux and very campy—at the Cabin Inn inspired male prostitute and gambler Alfred Finnie to begin holding masquerade balls in Bronzeville in the fall of 1935 specifically for African American female impersonators, their escorts, and their admirers. One of the couples to be married was "a midget dancer," Shorty Burch, who was one of the inn's performers, and his fiancée, Muriel Borsack. Burch was a well-known vaudevillian and had received acclaim in newspaper reviews as an "eccentric midget" as well as a "comedian and acrobatic dancer." He also bore the nickname King Kong "because of his size and sense of comedy." By the time of his marriage to Borsack, who was also identified as Vera Barsock, Burch had been in show business for two decades. His height was reported as anywhere from thirty-six to forty-five inches.

The other couple was female impersonator Jean Acker, who had taken her nom de theatre from Rudolph Valentino's first wife, and the "very handsome" Vernon Long. No sooner had the weddings begun than the police barged in. They arrested twelve of the employees, including "owners Nat Ivy and Jack Hardy, bartenders Dewey Parker and Bob Henderson, floodlight operator Carroll Joseph," and "seven female impersonators, three who worked at the Cabin and four guests at the wedding," charging them with "obscenity."

Brought into the morals court, they found themselves before what may have been an objective judge, Eugene McGarry. He said, "The testimony does not show any specific violations of ordinance," referring to the law against cross-dressing in public. "It appears," he continued, "that these men were dressed in female clothes. The testimony shows it was a masquerade party. Female impersonators appear on stage every day. . . . I have no choice but to find the defendants not guilty and that will be the order." Because Judge McGarry decided the female impersonators were cross-dressing for a *theatrical* performance, and not in public per se, they hadn't broken any law.

Finnie had initially held his masquerade balls "in the basement of a tavern" with a twenty-five-cent cover charge. They were not as well attended as those held at, say, the Coliseum Annex, and during the first eight years, he would sponsor the balls as often as five times a year at various venues. Nancy Kelly recalled that "they'd just pick out a random little shack" and "decorate it, put up some balloons." There would be "music" and "food," and "everybody'd be dancing with one another, they'd be drinking, they had tables like a cabaret, and you'd dance with a friend, you'd dance with somebody else's friends."

Although Finnie's masquerade balls were small events in their early days, they quickly grew—and grew very large. The night's entertainment did too, until it eventually included "a seven or eight piece" orchestra. By the late 1940s, the masquerades at the Coliseum Annex and other establishments gave way to Finnie's, which, although beginning as a venue for African American female impersonators, welcomed all of Chicago's queer community regardless of race. Unfortunately, Finnie never lived to see how dynamic and magnificent his masquerade balls became. He was killed in 1943 during a brawl while gambling.

The double wedding that had so inspired Finnie in 1935 wouldn't be the only time that the Cabin Inn's stars crossed paths with the police. One of the Cabin Inn's best-known female impersonators, the Sepia Joan Crawford (née George Manus), was living it up on the corner of Thirty-Fifth and State Street when police officer Sgt. Robert Harness asked the "tall and languorous" Crawford, who had had one "too many cocktails," to pipe down. When she "tossed back 'her' flowing hair" and threatened to slap him, the officer grabbed her blouse at the neck. Provoked by the police officer, she "popped a pair of manicured hands on 'her' shapely hips" and screamed, "Take your hands off my bosom!" The cop hauled her off to jail.

The Sepia Joan Crawford was freed by Judge Mason Sullivan a few days later but not without a warning directed at the now-male-attired entertainer to stop "displaying conduct unbecoming a gentleman, let alone a 'lady.'" The reporter who covered the case for the *Chicago Defender* noticed that Crawford had a black eye, and he was quick to point out that it wasn't Sgt. Harness who had struck her but her "boy-friend."

The storm of trouble that Mayor Kelly had unleashed on Towertown's queer and queer-friendly resorts soon drifted southward and anchored itself over Bronzeville. The Cabin Inn was his first target. It had fallen on hard times and had developed a seedy reputation. One report claimed that its female impersonators had become "notorious varietarist [*sic*] . . . willing to arrange sexual performances on occasion for a 'select few,'" and the police used them as an excuse to knock on the Cabin Inn's doors. At the nearby Club DeLisa, the police forced the female impersonator Peggy Hopkins Joyce, who was considered "one of the best in the business," offstage.

The Cabin Inn bounced back within a few days, offering customers more of the same "entertainment by female impersonators" as it had before despite the police's continued vigilance. However, the DeLuxe Inn couldn't withstand the threat of more harassment. "Several weeks ago police stopped shows at DeLuxe cafes," an article in the Baltimore *Afro-American* reported, "ordering impersonators into 'trousers or else!'" Unlike the Cabin Inn, the DeLuxe booted its female impersonator acts for good. The same befell other female impersonators after Police Commissioner James P. Allen instructed police to "rid the district of all female impersonators whose clan has grown to alarming proportions and caused considerable trouble and embarrassment throughout the Southside for the past eight years."

The *Chicago Whip*, an African American newspaper, was aware of the racist implications of the raids, and it charged that the police weren't just raiding "Cabarets" in general, "but . . . Black and Tan Cabarets." To cover their motives, the police claimed black and tans were the center of racial strife, when in fact nothing could have been farther from the truth. The *Whip* saw the situation with a clear set of eyes, noting how well blacks and whites got "along together after midnight," when the evening got into full swing. Another observer reported that when "ebony and white savagely sway in the semi-darkness, their bodies writhing and contorting to the rhythm of jungle blues," they are the same regardless of race, ethnicity, or sexual orientation.

Occasionally a scandal concerning the owners or managers of cabarets gave the police another excuse for padlocking their doors and threatening their entertainers or customers with jail sentences. When the African American owner of the Radio Inn was implicated in a scandal with an unidentified "young white girl," police raided the cabaret. The Sepia Gloria Swanson happened to be appearing there, and not satisfied with just closing the cabaret, police also ordered her "to keep out of female attire on threat of arrest." All "well known pansies" got the same "personal warnings" that had been handed out to Swanson. Police harassment became so bad and so overt that the Chicago correspondent for *Zit's Weekly* in New York wrote, "Censoring seems to be in vogue" in Bronzeville.

With Mayor Kelly's approval and help, official investigative bodies, principally the Committee of Fifteen, were eager to ferret out and expose those who were transgressing against the social standards of the time. Initially convened in 1911, just after the Chicago Vice Commission published *The Social Evil in Chicago*, the Committee of Fifteen's chief goal was to rid the Windy City of prostitution and the "'white slave' traffic," here referring not just to women and girls forced into prostitution but to young men and boys as well. Along with female prostitutes, female impersonators and pansies, who were more visible than other queer men, became the nominal target of the committee's investigations.

Mayor Kelly and the Committee of Fifteen's investigators used terms derogatory to queer men, such as *pervert* and *degenerate*, to inflame the public's moral indignation and to get Chicagoans to support their battle against queer Bronzeville. They also linked those terms to the very real and very specific statistics about the increase of syphilis cases throughout Chicago, using the disease as an excuse for their anti-vice, anti-queer campaign.

As in Towertown, Bronzeville was full of opportunities for all sorts of sexual encounters, whether between men or between men and women. Ben Reitman, by now a member of the city's health department, was enlisted to investigate illicit sexual activities on the South Side during the citywide upsurge in syphilis cases. His group focused a large part of their efforts on "targeting the Cabin Inn's" pansy staff and performers, as well as the "female prostitutes working out of other local cabarets." Reitman learned quickly that soliciting or cruising for sex wasn't restricted to cabarets. One day while "standing in front of a bootleg joint at Thirty-first and State," Reitman was "approached by several joyladies who mistook his look of investigative eagerness for passion. 'We were accosted by twenty-seven women who wanted to know if we wanted 'to get a little pussy' and five men who were solicitous in inquiring if we wanted 'to get a little ass.'"

Reitman wasn't the only city investigator to get propositioned by a male prostitute. An "undercover white anti-vice investigator" reported that a "black pansy" who called himself Norman had come on to him at Thirty-First and State Streets. The investigator reported that Norman had "'asked' him" if he was "'particular'" about which he would prefer to have sex with, a woman or a man, and then before the investigator could respond added, "WOULDN'T A BOY DO?" Norman was with two friends, and one of them coyly admitted to the investigator, "A lot of white fellows come to [our] apartment for 'pleasure.'"

As in other parts of Chicago, Bronzeville also had its share of bordellos that catered to queer men. According to Samuel Steward, a postal employee named Treville Holmes owned a large house on Fiftieth Street that served as a male bordello. Rumor had it that its clients included actor Montgomery Clift, playwright Thornton Wilder, and novelists James Purdy and Wendell Wilcox. Similar houses dotted Bronzeville and welcomed men from all over Chicago.

One night in 1930, a dozen members of the Seven Arts Club decided to visit a male brothel at 3549 South Park Way on the South Side. The group included Edward Clasby. They had just walked into the building, were "still in the entrance hall of the house" in fact, when the police swooped in, hauled the group off to jail, and "charged [them] with being inmates of a resort." Clasby, who identified himself as Edward Crane, explained to the judge, Charles McKinley, how they happened to be at the bordello. After their meeting earlier that evening, he testified, they decided to head to Bronzeville to investigate "negroid temperament and mysticism." The twelve took off for South Park Way, where "a Negro medium was supposed to reside."

Besides Clasby/Crane, only two other men were identified by name in the news article. Dr. Benjamin Krohn, whose last name the reporter misspelled, was a twenty-six-year-old dentist who lived with his parents and three brothers at 4616 North Western Avenue, and Dr. Charles A. Lapin, a physician who was married and the father of two children, lived at 4452 Woodlawn Avenue. Dr. Lapin explained the group's purported purpose to the judge. The Seven Arts Club, he said, "is devoted to the study of psychology, sex, and other modern problems." They had heard that the house at South Park Way was a "psychological mixing place" and decided to visit it. Dr. Lapin didn't bother to define what a "psychological mixing place" was, and Judge McKinley never asked. Because he had been on the bench of the morals court for quite some time, McKinley probably knew exactly what it was and didn't need to ask Lapin to clarify. Since the dozen were stopped at the house's entrance before they could actually engage in any licentious behavior or perhaps because two pillars of society, the dentist and the physician, were among those arrested, McKinley banged his gavel, dismissed the charges, and set the group free with a warning: "Next time be more careful where you pursue your studies."

The South Park Way male brothel was one of the South Side's most popular, although Madam Brock's ran a close second. She might hold séances and read fortunes at her place at 5519 Drexel Boulevard, but those activities camouflaged other goings-on in her establishment. She opened the doors to her "enormous three-story" house every weekend to queer men who could "stay all night and drink all you wanted" and have sex with any of her "employees and other patrons in one of the house's many rooms."

The anti-vice campaign took its toll on Bronzeville as it had on Towertown. It became obvious to queer men—and to the owners of cabarets and other establishments that welcomed them—that their very existence was in jeopardy. The men who would like to drive them from Chicago had suddenly gotten the upper hand politically. The United States was gearing up for another world war, and Chicago's city fathers were convinced that there was no place in society for men who weren't *really* men, whose very existence seemed to corrode society's democratic foundations. The dimming of the bright lights of Towertown and Bronzeville, combined with the shadow of war that now fell across Chicago and the rest of the country, lead one writer to complain, "How naked it now looks and forlorn! The blinking lights from scattered shops are sparks from dying embers which reveal yesterday's dead pleasures as shadowy specters."

13 | Play It, Whip It, Pat It, Bang It

Mr. and Mrs. Frankie (Half Pint) Jaxon are
expecting a blessed event . . . in the near future.

ANYONE IN CHICAGO who had an ear for the new music or a taste for
bathtub gin had heard of Frankie "Half-Pint" Jaxon, and thousands had been
in the audience of at least one of his many performances. Jaxon wasn't the
typical ragtime-blues-swing-jazz performer of the first half of the twentieth
century, although he was an impresario of each. He was a great deal more.
He was known as a go-getter, recording dozens of 78s during his career, and
a jack of many trades, which included serving as the star of several radio
programs on Chicago's most popular stations; a successful producer of the
revues of up-and-comers Ethel Waters, Bessie Smith, and dozens of others;
and even a respected actor with roles in several films, one of which starred
the legendary Duke Ellington. To top it all off, Jaxon was a highly respected
and quite unique female impersonator.

Slim and baby-faced with a single, deep dimple on the left side of his face,
he stood five feet, two inches tall, thus the moniker "Half-Pint." Although
physically diminutive when compared to most of the era's male headliners,
he was a powerhouse of talent onstage: energetic, involved, captivating, and
more often than not, funny as hell. He wrote many of his own songs, but
he was also skilled at rewriting many songs already known to his audiences,
substituting his own risqué lyrics for the cleaner originals. His version of the
blues standard "How Long, How Long," for example, evolved from a complaint
about the arrival time of a train in the original lyrics to, in Jaxon's version,

a meditation on the size of a man's penis. One reviewer succinctly explained Jaxon's success. "Frankie has an individual style that registers with the cash customers," he wrote, but the reviewer didn't bother to explain what Jaxon's "individual style" was. He didn't have to. His readers knew. For his devil-may-care Jazz-Age audiences, Jaxon's renovated songs were crowd-pleasers, became some of his most popular recordings, and brought down the house during live performances.

Born Frank Devera Jackson on February 3, 1895, in Montgomery, Alabama, Jaxon and his sister, Rosa, were orphaned at an early age and went to live with their widowed aunt Rosa Taylor and her children Viola and Thomas. Around 1910 Taylor moved to Kansas City, Missouri, to live with another daughter, Willie Frazier, and Frazier's children, Ima and Vivian. She took the Jackson children with her. Shortly after Taylor died on December 5, 1914, Frazier packed up her children, moved to Chicago, and bought a house at 435 East Forty-Eighth Street. Although he had already left to begin his music career, Jaxon had grown close to Frazier and would live in her Chicago home off and on for many years. Their ties were so strong, in fact, that in 1942 he listed her as the person who would always know his whereabouts on his World War II draft card.

The fifteen-year-old Jaxon set out on the road in 1910, touring with the Henry McDaniel Minstrel Show, a troupe lead by the father of future Oscar-winner Hattie McDonald ("Mammy" in *Gone with the Wind*), who also toured with the group. Other troupes and other tours followed. Within a few years Jaxon was performing in Atlantic City's Paradise Café during the summers and spending his winters at Chicago's Sunset Café. After a stint in the army that lasted only eleven months (April 22, 1918, to March 31, 1919), during which he rose quickly to the rank of sergeant and then earned an honorable discharge, he landed a job in Atlantic City's New World Café as a singing, dancing, and comedic female impersonator. At twenty-four years old, he was a huge hit, his brand was created, and in 1919 he returned to Chicago, Bronzeville to be exact, which would be his home base for the next two and a half decades—and the perfect place for a man with his talent and a queer sexuality.

Only three years after his homecoming, Jaxon was again performing at the Sunset Café, and a reviewer for the *Chicago Defender* dubbed him "one of the greatest entertainers in the business." Other performers may have been satisfied with being adored by audiences just past the stage lights, but Jaxon wanted more, and to get more, he realized that he needed to expand his fan base. Having toured extensively as an adolescent and young adult with various vaudeville troupes, Jaxon understood the need for touring in developing a following. He began going on the road again, short trips at first with small companies of African American performers, but in March 1925, he joined Mae Dix's Chicago Harmonaders, "a big-time ofay act," who traveled west then southwest from Chicago.

Jaxon was the only African American, and the only known queer man, in the troupe of ten male musicians and Dix, and while none of the members of the all-white orchestra were racially prejudiced, the group traveled "over some very treacherous ground," as one reporter for the *Chicago Defender* revealed. Another explained that the tour had taken Jaxon to towns and cities in the grip of Jim Crow laws, and "he had to have special escort to and from the theater and . . . every time it became necessary for him to leave the hotel."

While he may have been rattled by the overt discrimination he faced, Jaxon's talent won out. He received rave reviews wherever the Chicago Harmonaders appeared. The outstanding reviews not only underscored his talent and appeal to a broader audience than he'd ever had before, they also translated into excellent publicity, which resulted in more bookings back home in Bronzeville. In fact, Jaxon, the "clever little entertainer," became very "well known to the theatrical profesh," and his demand in Chicago was huge. He headlined at all the Windy City's major hotspots, from the popular Plantation Café on the South Side to the North Side's posh Club Villa Maurice, developing into one of the superstars of the Chicago scene and packing in standing-room-only crowds at all of his performances. When its owners asked him to appear at the faltering Grande Theater on South State Street, Jaxon's performance brought in enough revenue to keep the theater's doors open for months and saved its owners from bankruptcy.

Despite Jaxon's ability to draw audiences to cabarets and theaters, it was the radio—initially his appearances on WJJD from the Palmer House six nights a week beginning February 15, 1933—that made him a household name. After he left WJJD, he appeared on other stations, including WBBM and WMAQ, guaranteeing his fans wouldn't "lose little Frankie Jaxon" from the airways.

Jaxon had struck gold when he returned to Chicago permanently because the Pansy Craze was taking hold in most entertainment venues. The flair of Jaxon's performances fit right in to the Pansy Craze scene, especially in the black and tans. Although no photographs or film clips of him performing in drag exist, and although no one ever described it in newspapers or diaries, the recordings Jaxon made give a good sense of what his performances must have been like.

On many recordings Jaxon used his trademark falsetto, which many claimed was his real, high-pitched voice, either to develop dialogues between a man and a woman—one begins a conversation, the other replies, then the first reacts, and so on to the end of the song—or simply to sing as a woman, usually about sexual topics. His dialogue songs were one of two types: actual duos with another man or solos in which he sang both the man's and the woman's parts. When singing with another man, Jaxon always took the female role.

Jaxon's unique approach to performing is evident on his very first recording, on which he performed alone in a duet. Titled "Hannah Fell in Love with My Piano," its narrator, a man, begins the number by relating his history with Hannah. They were children who played together as children do, but then, like all children, they grew up. He got a job as a piano player, and she became one of his fans. She was such a diehard fan, in fact, that she slipped from being a devotee to being an addict of his playing style. He tried to take advantage of her devotion and seduce her, but she was having none of it. She wanted his music but nothing else from him. Portraying the male character, Jaxon told his audience that Hannah ordered him to "play it, whip it, pat it, bang it, / Play it, oh, papa, play it for me!" The verbs suggest the possibility of a wild sexual encounter between them.

Then Jaxon lets out all the stops. The male character steps out of the spotlight, and Hannah takes over. She rambles through a long narrative, sometimes speaking clearly, sometimes mumbling. The male character had offered to see her home and to give her the money that she otherwise would have spent on taxi fare. She realizes that he had assumed that she would have sex with him because she's such a huge fan, and by offering to give her the money, he hoped to seal the deal. She admits that her boyfriend is out of town, but she tells him that she adores his piano playing, his talent—but not him. "Hannah Fell in Love with My Piano" became a portent of what was to come in Jaxon's future recordings.

In later solo duets, Jaxon switches from the male role to the female much earlier in the song. In "I'm Gonna Dance wit de Guy Wot Brung Me," for example, Jaxon first takes the role of a young blood out on the town, visiting the "Palais de Danse," a public dance hall, looking to pick up a woman. Suddenly he spies one. She is alone and attractive. He approaches her, asking her to dance.

No sooner did the invitation leave his mouth than Jaxon switches roles, becoming the young woman who is insulted by his come-on. He hasn't followed convention. They hadn't been properly introduced. She doesn't like his looks, thinks he's rude, and tells him she follows customs rigorously. What's more, she guarantees that "I'm gonna dance wit de guy wot brung me." The song, with its takedown of a man on the make by a strong woman, is a comic self-duet, and Jaxon's shifting roles from man to woman and back again throughout the number must have delighted his audiences.

One of Jaxon's most provocative dialogue songs is "Operation Blues," in which he pairs up with Thomas A. "Georgia Tom" Dorsey, leader of the Harlem Hamfats, who accompany the two men. Dorsey takes the role of Doctor Eazit, pronounced "ease it," and Jaxon assumes the female patient's role. Interestingly, the lyrics were written without rhymes, for the most part, and they are actually spoken not sung, both of which underscore the song's conversation-like quality. The song begins with the female patient (Jaxon) asking for the male doctor (Dorsey), the doctor's name establishing sexual innuendo from the get-go, which continues nonstop throughout the recording.

Once the doctor and the patient get down to business and discuss her ailments, the doctor tries to talk her into removing her clothing so that he can "operate." She demurs. He tells her not to be shy, and in the meantime, he has pulled his penis from his trousers, shocking her. When she asks him what he's holding, he tells her it's his "tool" and for her to relax.

Suddenly she's over her bashfulness and eager to cooperate with him. She asks if she's lying in the position that he wants her in, and although now willing to have intercourse with the physician, she warns him that he better not "hurt" her. As he enters her, she feels pain, but it soon turns to pleasure. After the doctor has finished, he asks, "Is there anymore that the doctor can do?" to which she replies, "Oh, doctor, doctor, one more kiss. . . ." Their conversation fades out into a series of giggles, sweet nothings, and groans as they resume their lovemaking.

One of Jaxon's biggest hits, "My Daddy Rocks Me (with One Steady Roll)," wasn't one of his originals. Trixie Smith recorded it seven years before he did. Smith's lyrics are risqué and don't hide the fact that she's singing about making love with her man, but they're tame compared to Jaxon's renovation. On his recording of the song, Jaxon sings it as if he were a woman from beginning to end and retains two distinct aspects of Smith's version, the structure of her lyrics and the use of the word *daddy* to refer to her lover.

The first, five-line stanza of Smith's version becomes the template for each stanza that follows. The first two lines briefly contextualize the song: she's in bed, making love with her lover. In the third line, she looks at the clock and mentions the time, which reveals to her audience how long she and her man have been making love. She wants her audience to know that her lover isn't a wham-bam-thank-you-ma'am kind of man. By the end of the song, we learn that their sexual tryst lasted an amazing nine hours, from one o'clock in the afternoon until ten that night.

Jaxon rewrote Smith's lyrics to heighten the already substantial sexual content of the original. To make the song more risqué than Smith's, he added grunts, groans, and other sensuous sounds, which were the female character's reaction to the male lover's sexual prowess. These interrupt the narrative at several points and fill the musical bridges between each stanza. The musical bridges also include the woman's instructions to her lover: "Right there! Uh! Uh, huh!" As with Smith's version, Jaxon's female persona keeps an eye on the clock during this escapade with her lover, although their rendezvous lasts only three hours. Nevertheless, at the end of the song, Jaxon's persona tells her "daddy," "Ow, baby, let's have some more." We're left knowing the female character and her man continue to make love, but if they fail to tie Smith and her lover's record, or succeeded in outdistancing it, we'll never know.

It's important to remember that by the time Jaxon recorded "My Daddy Rocks Me," the word *daddy* had already been used as code by queer men for many decades. Like John Wing, Walt Whitman, and many others before him, Jaxon was following an age-old convention through which a queer man could refer to his beloved by borrowing a term used in a typical family's life, in this case *daddy*, inferring a father/son relationship. This appropriation wasn't necessarily meant to suggest sexual performance, with the daddy taking the active role and the son accepting the passive, although it could have. It also didn't necessarily mean that one partner was much older than the other, although because woman have traditionally married men older than they, it definitely could have.

Complicating the issue even more is the fact that, more often than not, a queer man might use the daddy/son binary to suggest that one of the men—*daddy*—was financially and socially better off than the other. Of course, some women have used the same word for the same effect, as Smith does in her version, but given the fact that Jaxon is a queer man impersonating a woman who tells her man that she not only enjoys sex with him but doesn't want him to stop, the term throws a distinctly gender-bending, homoerotic cast onto the lyrics—and onto Jaxon's performance of them. This is underscored by the fact that, besides the song's title, Smith only uses *daddy* once, while Jaxon uses it four times in the actual lyrics and several other times when he makes sexual noises during the musical bridges and at the song's end. The many repetitions of *daddy* in a song sung by a man, regardless of his being a female impersonator, would have spoken volumes to any queer listener, who would have appreciated its irony and sly ribaldry.

Interestingly, many musicologists believe Jaxon's version of "My Daddy Rocks Me" not only gave another genre of popular music—rock and roll—its name but is the first musical recording to include an orgasm. Jaxon's song was so erotic that ads for the song used its carnality to entice people to buy copies. One ad even exclaimed that Jaxon's song had "more heat in it than a steel mill."

Jaxon wasn't limited to adopting a female's role during his performances. In his version of "Willie the Weeper," for example, which was recorded and performed by countless others before he rewrote its lyrics and recorded it, he spoke loud and clear to a queer audience without using a female persona. Jaxon's Willie is a chimney sweep who's addicted to drugs. He doesn't identify which drug Willie prefers, but by referring to Willie's hallucinations in the song, he suggests opium. Opium dens were very popular in large urban centers and were the rage just before and during the Jazz Age—and Chicago had its share.

As the song opens, Jaxon gives a brief glimpse into one of Willie's hallucinations. He's standing in an Artic-like landscape when someone behind him calls him by name. He swivels around to find out who's calling him and sees a "nudie chump . . . dancing in his BVDs." If the nearly naked man didn't grab the attention of queer men listening to the song, the Freudianism of what he wanted to eat—"biscuits eighteen inches long"—certainly would have. Four years after Jaxon recorded "Willie the Weeper," Cabell "Cab" Calloway heterosexualized the lyrics, changed "Willie" to "Minnie," and released "Minnie the Moocher," his signature song and a huge hit.

Jaxon didn't always add a queer element to his songs. Years before it was acceptable, he wrote and recorded a paean to being African American, "Chocolate to the Bone (I'm So Happy I'm Brownskin)." In it he characterizes the world in which he lives as being "brownskin," not just the most obvious aspects of it but *all* of it, from the "bed" in which he slept to its "bugs" that nibbled on him. Most important to the song and its audiences, however, is the note of acceptance and even joy that he feels over being African American, and he includes at the end of each stanza, "I'm so glad I'm brown skin, chocolate to the bone."

Months before the end of the 1920s, Jaxon was set to appear as a leading character in a politically charged motion picture. Cartoons, films, novels, and other forms of entertainment had already begun to address the plight of the common people—black and white—who were defenseless against those in power, and in August 1929, Jaxon signed with Tricolor Picture Corporation to produce and to star in *The Mortgage Man*, a "talkie." "The show is a mixture of mirth and pathos," according to one report, "and shows life as it is with a couple at the hands of the mortgage shark." Jaxon was scheduled to appear in drag in the role of the Old Woman, who with her husband, played by Floyd Cardwell, were the targets of an unscrupulous banker. This wouldn't have been Jaxon's first celluloid performance. He had had a bit part in King Vidor's *Hallelujah* in the cabaret scene and a small role in Duke Ellington's *Black and Tan Fantasy*, both released in early 1929. In fact, Jaxon thought of himself as an actor and would continue to claim that occupation, not musician, on a number of official documents, such as the census, for much of his life. Perhaps he believed his female impersonation, certainly a form of acting, was more important than his role as a musician.

Unfortunately, *The Mortgage Man* was never produced, probably because the Great Depression struck the United States two months after Jaxon signed the contract. Had the film been made, he could have combined his female impersonation abilities with his concern for social justice on film as he had already done on vinyl with "Chocolate to the Bone" and "Mortgage Blues," which, as one musicologist noted, begins with "a brusque and spirited reference to Marcus Garvey, founder of the Universal Negro Improvement Association and spokesman for the Back to Africa Movement" that "probably got by any Caucasians but without a doubt resonated among his . . . African-American audience."

As the 1920s ended, Jaxon's popularity skyrocketed. One of the best indicators of Jaxon's tremendous popularity was his invitation to perform at the opening night ceremonies for the Chicago World's Fair on May 27, 1933. He

was the only African American, as well as the only known female impersonator and queer man, hired for the $7.50 per-person dance ($137 per ticket in
today's money) held at the Streets of Paris exhibition.

A month later a peculiar piece of information, the only bit of personal news
about the star that was ever to be published during his lifetime, surfaced in the
Chicago Defender. Columnist Allan McMillan announced, "Mr. and Mrs. Frankie
(Half Pint) Jaxon are expecting a blessed event . . . in the near future." As it turns
out, Jaxon's marriage and baby-to-be are shrouded in mystery and may have
been a ruse to protect Jaxon's career, similar to the ploy that Flo Ziegfeld created
to divert attention from Eugen Sandow's relationship with Martinus Sieveking.

The U.S. Census for 1930 includes the only other mention of Jaxon's wife.
Then thirty-eight years old, Jaxon lived, it claimed, in a house he rented at 5149
Calumet Avenue with Evelyn, a thirty-six-year-old white woman identified as
his wife. In fact, Evelyn was home on April 11 when the census taker, Magnolia
S. Green, knocked on the front door and asked Evelyn for the information the
census form required. Evelyn told Green that she and Jaxon were married in
1922, that he was an "actor" in a "theater," and that they had two "lodgers."
One was thirty-year-old Cliff Oliver, an African American and a cook for a
railroad (probably in a club car like Henry Gerber's friend Abraham Sutton),
and the other, twenty-six-year-old Helen McGinnis, was a telegraph operator.
Evelyn added that Oliver and McGinnis were single. The census report also
reveals that, like Evelyn, McGinnis was white. If Jaxon had been married for the
previous eight years, it seems likely that at least one of the scores of newspaper
articles written about him would have mentioned his wife at some point. The
Chicago Defender, which ran scores of articles and brief mentions about him,
often mentioned the spouses or children of similarly well-establish performers,
but it never included a word about Evelyn in any of the many articles and
notes it published about Jaxon. In 1929, for example, the *Chicago Defender*
listed Jaxon's address in Bronzeville as 220 E. Garfield Boulevard, Apartment
21, an appropriate place to mention a wife, but it didn't.

Making matters even more interesting is the fact that Evelyn and Jaxon's
marriage was never recorded—at least not in Illinois, where the couple lived; not
in New Jersey, where Evelyn was born and raised; and not in New York, New Jersey's neighboring state, where Jaxon often performed. While interracial marriages
were outlawed in many states at the time, they were legal in all three of those,
and were the two actually married, there would have been some legal record of it.

Complicating the information in McMillan's article is the fact that by 1930 births had to be recorded via official forms in every state throughout the United States, and yet there is no birth certificate in the records in Illinois or any other state for a child born to the couple. Nor is there any record of the death of a child associated with them. Because there is no documentation of Jaxon's marriage or the birth of his child, it seems likely that Evelyn and the baby were camouflage, diverting prying eyes from what might have been two queer men, Jaxon and Oliver, and two queer women, Evelyn and McGinnis, living under the same roof.

There was good reason for the camouflage too. By the time the birth announcement appeared in the *Defender*, the police were already raiding and shutting down many of Towertown's queer resorts, and they had begun targeting the Bronzeville cabarets that were known for their female impersonator shows. It seems plausible that, aware of Mayor Kelly's crackdowns on entertainment venues, Jaxon believed his career—his livelihood—was in jeopardy. The sudden appearance of a missus in his life would have served to deflect attention from his queer performances, and the promise of a child in the future would have added another, even thicker layer to the camouflage. With a note in widely circulated newspaper like the *Defender* claiming matrimony and parenthood, Jaxon transformed himself from a cross-dressing deviant to a respectable *real* man, even if he pretended to be a woman onstage or on his recordings.

The political pendulum that had swung to the left at the beginning of the 1920s, not long after Jaxon had debuted in Bronzeville, swung to the opposite direction by 1939, when the Nazis marched into Poland. The clubs in Bronzeville and Towertown that had openly staged female impersonator acts and welcomed queer men into their audiences had all but disappeared. Any man not exhibiting masculinity—and *masculinity* meant *heterosexuality*, a necessary quality, or so the majority of society believed, for the nation to be successful in a war—was anathema to the country. The year 1939, which marks the beginning of World War II in Europe, also denotes, for all intents and purposes, the end of the Pansy Craze in Chicago. It was also the year in which one of Bronzeville's most charismatic ministers struggled to retain his place in his church and in his neighborhood.

Eight-year-old Clarence H. Cobbs moved to Chicago from Memphis in 1916, following his mother, who had moved there a few years earlier. After attending the Pilgrim Baptist Church for a number of years, Cobbs felt himself drawn to the ministry, and William F. Taylor, founder and head of the Metropolitan Spiritual Churches of Christ (MSCC), ordained Cobbs when he was twenty-one. Located in Kansas City, Missouri, the MSCC was the mother church for a number of other churches, and the following year Cobbs founded his own house of worship, the First Church of Deliverance, in Bronzeville.

In its earliest days, Cobbs's church held services in the basement of his home at 3663 South Indiana Avenue, using his mother's ironing board as an altar. Initially, his congregation numbered less than a dozen people, but it grew, and as the congregation grew, it needed more space. Cobbs moved services to a building on South State Street and then, in 1933, to an abandoned "hat factory" at 4315 South Wabash. Once the church's finances stabilized, Cobbs converted the factory into the building that is still used by its members. The following year Cobbs took his message to the airwaves and held Sunday-evening services over the church's own radio station. By then he had "nine thousand congregants" and a "200-member choir."

In 1939, at the height of his career and one of the most powerful men in Chicago, Cobbs found himself the focus of an investigation "by state's attorney's police concerning wide-spread rumors of a scandalous nature"—as the *Chicago Defender*, which broke the news on November 25, 1939, reported. Speculations about Cobbs—that he was involved in a sexual relationship with his secretary, Edward Bolden, with whom he vacationed every year—had been swirling around the preacher for years. Cobbs and Bolden's trips together included several weeks in Argentina that same year. Given Cobbs's status in the community, most of his congregants and Bronzeville residents as a whole had simply ignored the gossip, but the *Defender* decided to make it public.

No sooner had the *Defender* published the news about the investigation and its insinuations about Cobbs's sexuality than another minister attacked him verbally. During one of his sermons, the Rev. William S. Bradden called Cobbs "a travesty on the sacredness of the Christian church." Attention to Cobbs's relationship with Bolden become so intense that Cobbs began to defend himself from the accusations during his live radio broadcasts. "I am full man," he claimed over and over again from his pulpit, suggesting he was not a pansy, one of the part man, part woman denizens who had become so evident on the sidewalks and in the cabarets and cafés of Bronzeville.

Fig. 18. The Rev. Clarence H. Cobbs (1907–1979), one of the most powerful voices in Bronzeville, was dogged by rumors of his relationship with R. Edward Bolden, his secretary. *Virginia G. Harsh Research Collection*

The *Defender* never bothered to give any evidence to support the rumors it was helping to spread, and it would only report that Cobbs had been involved in an "unsavory incident of serious proportions." It did add that a number of "well known citizens, some of the prominent politicians and holders of high city officers [*sic*]," were also involved, but it never identified them or what their involvement was. When Cobbs demanded that the *Defender* reveal its evidence of his—supposed—sexual activity with Bolden and perhaps with other men, it admitted it had none, and Cobbs sued the paper's publisher for libel, asking for $250,000 in damages ($4.5 million in today's money).

Five months later Cobbs's suit was dismissed by the courts. He appealed. Two months after that, he lost his appeal and was ordered to pay one hundred dollars in court costs. Then on March 22, 1940, the *Chicago Defender* surprisingly reported that Cobbs had somehow won his suit after all. Having been exonerated, he shelved his claim of $250,000, and yet not all was forgiven. When he spotted a reporter from the *Defender* among his congregants one Sunday morning a few months later that year, he stopped the service and wouldn't continue until the man left. Public accusations about Cobbs's sexuality ended, but the gossip did not—and with good reason. He and Bolden continued their trips together, even spending a lengthy vacation in Paris.

Frankie Jaxon would have heard all about Cobbs and his relationship with Bolden and the troubles that Cobbs faced because of it. That, along with all of the closings of Bronzeville cabarets, undoubtedly helped convince Jaxon to abandon show business and public life. Despite his camouflage, the handwriting on the wall became too threatening to him, and rather than allow his career to be killed off slowly, police raid by police raid, jail sentence by jail sentence, he simply walked away from it. It took him three years, but in the spring of 1942, he chucked it all, leaving the stage and fame, the music, the bright lights, and the hoopla. He moved to 922 French Street, N.W., Washington, DC, without a wife and without a child and began working for the federal government. Some claimed that he had a post at the Pentagon. Leaving that job two years later, he transferred to Los Angeles, moving into 1113 E. 119th Street. Although only sixty-one years old, his health began to fail, and on May 15, 1953, he died in a Veterans Administration hospital, but not without leaving his queer fans a message.

In one of his last recordings, "Be Your Natural Self," cut on April 17, 1940, Jaxon seems to be giving advice to those who, like him, had once been open about their queer sexuality but now felt the very real need to hide it. He relied on ambiguity to communicate his message. While on one level he seems to be cautioning listeners about the ease by which the famous can fall, and with them their money and prestige, Jaxon is also warning men in his audience to be "careful" because of the political climate in which they were living. He tells them, "Watch your step" and "Be careful in what you say," counsel that seems unnecessary to the once rich or famous but very important to the sexually transgressive. Yet no matter what, they must be their "natural self." In other words, while warning them to play it safe during the crackdown on cabarets and the arrests of the performers and patrons, Jaxon also advised queer men not to hide their identities. It was a thin line he was suggesting they walk, a complicated way to live. Some were able to follow his advice. Some were not. Some never had a brush with the law. Others weren't so lucky.

14 | Once a Bitch, Always a Bitch

Queers were born that way.

THE IDENTITY OF THE YOUNG MAN called "Herman" is a mystery. That may have been his real name or simply the one he assumed when, in the early 1930s, Earl W. Bruce, a graduate student in sociology from the University of Chicago, began interviewing him. As part of their course work, the sociology students were sent into the streets of Chicago to study individuals whom they considered examples of "social disorganization," compiling the individuals' life histories and sometimes writing follow-up reports about them. As far as the head of the University of Chicago's sociology department, Ernest W. Burgess, was concerned, homosexuals were perfect examples of the disruption in society that he believed had infected Chicago for decades.

Still feeling somewhat empowered and safe from legal prosecution within the bubble created by the Pansy Craze, the queer men with whom Bruce became acquainted were often very candid about their lives and often included extensive explanations about their sexual experiences, and he was able to compile scores of their personal histories, all saved by Burgess, who donated them to the university's library. Yet despite the fact that the queer men were quite open, their identities were disguised—just in case. They became known simply as "Chickie," "Mr. X," and other names.

Herman appears to have been one of the fair-haired boys of a group of queer men, many of whom lived on the North Side in and around Towertown. Herman, however, lived with his parents on the South Side and worked in the Loop. Plenty of the group's dramas involving boyfriends, sex, rivalries, and petty jealousies revolved around him. Born in 1903, Herman was first interviewed in 1931, and the interviews continued off and on for the next two years. He was in love with an older man, Harry Lipson, a dress designer who lived with his elderly parents on the Northwest Side, supporting them financially, but at the same time, Herman also had a boyfriend known as "Clarence."

Herman's sexual activities with other men began when he was a child, a fact common among many of the queer men Bruce interviewed. Robert was five years old when he had his first same-sex sexual experience. "Lester" was six. "Jimmy" was seven, and "Harold" nine. Older boys or men coerced some into sex. Others agreed willingly, even eagerly.

Bruce wrote that because of some of the comments that Herman had made, he believed that when he was a child, Herman had been "acted upon by the other boys" in his neighborhood, but Herman also admitted that he had freely engaged in sex with "a cousin" who was "twice his age." At the same time, he insisted that his cousin wasn't queer but simply wanted sex and didn't care who his partner was. Herman added, "I do not care how straight a person may be but when he gets in passion he will start fooling around" with anyone, male or female.

A short time later, Herman began exploring his sexuality with a neighbor girl, playing "doctor and nurse" with her. Then when he was eighteen, he "kept company with a girl" who was two years younger than he. He often visited her home on the North Side, where they listened to music. One night while they "were sitting very close to one another," his "sexual passion was aroused" and he "lost control" and "tried to get her to have sexual intercourse." She rebuffed his advances. It didn't take long for her father, who "wanted a man for her with money," to tell her to break it off with Herman, but the two continued to meet "on the sly." Eventually the father discovered their secret rendezvous, packed the family up, and moved away. Herman didn't grieve over the breakup because, as he explained, their relationship "was just a friendship," nothing romantic or even sexual, and shortly afterward Herman began seeing a man.

He was working behind a counter at Mandel's, the department store where, decades earlier, James Janes and Frank Smith were caught and arrested for shoplifting women's clothing. One day one of the store's executives dropped by unexpectedly and began talking to Herman. He asked Herman about his work, how long he had been employed at Mandel's, and other job-related matters. The older man was very serious, the eighteen-year-old Herman later recalled.

A month or so later the executive appeared at Herman's counter again, but this time Herman noticed the exec spoke "in a more friendly manner." He asked Herman if he would like to visit him at his home. Herman agreed. A few days passed before Herman found his way to the executive's house. The man led Herman to the sunroom, where they sat down side by side on a sofa to talk. Only a few minutes into their conversation, the man began to grope Herman, who "moved away" to another sofa.

The man followed him, and as he put his hand on Herman's lap, he asked, "Do you mind?"

Herman said yes, he did mind, but that didn't stop the executive, who then told Herman to lie down on the sofa. When Herman did, the older man began caressing him through his trousers, saying, "Don't mind what I do. We are all human." He *frenched* Herman (performed fellatio on him), and when he was done, he paid Herman five dollars and told him to keep what had just happened between them a secret. He also asked Herman to drop by again the following week. Herman took the money and agreed to return.

Herman kept his promise and showed up at the executive's the following week, but when he walked into the living room, he found another young male employee already there. Almost immediately the other employee began groping and kissing Herman in front of their boss, embarrassing Herman so much that he "became nauseated." He explained, "It was the first time that a man had ever kissed me." The executive fellated Herman again and gave him another five dollars.

Herman was wracked with guilt and disgust. On one hand, he got a "thrill" out of sex with the older man, but at the same time, he "felt like a prostitute." Herman kept away from the man for about three months, but then he found himself at the man's home again, and this time the man asked Herman to "reciprocate," promising to "double the amount of money" if he would. Herman refused, but he did allow the man to french him again and accepted money for it—another five dollars. Herman later admitted to Bruce, "I did not care to go to his place unless I received money."

Herman visited the executive's home several more times, but eventually the man decided not to pay Herman the usual amount. The older man must have seen the look on Herman's face when he handed the eighteen-year-old two dollars instead of the five he was expecting. "You are getting the same enjoyment that I am getting," the executive explained to Herman. "I do not see why I should pay you." Then after a half a dozen more trips to the executive's home, Herman stopped visiting him altogether and kept away from him for two years; however, then he made his way back to the older man's home. They picked up where they had left off.

Some of the queer men who traded sex for money learned the logistics of prostitution from other queer men. One, an unnamed soldier, told Bruce: "I met a fellow from Morgan Park. He said if you ever want to make money come down to Randolph and State in your uniform and stand with your arms crossed. That was a sign that you could and wanted to be picked up. You can make five or ten dollars easy that way." The stretch of sidewalk along State Street from Randolph down to Washington—in front of what was then Marshall Field's department store—had long been cruising grounds for Chicago's queer men, who used a variety of signals and codes that told those in the know who was on the make. As the investigator for the Chicago Vice Commission learned two decades earlier, wearing a red necktie was a dead giveaway. By the mid-1930s crossed arms had become another signal.

Nineteen-year-old Alexander Stahl, who claimed not to be queer, swore he discovered sex for money by accident. He told Bruce that he was in a striptease joint, one of the many just south of the Loop, when a man sitting beside him began chatting with him. That made Stahl laugh because "he had a high-pitched voice just like a girl." The man asked Stahl if he had a place to stay for the night. When Stahl replied that he didn't because he was on his way out of town, the man took him to his home on Delaware Place in the heart of Towertown. Stahl continued: "He cooked a meal for me and I was wondering why he was so big-hearted. I wondered about it while I was eating. After eating, he put his arms around me and began kissing me."

Stahl pushed the older man away and told him that he didn't want to "'punk' around" and grabbed his hat as if to leave. Unwilling to end his evening with Stahl, the older man invited Stahl to a party a short walk away. They arrived at the party around eleven o'clock. As it turned out, a large number of the men at the party were in drag, and many of them were with "their husbands." Unfortunately, Stahl didn't mention if the female impersonators' escorts were trade, "normal" men, or masculine-acting queer men.

Stahl had been drinking for some time when he spotted "a beautiful young girl. She was a bitchy thing. The shape she had you couldn't beat, so I asked this man to introduce me to her." Her name was Gertie, and as Stahl recalled, "Gertie sure looked good." He continued to drink and began kissing her.

It turns out that Stahl was an ill-tempered drunk, and he got into a fight with the "husband" of one of the female impersonators. Their friends stepped in and separated Stahl and the other man. After that, Stahl recalled, he led Gertie into a bedroom, "laid her on the bed," and "pulled down her pants. Here was a goddamn prick staring at me," he told Bruce. "That was the goddamnest shock of my life." Disgusted, he "began spitting. . . . To think that I had been hugging and kissing Gertie before—I was so damn sore that I hit Gertie one on the jaw." She screamed, which brought the other partygoers into the bedroom. Stahl slung his fists at anyone near him as he ran out of the apartment.

Stahl ended up at Bughouse Square, but he never told Bruce why he ended up there and not someplace where men didn't congregate to solicit others for sex. Perhaps it was just coincidental. Regardless, it was about three o'clock in the morning when he sat down on a bench. He found twenty-two dollars ($312 in today's money) in his pocket, far more cash than he had had before the party, but he had no idea how it got there. He began to notice men in the park who were slipping in and out of the bushes and behind trees with one another. A man sat down beside him, and Stahl, still shocked by his experience with Gertie, couldn't help but spill the beans to him.

As it turned out, the man was a prostitute, and he gave Stahl the lowdown. "This guy told me," Stahl said, "that if I worked it right with these queers I would make a lot of money." After talking to the prostitute, Stahl realized what the twenty-two dollars was all about. He decided that someone at the party must have thought he was trade and hired him for sex, although he was too drunk to remember who. Stahl resolved then and there that if he could make so much money just for sex, he would begin selling his sexual favors to men who could afford him.

Similarly, after fending off the advances of an older man at a movie house, "Carl" went home and described his experience to his roommate, who worked as trade. Carl remembered that his roommate "poked fun at me & told me what a great chance I had missed and wished that he was in my position." Then he instructed Carl on how to conduct himself to attract men in the future: "He told me to act dumb," pretending as if he knew nothing about queers or trade, and to act as if he wouldn't engage in sex with them before they agreed to his price.

The roommate also told Carl the two cardinal rules of the profession. First, once Carl had agreed to have sex with the man, he was to make sure that the man understood he had agreed to sex only to make money and not for his own satisfaction. Second, after he undressed, the man was to give him the money they had agreed on before anything happened between them. To make sure Carl got off on the right foot, the roommate even took him to the "busy section" of Chicago, probably Towertown or the Loop, to teach him how to spot and then to come on to queers.

"J.B.," also called "Jack," explained the "Queen Racket," as he called it, to Bruce. *Queen* referred to effeminate queer men. Regardless of whether or not the prostitute was queer, he must remain "aloof" and "pretend to be a dummy" about queers and their sexual activities so that he appeared to be "a real he-man" and not queer at all. Queens, J.B. said, could easily have experiences with other queens if they wanted, but most preferred finding a man who wasn't queer but who was willing to have sex with them even if they had to pay for it. Mr. H, who was a queer prostitute but pretended not to be, called the queen racket "playing trade" or, in other words, *pretending* to be trade. There were also other tricks some queer men played.

A young man recalled how another young man known as "C" showed him the easiest way to make some extra money in Chicago's movie theaters, including the Astor in the Loop at 12 S. Clark Street and the La Salle at 110 W. Madison Avenue in the West Madison Street vice district. The young man explained that he and C were in the Astor when a man beside C began to caress C's legs. C objected and stood up, saying he was going to "report him to the management," but the man pulled C back into his seat and offered him a dollar to keep him from complaining. Then to the young man's surprise, C "began to unbutton his pants and pulled his penis out" and asked the man if he still wanted to feel him up. C explained to the man that he could, if he still wanted to, "because it was worth the dollar."

A second man, who was sitting next to the young man, noticed that C and the first man were carrying on and began craning his neck, trying to get a better view of their sexual encounter. The young man told him to mind his own business, and after "this was over," the young man and C "managed to ditch" the first man, who had given C the dollar. On their walk home, C gave the young man the money he had just earned because the young man needed it more than C did. C told him that "there were quite a few Queers that would take in this particular show just to make some rough trade and if I would go there every day in the week and change from one seat to another and remain there for the whole day I would run into some queer" who would be willing to pay him for sex.

"Ted," another young man Bruce interviewed, revealed how he met a man at the Thompson's Restaurant at 27 West Randolph Street who was willing to pay him for sex. Thompson's Restaurant was a chain that was popular among queer men in Chicago. Ted and his friends "Sidney," "Stoney," and "Jack" were eating a meal there one night when Sidney noticed a man looking at them. Sidney told Ted that he could earn "$5.00 or more" from the man if he were interested in having sex with him. He was, and so Ted walked over to the man's table, sat down, and introduced himself. They began to chitchat. Then the man got down to business and asked Ted if they could "put on a party for tonight," to which Ted replied, "Well, name your price." The man offered him three dollars, which Ted accepted.

It was three o'clock in the morning when they left Thompson's. They began walking up LaSalle to the Lincoln Hotel at 1816 North Clark Street. It had a popular bathhouse in the basement with private rooms. On their way, the man admitted to Ted that he was afraid that Ted's friends might be lying in wait somewhere along the way to "jump him." Ted assured him he had no reason to be afraid. Once they arrived at the Lincoln Hotel, several miles north of the restaurant where they had met, the man got into an argument with the desk clerk, who was trying to overcharge him for the bathhouse room. Finally the price was settled. The man got two keys, and he gave one to Ted, who went to the room first. The man followed a short time later. Once behind closed doors, Ted explained to Bruce, "I stripped and he stripped."

Not all of the young men who indulged in prostitution were successful at it. One such young man, known only as "Harold," was arrested for selling his sexual favors. "Harold was picked up by the police at 4:00 a.m. at Bughouse Square," one of Harold's friends recalled, "and sentenced to 30 days in the House of Correction for loitering and soliciting. When he was released, Max," who was Harold's lover, "made arrangements for them to go to Elgin," a small city west of Chicago, "to live." Max hoped the move would keep Harold on the straight and narrow.

However, not all queer men who were strapped for cash resorted to prostitution. As the Great Depression raged and unemployment reached 25 percent of the US population, many queer men found work in the Works Progress Administration. Some helped to repair roads or bridges and to construct libraries, schools, or other public buildings. Those with artistic abilities—musicians, playwrights, painters, writers, and so on—were hired to work for the WPA's Federal Project Number One. John D. Hagenhofer was only one of many who did.

Fig. 19. John D. Hagenhofer
(1913–1980) gained attention
for his paintings, illustrations,
cartoons, and modern designs
after moving from Chicago to
Boston, but despite exhibiting
at the Museum of Modern Art,
he never realized the promise
of his early work. *Courtesy of
Gerber/Hart Library and Archives*

The facts of John David Hagenhofer's life are few and far between. Born in Chicago in 1911, he was only eighteen when the Great Depression enveloped the United States. During high school, his talent as an artist blossomed, and after graduation in 1929 or 1930, he enrolled in courses at the Chicago Academy of Fine Arts and the Art Institute and immersed himself in painting, drawing, and photography. In the summer of 1933, he took a series of photographs of his friends Mikey and Heine and a young man called Corswandt.

By 1935 the twenty-four-year-old Hagenhofer had moved to Boston, and after living in several different rooming houses, he moved into Prescott Townsend's home on Beacon Hill, where six other men also lived. A scion of one of the city's leading families, Townsend was a queer activist, lecturing various legislative bodies and other organizations on homosexual rights, but he was only tolerated by the city fathers and others in power because of his family name and his position in society. Otherwise, his comments fell on deaf ears.

While living in Boston, Hagenhofer began working for the WPA, but unfortunately no one recorded what his actual job was. It appears that he may have already shifted at least some of his attention from photography to paint-

Fig. 20. Hagenhofer's friends Mickey and Heine posed for several of his early photographs. Some slang dictionaries define *batey* as slightly or vaguely obscene, as Heine's pose suggests. *Courtesy of Gerber/Hart Library and Archives*

ing by this time, and he identified his occupation in the 1940 federal census as "artist." In that same year, judges for an exhibit at the Museum of Modern Art in New York selected his painting *The Sunken City (Shenendoah) [sic] or "Surface Rights"* in the PM Competition: The Artist as Reporter. He received a fifty-dollar finalist prize for it.

Shortly after the outbreak of World War II, Hagenhofer decided to return to Chicago and enlisted in the army to "kick Nazi ass," as he put it. According to his niece, Hagenhofer was "loud, expressive, opinionated, very funny in an effete, dry, and cutting way. He was opposed to fascism in all its forms from a very young age." His military service began on April 30, 1942, but he spent the war stateside until a month before the armistice, when he was sent to Germany. He was released from active duty on January 9, 1946, and he returned to Chicago to live for a few years. In the mid-1950s, he taught at the Rhode Island School of Design for a short time before he returned to Chicago,

"old boy" Corswandt.
6.11.33.

Fig. 21. Another of Hagenhofer's friends posed for him wearing men's clothing while donning a pair of women's dangling earrings. *Courtesy of Gerber/ Hart Library and Archives*

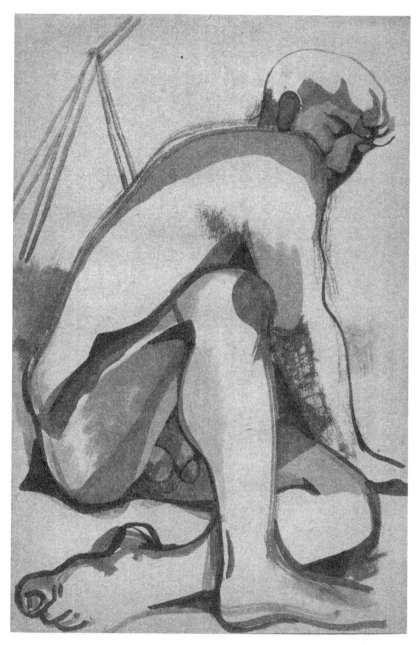

Fig. 22. Hagenhofer's paintings often employed very lush colors, which heightened the sensuality of their subjects, as in this untitled piece. *Courtesy of Gerber/Hart Library and Archives*

where he ended up living "from social security check to social security check." He died in 1980 from liver cancer. Unfortunately, he never fully realized the promise of his artistic talent.

Like Hagenhofer, photographer Edmund Teske also worked for the WPA, but Teske's art was far more daring than Hagenhofer's. Teske became interested in photography in 1923, when he was twelve years old, through the mentoring of one of his teachers, Mabel A. Morehouse. He left high school in his junior year, 1927, and spent the next fifteen or so years sharpening his talent. In the meantime he began a series of odd jobs, which included a stint in the stock room of Mandel's department store.

The 1930s were a decade of exploration and networking for Teske. He became acquainted with some of the nation's most noted artists, among them Alfred Stieglitz, Georgia O'Keeffe, Ansel Adams, and László Moholy-Nagy, as well as architect Frank Lloyd Wright. He also met a number of Chicago's movers and shakers in the local art world, including Nathan Lerner, Henry Darger's landlord, who became a close friend. Like Lerner, Teske began teaching at the New Bauhaus School of Design, where he also sat in on classes.

Perhaps more important, Teske became a close friend of photographer Edwin Bolan, whose nude photographs of men were "unabashedly erotic." Teske believed that Bolan "was very much into the wonder and the beauty of the athletic male being and he emulated the beauty of the male form as it was emulated in ancient Greece." It was probably through Bolan's influence that Teske took a series of nude photographs of several of his friends in the studio he had built in his family's basement, among them *Harry Gillies and Raymond Hammond* (1933–1934). One critic has declared that in the Gillies and Hammond photograph, "the glinting torso of the youth in the background upstages his face, which offers no eye contact—or ostensible personality." The photograph, he continued, is "bravely openhearted and candid . . . designed only for the photographer's personal enjoyment and for sharing with an intimate circle as expressions of youthful carnality and the bonds of same-sex friendship."

Shortly thereafter the twenty-three-year-old designed sets for the theater department of Jane Addams's Hull House for several weeks and occasionally even acted in its productions; he organized his first solo show at the Blackstone Theater (now the Merle Reskin Theatre); and he became assistant to photographer A. George Miller in his studio, Photography, Inc. Near the end of the decade, Teske designed sets for the WPA's Theater Project in Chicago and took the photographs that would become one of his most important early projects, a series of black-and-whites titled *Portrait of My City* through which he emphasized day-to-day life in Chicago. Unfortunately, he didn't complete the series but incorporated it into another, *Song of Dust*, later in his life.

As the 1930s drew to a close, Teske took a number of striking black-and-whites, many nude, of his then lover, Richard Soakup. In one, *Richard Soakup, Chicago* (1940), the younger man, "bare-chested and grease-covered, emerges from a dark interior, an automobile in the background, which he has clearly just been repairing. The natural light is focused on Soakup's tousled, curly blond hair and smooth chest." The effect of the photo is noteworthy: "Although Soakup is engaged in labor usually associated with men, the intimate image has a soft, almost feminine, quality to it."

Like many young men of his generation, Teske was drafted for military service at the outbreak of the Second World War, but he failed the medical examination because of his "asocial tendencies, psychoneurosis and emotional instability," a coded indictment of his homosexuality. Nevertheless, the government took note of his talent and offered him a job with the Army Corps of Engineers on Rock Island, near the Illinois-Iowa border, assisting in the production of aerial photographs for the war effort. While working for the government, he lived across the Mississippi River in Davenport, Iowa, and took a series of nude photographs of two of his coworkers, one of whom modeled for *Nude, Davenport, Iowa* (1942), a triptych of photos of the same young man. One critic has noted that

> there is an obvious delight taken in the sculpted contours of the young man's muscled physique, as well as a sense of Teske's careful direction of the sitting, with the model shifting the position of his head slightly between exposures. While the sitter initially had his hands crossed in his lap, he has revealed himself completely to the photographer

by the last of the photographs. "It is a bold and forthright appreciation of the nude male form," the critic continued, "though there is a lingering tentativeness in Teske's decision to truncate the composition above the genitals, which mitigates the subject's full erotic potential."

At about the same time, Teske came to a conclusion about how to deal with his homosexuality within the context of his life as an artist. He wrote in his journal that he meant to

> accept the facts of life with courage and serenity to develop talent, as an outlet for emotion, and to find happiness in the world of the mind and spirit. In the days when Greece and Rome ruled the world in arts and letters and philosophy, love of man for man reached openly its pinnacle of beauty. Civilization today, moving forward, must eventually recognize these true facts of love and sex variations.

In early spring of 1943, Teske had had enough of the mind-numbing job with the Army Corps of Engineers and resigned. He returned to Chicago briefly, and that summer he packed up his things and moved to Los Angeles. He would live in California for the rest of his life, often hand to mouth, creating the photographs for which he would achieve critical, if not financial, success.

Unlike Hagenhofer or Teske, Herman had no artistic aspirations, and having landed himself a job, he wasn't compelled to offer himself to men at Bughouse Square as Harold did. Herman's relationship with the Mandel's executive was a private transaction held between two men who knew one another, so there was no chance of his being arrested as Harold had been. Nevertheless, guilt consumed him after the exchange of sex for money was over, and he eventually left Mandel's and began working at *Collier's*, a national weekly magazine with a branch office in Chicago at 110 S. Dearborn Street, the same magazine for which J. C. Leyendecker had created a large number of covers. At what must have been a party composed of at least some queer men who also worked at *Collier's*, Herman was sitting down, enjoying himself, when a "nice looking clean cut fellow about 38 years of age" approached him and asked if he could sit on Herman's lap. After a brief chat, the man asked Herman to go upstairs with him. Herman did and later confessed to Bruce that although he "did not strip completely," he and the older man had engaged in sex.

Although he had experienced sex with men for the past five years, Herman wouldn't actually be considered a part of Chicago's queer community until 1925, at the height of the Pansy Craze. He was twenty-two years old and had stopped off at an elevated train station men's room where he noticed a man at the sink, washing his hands. Herman took a long time to urinate, and the man, who had begun staring at him, finally asked Herman, "What is the matter?"

"I am very self-conscious when somebody's in the room. I can't take a leak," Herman told the man, whom he identified as "Mr. L."

Apparently nothing happened between them then, but Herman had enchanted Mr. L., who didn't want to let the younger man slip away. To forestall their separation, Mr. L. accompanied Herman on the train when it arrived and talked with him about anything that happened to pop into his head. For example, out of the blue he asked Herman if he happened to be Jewish. Herman was, he said, and then Mr. L. mentioned having Jewish relatives and "loads of Jewish friends." Mr. L. offered to buy Herman a cup of coffee, and during their time together at the café, Herman began to warm up to the man. He agreed to meet Mr. L two days later.

That evening, Mr. L took Herman to Oak Street Beach, a popular gathering place—and a major cruising area—for queer men that stretched along Lake Michigan in Towertown. Herman had never been there before, and being a fresh face, he quickly became the center of attention. He met "Maxie," who "took a liking" to Herman instantly. Their conversation turned to men and sex, and they "started talking about affairs." Herman admitted, "I did not know what a love affair" between men "was at this time." He had never even considered the possibility that men could fall in love with one another. "I only wanted friendship," he told Maxie. For Herman, *friendships* were relationships based on love without sex, while *affairs* were simply sexual encounters regardless of whether they lasted only a night or for months.

Maxie explained to Herman that "fellows fell in love with one another" all the time.

Herman was skeptical about whether or not queer men could develop a relationship built on love that also included sex. Sure, sex alone could be the basis of a relationship. Love could too. But sex *and* love? He wasn't convinced.

Herman's skepticism about relationships and intimacy between men jibes completely with the mainstream's views of queer men. By the mid-1920s many people had become aware that some men were sexually involved with other men, but only a few—like the *Tribune* editor who understood that Guy Olmstead had loved William Clifford—could imagine that one man could actually fall in love with another. Herman even went a step farther. Even as he became more and more involved in the queer subculture, he was adamant that the only relationship that was possible between queer men was what he called "friendship." He believed men could be strongly attached to one another but only if they didn't have sex. Sexual activities, he thought, should take place outside of the relationship.

After his evening at Oak Street Beach, Herman's life changed drastically. As the months passed the men he had met that night introduced him to other men, and they introduced him to still others. One day Herman went to a restaurant with one of his new friends and noticed a "fellow [who] eyed [him] quite a bit." Herman's friend knew this man and ended up introducing him, "Ed," to Herman. Ed was around forty-five years old and blond. He took Herman out to dinner and introduced him to "many of his friends who were temperamental," a term often used among Chicago's queer men for *queer*. Their "affair" lasted nine months, and as far as Herman was concerned, it was "nice while it lasted," but they broke up over what Herman called "sexual disappointments" and "disillusions," although he was never clear about what those where.

While dating Ed, Herman met "Mr. J.," who became his best friend, as well as several couples: "B & B," "who were very nice," and "M & J," who lived in "a nice hotel." M. and J. had Herman to their home for dinners and invited him to their parties, where he would meet other men. He had "many wonderful times" with them. J. introduced Herman to Mr. J., Herman's "staunch friend." Herman recalled that Mr. J. gave him a "lovely set" of brushes and a "silk scarf" on his birthday.

Other friends included a physician, Doctor G., who lived at the Great Northern Hotel in the Loop, and Mr. M., who was "an accomplished musician," a "genius at the piano." It was with these friends that Herman attended his "first drag," one of the Halloween masquerades that was held "at the Armory." He said very little about the event, but evidently it impressed him. "What an unusual sight I beheld," he told Bruce. "It was very interesting."

After he and Ed broke up, Herman had "a perfectly legitimate friendship" with one of Ed's friends, the forty-year-old "Mr. R." Their "friendship" lasted a year, and Herman was quick to point out to Bruce that during that time, they never had sex but "merely kissed."

It's unclear whether or not he realized it while it was happening, but when Mr. L. took Herman to Oak Street Beach and introduced him to some of the other men who happened to be there that night, Mr. L. was bringing Herman out into Chicago's queer community. As Chauncey has explained, in earlier decades a queer man didn't come out by making a statement about his sexuality to his friends or family. Instead, a member of the queer community would introduce him to the men in his social circle, perhaps at a party, at a drag ball, or at some other social gathering. They would then befriend the man just introduced to their circle, offering him information about where to find queer-friendly housing, entertainment, and work, as well as sexual contacts. They patterned this practice of introductions after the age-old debutante balls, during which a young woman of marriageable age was introduced to society in general and, specifically, to eligible bachelors.

During his interviews with Bruce, Herman often mentioned Harry Lipson, who represented Herman's ideal mate and in whom he found a kindred spirit. Like Herman, Lipson was interested in "art and music." "His interest are my interest [sic]," Herman explained. "My liked are his liked [sic]." He added, "I like a person who is a good sport, not small in things." Of course, there were physical attributes that Lipson had too that attracted Herman. He was "pleasant looking" with a "fairly good physique." Herman eventually came to realize that "I love Lipson and would leave Clarence," his nominal boyfriend, "if I had to choose between" them. And yet regardless of whatever feelings he had for Lipson or for Clarence, Herman was never faithful to either.

In fact, Herman met Lipson through his boyfriend Clarence. Herman and Clarence were walking down Michigan Avenue one evening when they ran into Lipson, and Clarence introduced the two. Herman "fell for Harry Lipson at first sight," according to Herman's friend "Harry S." It took Lipson a little while, but he eventually developed feelings for Herman too, although he was already "going around with a fellow steadily and had a great love for him." After Lipson and his boyfriend got into an argument and broke up, Lipson was free to pursue Herman. He visited Herman's father's fruit stand, where Herman was then working, to get to know him.

Herman couldn't hide his feelings for Lipson from Clarence, and they created a considerable conflict in his and Clarence's relationship. Not long after Lipson and Herman began seeing one another, Lipson hurt his foot, and Herman visited him at home one day and "began to bandage it up" for him. Clarence walked in on them and was angered by the attention Herman was paying

Lipson. The following evening Clarence sarcastically asked Herman, "How is Harry L.'s foot?" and an argument about Lipson broke out between them.

Clarence's jealousy exploded time and time again during the next few months. Finally, the two had a showdown one night after Clarence got off work and broached the subject once again.

It was about twelve thirty in the morning. Clarence said that if he could afford to give Herman "gifts and clothes" as, he inferred, Lipson had, maybe Herman would love him again instead of Lipson. At the same time, Clarence insisted that Herman couldn't go out with anyone except him, but he reserved the right to date other men.

Weeks later Clarence and Herman went out to a cabaret in Bronzeville. No sooner had they been seated at a table by the maître d' than Clarence jumped up and walked over to another table to speak to a man called "Arnold." Clarence sat down and began to drink heavily and kiss Arnold passionately. In retaliation Herman went to a different table and began a conversation with a man there. Clarence became furious, and he and Herman began arguing loudly in the cabaret.

On the streetcar going home, Clarence stood on the rear platform because he was sick from all the alcohol he had drunk and needed fresh air. Herman ended up sitting beside a man who, Clarence believed, gave Herman a slip of paper with his address on it. Clarence walked over and slipped his hand in Herman's pocket to get it, causing another loud argument to break out between them. Then several days later, Herman discovered that Arnold, who was from out of town, was staying at Clarence's apartment and the two were sleeping together.

Herman shared the difficulties that he and Clarence were having with Harry S. "Don't see Clarence for a month," Harry S. advised Herman, "and then you will know your true feeling for one another." Herman was too concerned about what Clarence might do if they separated for that long to take the advice to heart.

Bruce also interviewed a number of Herman's other friends, who gave Bruce important insights into Herman's life and behavior. Harry S. complained that Herman talked about nothing but Lipson when they were together and described Herman as "very effeminine." Max described how Herman carried on at parties. Herman was self-centered and not a little bit hypocritical.

Mr. Nathan arrived at one of the parties given by one of Herman's friends and brought a newcomer with him, whom he introduced to the group. The newcomer was a man in his early forties and "rather manly," and because of his masculinity, he drew a great deal of attention from the men already there. Many in the group were queens who were especially attracted to masculine men. As Max explained, "Queens will not pay any attention to a queen of 42 years of age, but a man"—that is, a *masculine* man who may or may not be queer—"of that age they will pay attention to." Max revealed that "the minute the door . . . opened" and the new man walked in, Herman set his sights on him. The newcomer noticed Herman too, and despite having arrived with Nathan, he eventually holed up in a corner with Herman where, to the consternation of the other partygoers, they began "kissing" and "feeling up one another."

Nathan became extremely jealous of Herman's advances on his date, and the rest of the men did their best to separate the two from one another. Lipson stepped in and told Herman "to stop it," but Herman didn't care how he was making Nathan feel. Undeterred, Lipson said "in a nice way" to them, "Why don't you kids break it up and come out and dance with me?"

Max wasn't as diplomatic. He called Herman "vulgar," certain that Herman would have taken the newcomer into a bedroom if one had been available to them.

Nathan took his date aside and told him that Herman was superficial, only out for a good time, and that whatever sort of relationship they managed to develop, it would be short lived. The newcomer promised to ignore Herman, and yet when Herman left the party, the newcomer followed him out the door. The two ended up waiting on a corner for the streetcar together. Herman admitted to Bruce that he gave Nathan's date his address and told him to stop by his place. Bruce never recorded if the new man contacted Herman or not.

Despite the blossoming of the Pansy Craze in Chicago, Herman was concerned about being labeled queer. One day an acquaintance, "John S." visited him at his home. At the time Herman was living with his parents, and because John "acted very effeminate," Herman became extremely nervous. He explained to Bruce, "I was afraid of my father coming into the parlour and seeing him." Herman was concerned that his father might realize he was queer because of his association with John S., but Herman wasn't only afraid of his sexuality being found out by his family. To cover up his homosexuality when he was in public, Herman adopted what he considered a masculine demeanor. Harry

S. described Herman's public persona: "When Herman walks down the street, he throws back his shoulders. I am a man," his body language told anyone around, and "I am certainly glad of it."

Like many of the men in his group, Herman often thought about being queer, trying to understand why his sexuality veered so sharply from what the mainstream thought it should be. He recalled that one of his friends, a physician, told him that "queers were born that way" and explained that it could happen in one of two ways, either "the husband sucked wife virgina [sic] during intercourse" or during her pregnancy the "mother wanted a girl" so strongly that the son she bore was queer.

Many other theories of why some men were queer while others weren't circulated among Herman's friends. One young man simply believed that "homosexuals are born that way," while "Robert" was perhaps the most diplomatic of all. "My opinion," he said, "is that one is born homosexual and doesn't acquire it through influence from other people. However, this is a very debatable subject, so I will not get into it as I know nothing about it from the scientific angle."

Herman even discussed homosexuality with some of his non-queer friends. "One day," he said, "I drew out rather indirectly some Jam friends regarding Homosexuals. One said he would like to kill one. I told them that my conversation with the doctor was that a Homosexual could not help himself, and I convinced them." *Jam* was used by Chicago's queer men to refer to non-queer people, male or female.

Despite hiding his homosexuality in public, Herman didn't want to live a dual life, unlike many of the men he had met. He decided that to date and perhaps even marry a woman but to sleep with men on the side wasn't for him. It "is not wise to go with girls as long as you are in this sort of life," he explained. He even asked a doctor how to cure himself of his sexual interest in men, and the physician told him to "get married." Herman told the physician that he couldn't, and so the doctor told him to "go out with prostitutes."

Herman wasn't the only queer man to be advised to have sexual intercourse with a woman in order to rid himself of his sexual attraction to other men. "G.," as he was identified, lost his boyfriend "Bob" to another man, and although he contemplated suicide, he also hoped Bob would tire of his new love and return to him.

G. had been involved in the queer community for ten years and took what he called the "feminine role" in sexual relationships, but having lost Bob he decided to abandon it for the "masculine role" and have sexual relationships with women. Bruce advised G. on how he might downplay his effeminacy. He told G. to lower his voice, keep his hand gestures to a minimum when he spoke, and smoke cigarettes. G. was only able to follow Bruce's advice for two weeks before he gave up.

Even his friends told him that they doubted that he would succeed in the experiment with women, telling him that they too had tried to change but failed. Chickie emphatically told G., "Once a bitch, always a bitch," and an empathetic sixty-year-old man told G., "If God wanted you to be queer you would be queer, and you should take it as it comes and say, 'Thy will be done.'" Nevertheless, G. was dead set on getting rid of his same-sex sexual desires, so much so that he agreed to have intercourse with a woman known as "J." Bruce had procured her for G., sure that being with a woman sexually was all it would take to straighten G. out.

J. was aware of G.'s sexual past, and she worked diligently to help him through their sexual encounter. She acted as "feminine" as possible in bed with him so that G. could be "masculine." As he struggled to make sense of the situation and his role in it, she "kissed" him and "rubbed" herself against him, hoping to make him think he was exciting her. Time after time she thought he was about to "climax," but it took well over an hour before he did. That might have been considered something of a success had it not been for the fact that G. didn't have an orgasm until Bruce got into bed with them, an important fact that may have slipped by J. and Bruce but not G. He realized that Bruce, and not J., was the "stimulant" he needed to achieve orgasm and decided the experiment was a failure. He wasn't interested in having sex with a woman unless another man was also in bed with them.

Bruce never explained in his report why he decided to get into bed with J. and G. in the first place.

A few queer teenagers and men Bruce interviewed wished that they had been born female instead of male. While this might initially seem as if they were transgender, the context in which they admitted dissatisfaction with their sexual orientation had nothing to do with feeling as if they had been born in the wrong body. Instead, they were acutely aware that if they had been born female, their desire for men would be acceptable and they would not have to feel ashamed or to hide it. "James" admitted that, when he was eighteen, he "wished that I were a woman; maybe this idea came to me because I thought that a woman can pick out whom she likes" for a sexual partner or to love without being afraid of repercussions from the law, family, or friends. Comments by "Charles" illustrate a similar point of view. For as long as he could remember, he said, "I have always wished I was a girl. About my attraction for Lew, I was horribly shocked at myself. I didn't understand, I wished I was a woman so that we could do something about it. While I would liked to have touched him, I never did." Nevertheless, most in the community typically felt no desire to be female at all and agreed with "Mr. C.," who told Bruce emphatically, "I never wished that I was a girl."

Then as now, realizing one is different was often a disturbing and alienating experience. Some were able to recognize their difference on their own: "When I was twenty-three years of age," Mr. C. said, "I found that there were other people besides women who carried on with men. If I was not queer, how could I care for my own sex." Others needed the benefit of another person's perspective. In an effort to help "Mr. P.," an older man told him that the two of them were "the same type." When Mr. P. replied that he didn't know what the older man was going on about, the older man told him that he knew Mr. P. was "gay" the second he laid eyes on him and that "there is [sic] a lot of others like" them, especially in the "big cities," echoing what Shorty had told Nels Anderson.

Then as now, not everyone who discovered that he was queer accepted the fact readily, much less easily. Like numerous others before him and since, "Jimmy" decided early on to keep his sexuality a secret, and he used various tactics to deflate any suspicion about it. When his coworkers at a saloon accused him of being "queer," he agreed that he might be a "little bit effeminate" but "not queer," and he blamed his effeminacy on being the only son in a household full of women and on being forced to help his mother with the "house work," an excuse that recalls Frederick Thompson's claim about cross-dressing because his parents wanted a daughter and not another son.

To strengthen his assertion that he wasn't queer, he would tell his male coworkers off-colored stories, the "dirtier . . . the better," because he believed that they thought that "sissies" would never tell obscene stories. He also flirted with women. "I tease . . . the girls, love them, kiss them," he said, in order to camouflage himself, and he bragged about his sexual exploits with women to the "boys at work." He claimed that he was very popular with the other men at the saloon and that they "begged" him to come along on their outings because he was "lots of fun," and yet he was "afraid underneath it all," terrified that he would be found out.

Other young men, too upset with their lot in life and unwilling—or unable—to accept it, turned to self-hatred. "I used to go into the washroom," one recalled, "and hit myself and beat my face and scratched it, because I thought that I looked like a woman. Men and women would look at me and I would think I was a molly coddle. I wanted to be a man." A *molly coddle* was an effeminate mama's boy.

Regardless of how accepting a queer man was of his sexuality, he could easily maintain a jam facade if he wanted and, at the same time, hob-knob with other queer men at trendy cabarets that welcomed both queers and non-queers alike. The Ballyhoo Café was one such place. Located at 1942 N. Halsted Street, it had a cover charge of twenty-five cents and was known throughout Chicago for its cross-dressing entertainment. Not only did Herman and Clarence patronize it, but many in their group of friends did too

While at the Ballyhoo one night, Clarence ran into his cousin, "who is jam." The cousin was as surprised by running into Clarence there as Clarence was by running into him. "What are you doing here?" Clarence asked him. The cousin replied that "he was merely visiting this place with friends." Afraid that his cousin would guess that he was queer, Clarence told him the same thing. Herman had a similar experience one night when he and Clarence were at the Ballyhoo again, but this time the scenario played out differently.

He ran into "a girl who knew him quite well a few years" earlier, a married friend who didn't know he was queer. Clarence told Herman to lie to her about why he was there. Clarence said that Herman should "play dumb and not to let her know that he was queer," but Herman knew one of the men who had brought her. He was queer and knew that Herman was queer too. It was "inevitable" that their mutual friend would tell her all that he knew about Herman, and so Herman beat the man to the punch by telling her himself.

Earl Bruce visited the Ballyhoo on the evening of Wednesday, November 22, 1933, and he recorded that as soon as he walked through the door, he noticed a "good looking woman . . . in an evening gown." Bruce was "surprised" that she used his name when she greeted him. "Why, don't you know me?" she asked him, and when he told her he didn't, she told him she was Malliard, a man Bruce had "met a few months previous and whose drag name was Neomi." Bruce "congratulated him on his makeup, dress and his impersonation"—the "best" Bruce had ever witnessed. Then, in the middle of the bar, Bruce saw a "homosexual dressed in a costume made entirely of paper" performing. As "he sang in a deep voice," he pulled his "paper dress" up, revealing his "hips," and then "his back." The "crowd," Bruce reported, "gave him a good hand."

One of the evening's highlights seems to have been the cross-dressing MC, who stood "about six foot three inches tall" and was "very slim." She "walked gracefully about the room making wise cracks" to the customers, queer and jam alike. As she played the crowd, someone "called out" for her to sing her version of "Alice Blue Gown," a song from the Broadway musi-

Fig. 23. An unidentified female impersonator posed in drag for this photograph taken in Chicago in the 1930s. *Courtesy of the Special Collections Research Center, University of Chicago Library*

cal *Irene* (1919). Like many queer entertainers, the MC had rewritten the song, substituting her salacious lyrics for the originals. She accommodated the guest, singing:

> In my sweet little Alice blue gown
> was the first time that I ever went down.
> I was bashful and shy
> as he opened his fly,
> and the first time I saw it
> I thought I would die.
> He told me to lay on the ground,
> Then he shoved it up my brown.
> Till it wilted, I wore it,
> but I adored it—
> the first time I ever went down.

The MC hadn't been content simply to change the lyrics. She also "made gestures toward his lower extremities" as she sang. Adding to the hilarity of the lyrics is the fact that "Alice blue gown" was queer slang for a police officer.

Some customers arrived at the Ballyhoo dressed in drag, although they weren't performers per se. They did, however, take part in a "drag parade," which was in reality a contest for the best outfit of the evening. During the procession, the contenders "walked . . . in a circle" through the audience. The loudest applause indicated who the audience thought wore the best drag. One of the favorites on the evening of November 22 was Perley, whose demeanor reminded Bruce of a "French demoiselle, aloof, smart, haughty, charming and graceful, head flung back." Although the crowd approved of Perley, the loudest applause went to Neomi, who received the prize, which was "a bottle of gin." It was worth its weight in gold during Prohibition, but its value would drop tremendously when, less than two weeks later, the federal government repealed the law prohibiting alcohol.

15 | A Nudist Club for Boys and Young Men

Why they don't round us all up and kill us I don't know.

FOR YEARS, TEENAGERS AND YOUNG MEN had been visiting Frank Wiley's apartment at 123½ North Wayman Street in downtown Rockford, Illinois, a few miles west of Chicago, without anyone raising an eyebrow, but then a "youth who had visited the place" tipped off the police about the goings-on there. A few days later, on the evening of Friday, November 12, 1937, Detective George Morris and Officer George Albee knocked on Wiley's door. It took him a few minutes, but he finally answered it. Inside, Morris and Albee discovered a sixteen-year-old male and hauled the unidentified teenager and the forty-eight-year-old Wiley off to jail. The apartment served for what newspaper reporters would quickly dub "a nudist club for boys and young men."

That evening, Morris and Albee interrogated Wiley at the Rockford police station for hours, and what he told them raised the hair on the backs of their necks. He admitted that some twenty-five to thirty teenagers—"members" of the club, the press called them—visited his apartment "fairly regularly," some nights as few as "four or five" but other nights as many as a "dozen." They "stripped naked and played games" or "read books" or "took baths" and "gave each other rubdowns." Sometimes Wiley took whoever had come by out to a movie. He had met some of the boys at the public library, only a block from his apartment, and invited them to visit him, but some of the regulars had invited their friends to join them at Wiley's. In his defense, he claimed that he had made "'no secret' about the boys coming up to his apartment and going around in the nude" and swore that he never engaged in sexual activity with any of them. The police also questioned the teenager discovered in Wiley's apartment, but whatever information he told them went unreported, at least in the newspapers.

Wiley cooperated with Morris and Albee and gave them the names of from fifteen to twenty other teenagers and young men who visited his apartment regularly. Police immediately tracked down six of them, ranging in age from sixteen to twenty-one, and brought them in for questioning. They lived all over Rockford and even in the rural areas beyond the city limits. They corroborated Wiley's statements about the activities that occurred in the apartment, but they also "implicated" him "in immoral practices" with at least some of them.

The police charged Wiley with crimes against nature, and a judge set his bail at $5,000. Unable to come up with the bond money, he spent the night behind bars. The click of the key turning in the cell lock was the most terrifying sound he'd ever heard. The police also held the teenagers and young men they had brought in for questioning. They spent the night in jail too, each in his own cell.

The next day the police continued their search for the other boys and young men Wiley had named, rounded them up, and brought them into police headquarters for questioning. Some admitted they had been visiting Wiley's apartment for "as long as four years." The police put Wiley through a second barrage of questioning. Although he had claimed the night before that he had entertained young men in his apartment for only four years, which jibbed with what some of the boys and young men had said, he changed his mind. He had been "entertaining young men at his quarters for about 10 years," since the mid-1920s, he admitted to the authorities. During the previous decade, he had lived in at least four different apartments, all within Rockford's downtown district.

Wiley was arraigned in circuit court fifteen days after his arrest. During his arraignment, he said he would plead guilty to the charges and ask for probation. He couldn't afford a lawyer, so the court assigned one, Raphael Yalden, to his case. Wiley asked Judge Arthur E. Fisher for one favor. He wanted to be given a chance to tell his side of the story at his trial before he was sentenced.

The judge promised to let him speak but warned him he wouldn't have much time and would have to keep it short.

A few days later, the police hinted to reporters that Wiley wouldn't be the only man arrested in their investigation but that they would soon nab another. They mentioned this to reporters again a few days later.

The police kept their promise. On Monday, November 29, Morris and Albee drove to Chicago and took Raymond B. Carlson, who was forty-four years old, into custody on "morals charges." He was living at 6554 North Talman Avenue in Chicago with another man, Carl Kuehne. That night, as Morris and Albee interrogated him, Carlson confessed to having engaged in "immoral activities" at the "nudist club." That same evening police also arrested thirty-year-old Paul Tobin in Rockford. No sooner had police locked Carlson and Tobin behind bars than State's Attorney Robert Nash announced to the press that "the activity of a long established 'nudist club' for young men and boys necessitates a city-wide morals probe." Nash was out for blood.

The next day Morris and Albee hauled Ralph Wright into jail. A retired mail deliverer who now taught and performed music professionally, fifty-seven-year-old Wright lived in the village of Pecatonica, a short distance due west of Rockford. As it turned out, while being interrogated Wiley had not only identified the boys and young men who visited his apartment, he also named Carlson, Tobin, and Wright as three of the men who visited his apartment to enjoy the company of the club's members.

Both Wiley and Carlson pleaded guilty before Judge Arthur E. Fisher in circuit court three days later, and both filed petitions for probation.

Police promised reporters that they would be making a total of at least six arrests before they were done.

On December 9, nearly a month after Wiley was arrested, Judge Fisher sentenced him. But before he announced his ruling, the judge announced, "In cases of small pox and scarlet fever, they isolate cases. That's what I'm going to do in this case," and he gave Wiley a one-to-ten-years sentence to be served in the Illinois State Penitentiary in Joliet.

Two days after Wiley's sentencing, Morris and Albee told reporters they had tracked twenty-five-year-old James E. Deering, also known as Howard Craig, to Chicago, where they had arrested him. Deering wasn't one of the men who engaged in sexual activities in Wiley's apartment, but while questioning the twenty teenagers and young men who were considered the club's principal members, Deering's name popped up. Checking police records, Morris and Albee discovered that Deering had been in trouble with the law twice before. Police had taken him into custody because he engaged in a "series of immoral acts with young boys," some of whom now happened to be members of the nudist club, and the previous October, Chicago police had discovered Deering with a "boy in his room in a local hotel." He was brought into police headquarters and questioned in both incidents, but Deering was released. The same can't be said about Carlson.

Born in 1897, Raymond B. Carlson was raised in Rockford and graduated from Rockford High School in 1912. He had been a popular and active student. He played the clarinet in the school band, served as secretary of the literary club, took a role in the school play, and worked as the 1912 high school annual's art editor, contributing a number of sketches. His coeditors poked a little good-natured fun at him by nicknaming him "Terrible Swen" and by discussing one of his sketches in the annual's editorial:

> The original has recently been hung in the Louvre, Paris, and is closely watched by body guards [sic]. Two of Raphael's and several of De Vinci's [sic] have been taken down to make room for this priceless work of art, and an enlargement of the Louvre is contemplated to make room for the enthusiastic throngs.

Adding to the humor of the comment is the fact that none of Carlson's sketches appeared on the cover but were scattered throughout the yearbook.

After he graduated from high school, Carlson took on a variety of jobs—reporter, artist, and stenographer—and enrolled in classes at Lake Forest College. In 1917 he moved to Chicago, where he worked as a clerk for R. R. Donnelly while taking courses at the Art Institute. He rented a room in Harriet Montgomery's home at 1543 E. Sixty-First Street, a short distance from the art colony that Lorado Taft and others had established on the South Side when they left Towertown. In fact, Taft and other artists attended art-patron Montgomery's many salons.

In 1920 Carlson moved back to Rockford to teach art, science, and advanced math at the Keith School, a private institution. His colleague there, artist Lester Young Correthers, took the younger man under his wings, and the two are linked time and time again for a span of nearly ten years. Together they cofounded the Rock River Valley Artists (with the Keith School's founder, Belle Emerson Keith), exhibited their work in the same shows, and worked on community theater productions as both actors and scene designers. Establishing himself at the onset as an artist, actor, teacher, sometimes newspaper columnist, musician, and playwright, Carlson quickly became a favorite of the society pages in Rockford's several newspapers, which reported on everything they could about him, however trivial it may have been.

In the summer after his first year of teaching, for example, Carlson and Correthers took a canoe trip down the Rock River to Oregon, Illinois, with two other men, former sailors Ross Nelson and Cloy Chalmers, who were younger than the two teachers. For three weeks the four remained in Oregon, where Lorado Taft had founded Eagle's Nest, an art colony, twenty-three years earlier, sketching and painting the landscape. Carlson and Correthers spent the weekend of February 9, 1923, in Chicago, although the paper didn't explain the purpose of their getaway, and the following summer, Carlson and Correthers traveled together to Europe to gallery hop and paint. A few years later, when dance-duo Ruth St. Denis and her husband, Ted Shawn, gave a performance at a theater in Madison, Wisconsin, both Carlson and Correthers attended the reception that Karl Noble, an interior designer and former Rockford resident, hosted for the dancers. It was widely known that Shawn was queer and that most of the men in the dance troupe were too.

After teaching at the Keith School for five years, Carlson moved back to Chicago to teach at the North Shore Country Day School in Evanston, but his time there was unexpectedly cut short. He returned to teaching at the Keith School in September 1926. Two months later he and Correthers cohosted an "informal supper party" for the Rockford Players after their last performance of Jesse Lynch Williams's play *Why Marry?* After the 1930–1931 school year, Carlson took a leave of absence from the Keith School, but instead of returning after his leave, he left teaching altogether and found a job as a clerk with the city's water department until early 1935, when, during the height of the Great Depression, he began working for the Winnebago County Relief Department. The following year he became the Works Progress Administration director for arts projects for northern Illinois and, on March 9, was promoted to director of the WPA arts projects statewide. He moved back to Chicago again, where he lived with Carl Kuehne on North Talman Avenue. That's where Morris and Albee picked him up.

Carlson's day in court was Monday, December 13, 1937, and like Wiley he stood before Judge Fisher. Unlike Wiley, Carlson could afford a lawyer and hired his own, Charles S. Thomas, who defended his client as aggressively as possible despite the fact that Carlson had already confessed to committing "immoral activities." Thomas called four character witnesses to testify on Carlson's behalf, hopeful that their comments would soften Judge Fisher's heart. Thomas didn't want Carlson to share Wiley's fate.

First on the stand, City Engineer Morgens Ipsen was Carlson's former employer. According to Ipsen, Carlson handled all of the clerical work in his office during Ipsen's tenure as superintendent for Rockford's water department in 1934, and when Ipsen became director of the WPA projects in the district that included Rockford, he hired Carlson to supervise the local art projects. Ipsen testified, "I never had any man who did a better job," and he went on to say that Carlson's abilities were so well known that the officials of the Illinois branch of the WPA had asked him if he would release Carlson to run their much larger, statewide department of art for them. Ipsen readily agreed. That was in 1936, and Carlson held that post when he was arrested.

The next witness was psychiatrist, E. W. Fell, who testified that it would be preferable for Carlson to be "put on probation" instead of serving a prison sentence. Dr. Fell explained to Judge Fisher that it wasn't Carlson's "fault" that he was "abnormal" and that he had even gone to "doctors and psychiatrists" to try to cure himself of it.

During cross-examination, Assistant State's Attorney Max A. Weston asked Dr. Fell whether or not prison sentences cured men of their homosexuality.

The psychiatrist answered that incarceration would create "more harm than good" for Carlson.

Robert McKeague, business director of the WPA in Illinois, was the next witness to take the stand. He had known Carlson for a few years and testified that Carlson was a very talented administrator and artist, and he was prepared to hire Carlson to work in his department if the judge granted the prisoner probation. Carl Kuehne, whose relationship to Carlson was never clarified, was the fourth to testify on Carlson's behalf, speaking positively of the defendant's character.

Thomas, Carlson's lawyer, commented on his client's past behavior too. Carlson, he told the court, had never "had any contact with minors" and had been gainfully employed throughout his adulthood and supported his parents financially because his father was "unable to work."

When allowed to speak on his own behalf, Carlson admitted that he had gone to Wiley's apartment, but he also contended that he hadn't had sexual contact with anyone there.

To show the judge that Carlson was trying to govern his behavior, Thomas asked his client if his sexual "impulses" were "controllable."

Carlson replied that if put on probation, he would "try to control them."

All seemed to be going well or at least as well as could be expected. Four witnesses had spoken glowingly about Carlson, and one of them had shown that his trust in Carlson was so strong that he was prepared to hire him if Carlson were given probation. All things considered, Judge Fisher shouldn't have needed to hear any more support for the defendant to award him probation, but as McKeague was later to reveal, "the judge wasn't paying any attention to any character witnesses." Prosecuting attorney Weston rose from his seat and made a sharp and calculated comment about Carlson's sexuality.

He began by saying that he didn't want to bog the court down with all the disagreeable information he had gathered about Carlson, but he wanted the court to know that Carlson had engaged in same-sex sexual practices since his childhood. This suggested to the court that after several decades of engaging in "immoral activities" and despite the undisclosed amount of time that Carlson had been under psychiatric treatment, it might be close to impossible for him to control himself as he promised to do. In case that wouldn't sway the judge, Weston added that this case wasn't Carlson's "first offense," suggesting that Carlson had a record. Before he was finished with Carlson, Weston painted the portrait of a forty-four-year-old man who had been unable to control himself sexually for several decades, one who was so out of control that he had committed the same crime at least twice—or, at least, he had been caught twice. Weston sat back down to the stunned silence of the courtroom.

It was Judge Fisher's turn to speak, and Carlson's thoughts were caught up in a whirlwind of fears.

If Fisher decided not to give him probation, Carlson's life would be, for all intents and purposes, over. He would probably also be imprisoned in Joliet, where dangers lurked in every dark corner, and for the same period of time as Wiley. The penitentiary in Joliet, where Wiley would be confined, held some of the state's most hardened criminals, and they wouldn't take kindly to having a child rapist—that's what he would become in their minds—among them.

He was also concerned over the fact that there would be no one to take care of his parents while he was locked up. He was their only child, the only person they could depend on. Making everything even worse, his parents would have to deal with the shame of why he would be incarcerated in the first place. It would kill them to have their son branded a convicted felon *and* a pervert. If it didn't kill them, it would certainly destroy his relationship with them. Besides, even if he survived the brutality that he knew awaited him in prison, he'd never be able to get a good job once he was released. In ten years he would be fifty-four or fifty-five years old and an ex-con. No one would hire him, and he would have no place to go but West Madison Street, where he could blend in among the other unemployed or unemployable men, the "butt-ends of humanity."

Judge Fisher's comments about Carlson were even more condescending than his remarks to Wiley a few days earlier. Fisher began by claiming that one of the boys rounded up by the police had told them that he and Carlson had had sex "14 years" earlier and that experience had turned him queer.

Fisher was echoing a common belief that if boys, teenagers, or even adult men engaged in same-sex sexual activities, they could "catch" homosexuality as if it were a disease. Fisher would have known Carlson had taught, as records show, at the Keith School from at least 1925 to 1930, and he may have been suggesting that Carlson had sexually abused some of the students there. Perhaps that was the record Weston had suggested. Regardless, the proof of his involvement with a fourteen-year-old was never established, and surely, in Fisher's mind, it didn't need to be.

The way newspaper reporters dealt with the case, specifically the language they used, reveals volumes about the way people had begun viewing queer men in the last years of the 1930s, which would persist through the next several decades. Although initially reports about Wiley's apartment called it a "nudist club for boys *and* young men" (italics added), within a few days of the investigation, the reporters covering the case had dropped "young men," to make it appear that those who visited Wiley's apartment were no older than twelve or so, when in fact their ages ranged from sixteen to early twenties. The age of consent for boys in Illinois had been sixteen since 1920 and would remain so until 1999, when it rose to seventeen.

The effect of the omission was twofold. First, it pushed the "young men" so far into the background that they were no longer visible and so were forgotten. Second, it inflamed readers against queer men, who, they believed, were only victimizing the very young. In short, the consequence of Carlson's trial for a crime against nature, which was bad enough at the time, was accentuated by the specter of pedophilia that swirled around it. Apparently it loomed as large in Fisher's imagination as it did in that of the reporters and the reading public.

Judge Fisher claimed he didn't want to send Carlson to the "penitentiary," and Carlson must have jumped to the conclusion that he would, after all, get probation. Instead, Fisher said that he would like to send him to a "pest house," where he could be segregated from innocent, normal "people lest" his "contagion be passed to them," which must have sounded to Carlson like a contradiction. It was. Judge Fisher denied Carlson's petition for probation and sentenced him to one to ten years in the Illinois State Penitentiary in Joliet. He banged his gavel, rose, and left the courtroom for his chambers without another look Carlson's way.

It was eleven thirty in the morning.

Sheriff Paul Johnson led Carlson, in a daze, from the courtroom to his cell at the county jail and left him there. One of the guards, Ray Juhlin, told Carlson that he would be bringing him dinner in the early evening and would be back then.

At two thirty Carlson had a visitor from Chicago, Robert McKeague, one of Carlson's character witnesses. Juhlin brought him to Carlson's cell and let him in and then left. Later McKeague revealed something Carlson had told him that afternoon, but he didn't think twice about it then:

> Ray said to me, "Well Bob, I'll be saying good-bye." I said, "Well, you'll probably be here for awhile before they transfer you. . . ." He said, "No, I won't be here after tonight. I know these guys in prison. For this kind of sentence life would be hell, and I'm not going to put up with it."

No one recorded when McKeague left.

When Juhlin returned to Carlson's cell at five thirty with dinner, he first saw Carlson sprawled out on the floor and wondered why he was napping there instead of on his cot. Then he saw the pool of blood in which Carlson lay and the blade of a safety razor on the floor nearby. Juhlin ran for help.

During the probe of Carlson's death, which began the next day, coroner Dr. Warren C. Ives declared that Carlson had died about an hour before Juhlin discovered his body. He had slashed a deep gash in the right side of his throat with the razor blade and a shallower one on the left side. He also had sliced both of his wrists. The wounds were so deep, Ives stated, that Carlson had died within five minutes.

Juhlin and another guard, James Cassioppi, searched Carlson's cell thoroughly and found a pack of brand-new razor blades with one blade missing among his possessions. However, according to Juhlin and Cassioppi, Carlson had never had a safety razor in his cell, and neither of the men had "given anyone permission" to give him any. It's unlikely that McKeague brought razor blades to Carlson so that he could commit suicide, but who did remains a mystery.

What is clear is that if the guards were correct and Carlson didn't have any razor blades in his cell, he had somehow prepared ahead of time for a worst-case scenario.

Carlson didn't bother to leave a suicide note.

When police questioned the fifteen-year-old runaway in the cell next to Carlson's, he said Carlson hadn't uttered a sound as he was killing himself. Wiley and Tobin, who had been locked up in the same cell block but in different cells a few feet away, corroborated the runaway's comment.

When he heard the news, Wiley was unable to eat his dinner. To keep Wiley from the same fate, Sheriff Johnson assigned two guards to watch him whenever he shaved.

Carlson's family didn't give him a church funeral, and in fact they may not have been able to even if they had wished given the nature of Carlson's conviction and death. Instead, the Rev. O. Garfield Beckstrand held a service in Carlson's parents' home at 2020 Fremont Street at two o'clock in the afternoon on Wednesday, December 14. He was buried at Willwood Burial Park in Winnebago, Illinois.

The three other men arrested in the "nudist club" roundup faired far better than Carlson.

Although given a one-to-ten-year sentence, Frank Wiley remained behind bars for only a year before the court granted him probation. He disappeared from the public record for the next five years and resurfaced in 1943, when his draft card reveals he was living with his widowed sister, Lillian V. Washburn, in Kewanee, Illinois. It's possible he had been living with her since his release from prison. A college graduate who attended Illinois State Normal University, he had made his living as a draftsman at Barber-Colman Company in Rockford before his arrest. In 1948 he moved from his sister's home to Peoria, where he was a foreman at Thomas and Clark. By 1955 he had become a salesman for the Peoria Goodwill Industries. He died on February 24, 1978.

Paul Tobin, who had been arrested "on the complaint of a 21-year-old youth," an adult, on the same day as Carlson, received probation a little over four months after being arrested. Unlike Wiley and Carlson, he refused to plead guilty when Morris and Albee brought him to police headquarters, although he changed his plea to guilty on March 2, 1937. During Tobin's sentencing, Judge Fisher told the prisoner that he "regretted that 'Illinois doesn't have a whipping post where I could sentence you to the type of punishment you need.'" After his release Tobin lived with his mother and, several years later, began to work as a painter. He enlisted in the military in late June 1942, and during basic training, he became an expert marksman with the rifle and then rose quickly in the ranks to become a corporal. He was honorably discharged from the army in early November three years later, returned to work as a painter, and moved back in with his mother, with whom he lived until she died on Thanksgiving Day in 1960. Tobin died on September 6, 1986.

Ralph Wright appeared in Judge Fisher's court, as had the three others. He had been released on a $3,000 bond on the day of his arrest. Although he was charged with a crime against nature and had pleaded guilty to the charge, Judge Fisher decided to grant Wright's request for probation because, in Fisher's words, Wright had a "good record." Although it's unclear what Judge Fisher meant, he may have been referring to Wright's being a very active member of his church, the Pecatonica Methodist Church, where he had served as trustee, secretary, and organist since the mid-1920s.

Incensed by the judge's leniency with Wright, Max Weston blurted out, "This man is no more deserving of probation than Frank Wiley or Ray Carlson. . . . We have divided these people into two groups, the ones whose associations were with men of their own age and those who recruited the younger ones. Wright fell into the latter category." Despite Weston's outburst, Fisher's judgment in the case stood, and Wright left the courtroom on January 27, 1938, went home, and a month and a half later married Ethel M. Davis in Valparaiso, Indiana. He continued performing in public to favorable reviews for many years. He died on April 16, 1961.

Carlson's role in the case of the "nudist club for boys and young men" shocked many, but it paled in comparison to the hundreds of other cases that made the headlines in Chicago and elsewhere near the end of the 1930s. Stories of girls and women who were beaten, raped, and murdered flooded the national news and were reported in *Time*, the *Saturday Evening Post*, the *Christian Century*, and the *Nation*, among many other popular magazines, as well as in every newspaper in the country. In the year in which Carlson was arrested and committed suicide rather than face what the future held for him, the *New York Times* alone published 147 articles describing horrific murder-rapes—most perpetuated on women or girls and a few on boys—by men who were considered out of control. The entire country was alarmed, horrified, and anxiety ridden about the sex crimes, and terrified and angry citizens began holding rallies demanding the authorities—not just local law enforcement but the FBI as well—put an end to them.

Instead of trying to quell the alarm that had arisen over the sex crimes, FBI director J. Edgar Hoover fanned the flames of panic, pouring gasoline on them until they burst into a conflagration. He pointed his finger at an enshrouded monster that no one could actually define but that everyone was certain they knew: "degenerate sex offenders." According to Hoover, they attacked the inno-cent "every 43 minutes, day and night" in the United States.

In a similar vein, David G. Wittels announced in an article he wrote for the *Saturday Evening Post* that "sex killers are psychopathic personalities," and while he admitted that there were no statistics that revealed how many "such creatures" existed, he nevertheless estimated that "thousands . . . are loose in the country today." Like Hoover, Wittels had no statistics to back up any of his claims, but—again as with Hoover—his language inflamed readers, who were eager to blame anyone identified as a perpetrator of such crimes.

Central to both Hoover's and Wittles's reports was the idea that certain men—for Hoover, the "degenerate"; for Wittles, the "psychopathic"—couldn't control their sexual urges. Of course much of the general public already viewed queer men that way, which is why Carlson's lawyer asked him about being able to control himself. As early as the mid-1800s, Chicago sexologists Dr. G. Frank Lydston and Dr. James G. Kiernan had popularized the notion that queer men were little more than women, and like women they were unable to control their emotions, which included their sexual longings, urges, lusts. As words like *moron* and *psychopath*—terms used for people unable, through their mental disorders, to control themselves—became associated with the murderer-rapist, the queer man became, because of his presumed lack of control, the face of the even vaguer "sex moron," "sexual psychopath," and similarly hazy figures.

Calmer men who wanted to get to the bottom of the sex crimes and not stir up the anxiety rapidly growing across the United States published reports that exposed Hoover's and Wittles's claims as hokum. For example, after studying evidence in both police and FBI sex crime reports, Morris Ploscowe, a New York City magistrate, noted that queer men may have been considered "nuisances" because of the "scandal and annoyance" they left in their wake, but there was no proof that they were a "danger to . . . women and children." Even state-mandated investigative groups like the New Jersey Commission on Sex Crime countered the popularly held notion with its investigation's conclusion that the "thousands" of monsters that Hoover and Wittles feared were the products of a "well stirred imagination."

Despite such efforts, Hoover's agenda won out. The United States preferred a "well stirred" nightmare over fact, and all sorts of individuals came up with ways of controlling the sex moron, by which they invariably meant queer men. Although he wasn't convinced that they were "potential murderers," Dr. Thomas K. Gruber, for example, wanted to imprison the "floating populations of female impersonators" that, he believed, "roam at liberty" in large cities. Ideas such as his, Hoover's, and Wittles's helped to fuel the crackdown on Chicago's queer-friendly cabarets. The Chicago Police Department began investigating resorts that were accepting of, or dedicated to, queer patronage along with certain streets, alleys, parks, and other places that men used "to search for sexual partners." It also paved the way for unfettered raids on the homes of presumed-queer men and the confiscation of anything that might be used as evidence against them, as had happened decades earlier to Henry Gerber.

Fig. 24. Confiscated by Chicago police during a raid on a man's home in the 1930s or early 1940s, this photograph shows two "pansies" engaged in foreplay. *Kinsey Institute*

Resorts like the K-9 Club or the Cabin Inn had disappeared, and those queer men who were interested in a nightlife were forced to patronize taverns with entrances in the dankest alleys of the darkest parts of town—if they dared to patronize any. On a whim, the police could raid such places, arrest anyone there, and publicize their names in the *Tribune* or other Chicago newspapers. Those who were arrested would be branded and fired from their jobs. Their families would reject them. They would be pariahs in any and every social gathering to which they had once been welcomed, exactly what would have faced Carlson had he served his one-to-ten-year sentence.

The Pansy Craze, with its fifteen or so years of acceptance and visibility of queer men, was now not simply dead but in its grave, and the fear of queer men instigated by Hoover and his minions began to engulfed the United States. Given the threat of World War II, which was beginning to seem inevitable, the United States assumed a militaristic demeanor, as it had in the years just before the First World War. Society labeled any man who didn't fit into its idea of what a man was—typically the hypermasculinized model of the military—a "sex moron."

Historian Charles E. Morris has called this period the "post-pansy panic," which was full of paranoia that "gripped the nation, animating its quest to distinguish, and extinguish, the sexual deviant." The commissioner of corrections in New York summed up the situation, claiming that it was "sex in its abnormalities" with which authorities were dealing, "rather than in its normal expression and in its aberrations rather than in its natural course." The commissioner's words *abnormalities* and *aberrations*, like Hoover's use of *degenerate* and other words, targeted queer men, and the "innocuous pansy" was irrevocably linked to the "dangerous 'menace.'" The post-pansy panic would continue for many decades, becoming as fiercely destructive to the queer subculture of Chicago as the Great Fire of 1871 had been to the city's general population.

Chicago's queer men reacted despairingly too, as one man's letter to one of his friends reveals. He wondered if his friend had seen any newspaper reports "about the kidnapping and killing" of a "little girl" in Chicago. He wrote that the police had decided "(in their damned self-righteous way) that . . . a pervert had done it and they rounded up" any of the effeminate, and thereby easily recognizable, queer men they could find. "They blame us for everything," he continued, adding, "why they don't round us all up and kill us I don't know."

16 | Thank God I Got Only 60 Days and a Small Fine

If there were more people like you who cared to find out and write about their fellow-men and their innermost self this world would be a better place to live in.

HE DIDN'T KNOW IT AT THE TIME, but the summer of 1939 would prove to be a watershed in the career of the entomologist Alfred C. Kinsey, an authority on the gall wasp. He had taught in the Department of Zoology at Indiana University in Bloomington since 1920, and when in May 1938 the Association of Women Students there asked the administration for a course on marriage, Kinsey volunteered to teach it. Initially, only faculty and their spouses, graduate students, and undergraduates who were married or engaged or at least twenty-one years old could enroll in the course. Offered for the first time in July 1938, it was a success by all accounts.

In their evaluations of the course, students raved about Kinsey's manner (objective) and the course content (lectures overtly about sexual matters), claiming that it, and not the hygiene course that students were required to take and that they found steeped in Victorian prudery, offered what they needed. With the approval of the university president and its board of trustees, Kinsey began asking his students to give him their sexual histories.

The course wasn't the first instance of Kinsey's interest in human sexuality, and in fact his biographers reveal that he had sought answers to his own sexual questions through confidential discussions with male friends and colleagues. Since at least the mid-1930s, he had offered to counsel any graduate student or faculty member who needed advice on sexual matters and occasionally asked them to give him their sexual histories. Nevertheless, the course gave him a pool of individuals with whom he could take his time interviewing about their sexual experiences, instead of the all-too-quick, catch-as-catch-can "counseling sessions" he had previously offered. By the end of the spring semester of 1939, after teaching the marriage course four times, he had amassed some 350 histories from students who had been enrolled in his course. Interestingly, from the onset Kinsey questioned his interviewees about any homosexual activities they may have had.

As the number of sexual histories he obtained multiplied, so too did the number of people, both at the university and in the community at large, who opposed the course. One of their objections was, as might be expected, Kinsey's interest in the students' sexual histories. Finally, some faculty and local religious leaders and politicians became so loud in their complaints that President Herman B. Wells, who had supported Kinsey and the marriage course from the beginning, gave him an ultimatum. Kinsey could continue teaching the course after heavily revising the syllabus to placate the opposition or he could step away from it and focus his time on his research into human sexuality. Kinsey chose the latter.

In the meantime Kinsey had made the acquaintance of a gay student on campus. It's unclear how the two met, but after several conversations, the student told Kinsey that Chicago was home to a large community of queer men, and if Kinsey was interested in recording their sexual histories, the student was willing to introduce—and vouch for—the professor to some of his friends who lived in a boardinghouse at 711 Rush Street.

Kinsey made the first of his scores of trips to Chicago in June 1939, driving there from Bloomington, where he, his wife, and his children lived. It was a year and a half after Ray Carlson's suicide and at the height of the "post-pansy panic" that had forcefully gripped the United States. Kinsey's decision to begin his research with queer men and at that particular moment in time couldn't have been more poorly planned, and it shouldn't have been a surprise to anyone that his first research trip to Chicago was a disappointment.

Arriving in Chicago, Kinsey checked into the Harrison Hotel, a huge structure with four hundred rooms at the intersection of Harrison Street and Michigan Avenue. His contact person in Chicago invited him to visit the Rush Street boarding house, but the men who lived there were so suspicious of Kinsey that after nearly a week of trying to get them to open up to him, he had only been able to interview three of them, a less than promising start to his research.

Kinsey had not yet understood how completely Hoover's illogical ravings had turned Chicago, along with the rest of the country, into a "repressed culture, where homosexuality was both a crime and a disease" and where queer men could be imprisoned for up to ten years simply because their sexual desire was different than the dominant culture's. Chicago's vice squads actively hunted for men like those who lived in the Rush Street boardinghouse, hoping to find evidence against them that would destroy their lives, and for all the boardinghouse men knew, Kinsey was working for the Chicago police or, perhaps, even for Hoover's FBI.

To his credit, Kinsey quickly began to understand how difficult it was for the men to open up to him, but he persevered. In letters to the queer men who had initially spoken to him, he sent his thanks for taking the time to speak to him and for trusting him, but he also used the letters to flatter them. To "R.J.B." he wrote, "You are a distinctive creature," and he said to "E.B.," "You are an outstanding individual." While Kinsey undoubtedly meant his compliments, they were also very strategic. By the time he returned to Chicago for his second research trip, the men who had spoken to him on his first visit ended up vouching for him to their friends who, in turn, vouched for him to their friends.

It also didn't hurt when, during his second trip and thereafter, he began to insist to any queer man he met that his goal was to gain an understanding of their lives and not to gather evidence against them. He was sure, he told one of his contacts in Chicago, that the material he was gathering would, first, help him understand queer men and, second, be a boon to giving the country a better understanding of homosexuality. In Kinsey's words, "Folk as intelligent as yourself can help my thinking a great deal," and he followed that up by adding, "I can see no way of making social reactions" about homosexuality "more sensible unless we can bring this picture of reality together in an objective scientific study." To another he said that he strongly believed the country could be "made more tolerant" but "only if the facts" of homosexuality "are known." The repression under which queer men were living, he told them, would never disappear until society as a whole understood homosexuality. Once people did, they would view queer men simply as human beings—no more, no less—and not as the "depraved human beings, more savage than beasts" that Hoover had once labeled them. Kinsey repeated these and similar ideas over and over again to the men he met.

Just after his second research trip, the men's suspicion of Kinsey began to disappear quickly, and he wanted them to know that he understood their reluctance to talk to him. In July 1939 he wrote to "T.K.," "You had 'T.E.'s' word for it that I was safe, but I realize that it was asking a good deal to ask you to disclose all the details of your history." By the end of 1939, Kinsey could write to "R.B.," another of the men who had given Kinsey their sexual histories, "I appreciate very much the way in which you and so many of the others accepted me and helped." Within a very short time, the men Kinsey interviewed began to realize that they were contributing substantially to a project that might help change people's minds about them. One of them, "J.D.," wrote to Kinsey in 1940, "If there were more people like you who cared to find out and write about their fellow-men [sic] and their innermost self this world would be a better place to live in."

By the end of his second research trip to Chicago, Kinsey had interviewed sixty more men. Some were among the Rush Street crowd. Others were their friends, or their friends' friends, and they were from all over Chicago. Some lived in Towertown: "H.E." across the street from the boardinghouse, at 712 North Rush Street; "O.D." at 201 East Ontario Street; and "R.J.B." at 11 East Pearson Street. Many lived in other parts of Chicago. "H.B." lived at 3553 North Broadway Street in what is now Boys Town, as did "R.B.," who lived at 618 Roscoe Street. "J.F." lived on the South Side, at 514 East Thirty-Seventh Place, and "F.S.H." lived even farther south, at 5141 South Harper Avenue. "J.E.K." lived on the West Side at 3502 North Paulina Street.

During the first year of his research, from the summer of 1939 to the summer of 1940, Kinsey had even added the sexual histories of about forty male prostitutes. By Christmas of 1940, he had collected nearly six hundred interviews, a number that, over the next few years, quickly doubled and then quadrupled until he had taken the sexual histories of thousands of men. Kinsey wrote to his student acquaintance that the men had given him a very pointed and worthwhile "understanding of the problem" they faced. "It would have been [a] tragedy," he continued, "if you had failed to introduce me." From his research he was even able to estimate that Chicago's queer population was three hundred thousand—a huge jump from the twenty thousand estimated by the Chicago Vice Commission only some thirty years earlier.

During an early research trip, one of the men Kinsey met offered to give him a "sexual diary" and a collection of "love letters," which Kinsey gladly accepted. The diary and letters, along with some erotic photographs and other articles given to Kinsey by his interviewees, who were now eager to help him as much as they could, started him thinking about creating an archive of such materials. These were among the first items that would eventually become the Institute for Sex Research in 1947, now known as the Kinsey Institute for Research in Sex, Gender, and Reproduction. The archive would, of course, also include all of the interviews Kinsey conducted, but they would remain confidential and unavailable to anyone but Kinsey and his immediate staff. He wrote a letter to the diarist, telling him, "Your capacity for love is the thing that stands foremost in my thinking of you."

Several of the interviewees and Kinsey exchanged letters for some time after they had initially met, creating a series of brief, but often revealing, correspondences. In mid-December 1939 Kinsey wrote a thank-you letter to "P.'B.'J." in which he said, "The stuff of which you are made is so unusual that I shall always consider that you have contributed to our studies in a fashion that very few other people could." Two months later, P."B."J. responded to Kinsey from the Cook County Jail. In the letter he never mentioned the crime he committed, but he was happy to have gotten a light sentence for it: "Thank God I got only 60 days and a small fine." Evidently, he felt close enough to the researcher to ask to borrow two dollars, which he promised to return as soon as he was released, and he also told Kinsey how important the thank-you letter had been to him: "I shall all ways [sic] remember the nice things you said in your letter which will all ways [sic] make me feel good." He went on to tell Kinsey that he had had his photograph in the *Pittsburgh Courier*, had won first prize at the Cabin Inn on Halloween and at another time for "a ballet dance" there, as well as being "best dressed" at the Savoy Ballroom. Although he didn't mention it, these prizes were probably for female impersonation. A little over a week later, Kinsey sent the two dollars.

Another young man, "D.M.," felt that he had gained a sense of tranquility while he was being interviewed for his sexual history, and he wrote to Kinsey that "the confidence gained from your advise [sic] and experience has given me the assurance I was seeking." A third wrote to Kinsey after breaking up with his boyfriend, and he joked that he "had done little for amusement" afterward, "though if you call getting drunk amusement, I was very amused Saturday night." A fourth wrote to Kinsey about his lover who, after a "brief but intense" relationship, "disappeared," taking the young man's watch in much the same way that Tommy Phelan had stolen John Wing's ring. Kinsey counseled the young man not to let the experience sour him against relationships.

A fifth began what, for Kinsey, would be something of an extended correspondence. "T.K." had mentioned to Kinsey, perhaps while giving the researcher his sexual history in July 1939, that he often went to a nude beach near Chicago as his weekend getaway, and in his thank-you letter to T.K., Kinsey added, "Sometime I want to see your nude beach." A few months later T.K. wrote to Kinsey to tell him some good news. He had been hired to teach in the dramatic department of the Caskey School of Dancing in down-state Springfield, Illinois. He also recalled the evening during Kinsey's most recent trip to Chicago when the two of them looked for "various gay cocktail lounges"—they were especially set on finding a new place called the Club Gai—but had the "wrong house number" and so they were out of luck. T.K.'s letter also reveals a danger with which queer men had to contend. He wrote, "I don't know if saying too much in a letter" or waiting until they can speak face-to-face "is preferred. . . . I shall remain brief at presently [sic] until I have your O.K." He was concerned that someone might tip off the post office that he was queer and the authorities might begin opening his letters to look for evidence against him for sending what would have been considered obscene materials through the mail.

T.K. had a similar concern in November 1939. He had bought two photograph albums, which probably contained risqué snapshots of men, with money that Kinsey had given him for the purchase. They may have been the photos that were among the first items in the archives that Kinsey was beginning to create. T.K. wrote the researcher, "I've been thinking it over and decided that I shouldn't mail the albums to you on account of it being rather dangerous to trust the mail." He decided he would hold them until Kinsey returned to Chicago and could pick them up himself.

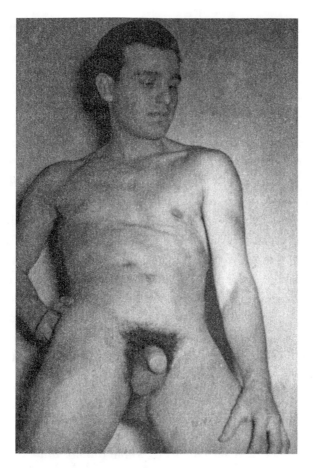

Fig. 25. Another photograph confiscated by
Chicago police in the 1940s. This one depicts a
masculine model, the opposite of the "pansies"
in Fig. 24 and a type more akin to Sandow.
Kinsey Institute

Four years later T.K. was still writing Kinsey, and in September 1943 he
revealed his sense of humor. However, even that had to be tempered with
ambiguous language. In the letter he promised to introduce Kinsey to some
potential interviewees. "There is so much ripened fruit around these here parts,"
he wrote, adding, "I will try and gather some species for you while you're here."
Then on a personal—and quite upbeat note for the times—he also told Kinsey

that he and his partner were doing well. "Nothing exciting has taken place," he wrote, "except that 'D.' and I are still enjoying our blissful life together." That was a huge achievement for two men in such a repressed time.

T.K. wasn't the only queer man in Chicago to take Kinsey out on the town. "J.P.B." took Kinsey to the Cabin Inn in late 1939 for drinks and to enjoy the floor show. Another man from the Rush Street house took Kinsey to an unidentified cabaret to watch another of the interviewees, called "J.J.," perform. J.J. must have had something of a career in local hot spots because Kinsey wrote him, "I was glad to have heard you at the club, but I wish I might have heard you sing at the theater."

While engaged in his research, Kinsey came to believe that Chicago's queer subculture was not actually one "community" but two. "First," he said, "was the . . . friend/lover networks" and the many "social institutions that catered to those men who" accepted themselves as queer. Kinsey recognized that the Rush Street boardinghouse had become "a haven" from the "social isolation and psychological marginality" that threatened them daily and that, behind its doors, "group acceptance could magically transform pariahs into human beings. In a society that spurned them," the men who lived there among others like themselves were able "to laugh, to dance, and to love." (Herman and his friends fit into this second category.)

The second group that Kinsey discerned was as opposite to the first as day is to night and included men who were sexually attracted to other men, "married and single men alike, many of whom did not think of themselves as homosexual" and rationalized their sexual exploits with other men "on liquor, cold wives, experimental urges, or the like." They met other, like-minded men during "brief, anonymous sexual contacts in dark places." This group had rarely been discussed by medical, legal, or religious authorities and never investigated by any of them because the heterosexual camouflage that they used had kept them hidden and safe from scrutiny, exactly as it was meant to do. Kinsey would be the first to shine a light on their activities.

The two groups, Kinsey believed, "did not really know one another," and their paths rarely crossed—at least socially.

Kinsey had gathered a huge amount of information on which he could base his claims about the second group, and some of that came from his personal experience. It had taken Kinsey only a few visits to Chicago before some of the men in the boardinghouse became "his private guide to their hidden world."

It included "city parks and public urinals" where he became involved in the "search for anonymous sex" with other men. If he hadn't already known it, he was beginning to realize that he belonged to the second group of men. He could enjoy his wife and children back in Bloomington "while preserving the perfect cover" of a non-queer, married sex researcher who had fathered children. Then, when he wanted, he could "engage in furtive, anonymous sex" in "tea rooms," queer slang for public toilets, while visiting Chicago. He lived this dual existence for nearly a decade, from 1939 to 1948.

In 1949, the year after he published the results of his research in Chicago and elsewhere in *Sexual Behavior of the Human Male*, Kinsey wrote to "J.F." that "it makes us home-sick to think of you and the rest of the folk who helped us in the early days of our study." His research trips, his acquaintance with thousands of queer men in Chicago, and his exploration of his own sexuality had meant more to him than he could have ever imagined when, ten years earlier, he was only able to convince three Chicago men to speak to him openly about their sexual experiences.

The men who trusted Kinsey—a hard-won trust that he achieved only because one man vouched for him to another, who did the same to someone else, who followed suit—unwittingly became part of a movement that was only just beginning, one that was little more than a hope for some, such as Henry Gerber two decades earlier, but a seeming impossibility to most. However small and obscure it was in the beginning, it would help to stoke the fires of the sexual revolution that would explode in New York in 1969 in what has been called the Stonewall riots and in the gay liberation movement that the riots spawned. It would be too late for Raymond Carlson and hundreds of other men like him who, caught up in the insidiousness of the time, took control of their destiny in the only way available to them. It also would be too late for those who, like Ralph Wright, charged into marriage to hide their sexuality. Others, like the men of the Rush Street boardinghouse, would make due, devise strategies that would allow them to survive the very real threats that surrounded them—threats not only to their bodies but also to their sense of self—while keeping what we think of as their sexual identity intact. Chicago was full of such men, all heroes and virtually all forgotten now or, if remembered at all, relegated to a footnote to the narrative of the period in which they lived and loved and over which, in time, they triumphed.

Notes

Epigraph

"Fairy Town, Fairy Town": "Songs," EWB.

Introduction: From Sodomite to Sex Moron

"She—Sometimes you appear": National Medical Association, Sketches from Life.
"manufacture, transportation": History Channel, "Prohibition."
"Some of my friends": "Visitors at the Subway," EWB.
"Two rooms": Blinstrub, "Follow-Up Work."
"post-pansy panic": Morris, "Pink Herring," 233.

1. Took Him Home with Me, and Love Him Better Than Ever

"Monday is a sort": Wing, *Chicago Diaries*, 29.
"fair": National Archives and Records Administration, *Passport Applications*.
"Diamonds are my delight": Wing, *Chicago Diaries*, 66.
"largely male frontier": Erenberg, "Entertaining Chicagoans."
"male prostitutes rented": de la Croix, *Chicago Whispers*, 20.
"whole souled boys": Wing, *Chicago Diaries*, 66.
"fell in with a bully": Ibid., 15.
"'youth' and an 'old'": Katz, "Coming to Terms," 218.
"child/parent": Ibid.," 219.
"my darling boy": Ibid.," 219–20.
"bully boy": Wing, *Chicago Diaries*, 93.
"a lucky boy": Ibid., 61.
"the younger": Gehl, "Making of a Chicago Eccentric," xii.
where he met the "boy": Wing, *Chicago Diaries*, 31.
"fell in love": Ibid., 45.
"d—d poor bed": Ibid., 38.
"Saw a boy": Ibid., 45.

"*enamorata* of last night": Ibid.
"I run against": Ibid., 31.
"When my newly found": Ibid.
"went to work": Ibid., 32.
"found to my great horror": Ibid., 33.
"I love the boy": Ibid.
"a horrible old suit": Ibid., 34.
"O, that I could help": Ibid., 36.
"stranger behavior": Ibid.
"a stylish boy": Ibid., 37.
"a brick": Ibid., 64.
"We did not": Ibid., 74.
"Monday is a sort": Ibid., 29.
"'the only girl'": Ibid., 53.
"by whether they served": Katz, "Coming to Terms," 216
"crime against nature so inexpressibly": Police Courts, *Daily Inter Ocean*.
"Porter and I": Wing, pocket diary, April 30, 1858.
"Geo W Porter": Ibid., May 20, 1859.
"I and Porter": Ibid., May 30, 1859.
"He has gone!": Ibid., June 1, 1859.
"Have been thinking": Ibid., November 18, 1859.
"I dreamed": Ibid., November 17, 1859.
"Ex": Ibid., July 5, 1861.
"bachelor by the Grace": Williams, introduction to *Chicago Diaries*, xlix.

2. The Most Effeminate Type of Sex Perversions

"The audience disturbed": Fleeson, "Gay '30s."
"ordinary-looking": "Who Runs the House?," *Daily Inter Ocean*.
"a woman's night dress": Ibid.
"Mamie Conley": Ibid.
"Boy houses" that catered: de la Croix, *Chicago Whispers*, 21.
"nameless ecstacies": Ibid.
"twenty-seven panel houses": Ibid.
"The method of negro perverts": Kiernan, "Classification of Homosexuality," 350.
"dancehalls attached to saloons": Sprague, "On the 'Gay Side,'" 7.
"by bad influences": Healy, *Individual Delinquent*, 584.
"had a dress": Ibid., 585.
"for the most flagrant": Ibid., 586.

"mutual masturbation": Terman and Miles, *Sex and Personality*, 301.

"peg house": Ibid.

"his father insisted": Ibid.

"Their disguise": Vice Commission of Chicago, *Social Evil in Chicago*, 297.

"the almost unbelievable": Friedman, *Strapped for Cash*, 48–49.

"whole theatre is an exhibition": Stead, *If Christ Came*, 248.

"jaded sex circuses": Bruns, *Damndest Radical*, 4.

"cafes, bars, baths": S. L. Lewis, "Gay Masquerade," 48.

"palaces of sherbet": Murray, *Homosexualities*, 189n172.

"A special factor": de la Croix, *Chicago Whispers*, 22.

"Turkish baths": Hirschfeld, *Homosexuality in Men and Women*, 625.

"certain smart clubs": Sprague, "On the 'Gay Side,'" 13.

"athletic societies": Ibid.

"adolescent boys and young men": Ibid.

"a doctor": Ibid.

"wealthy gay men": Ibid.

"homosexual atmosphere": Ibid.

"a busboy's jacket": Fleeson, "Gay '30s."

"had sex": Ibid.

"Officer's Club": Ibid.

"I worked in a men's club": Henry, *Sex Variants*, 432.

"They always kept": Ibid.

"infested": Decency, "Look Under the Bridges," 6.

New York had "beasts": "Bridge-End Dens," *Daily Inter Ocean*.

"how low men": Ibid.

"And what do": Ibid.

"dregs of filth": Ibid.

"foppish and effeminate": Junger, *Becoming the Second City*, 65.

"woman" beneath the bridge: "Bridge-End Dens," *Daily Inter Ocean*.

"band of dissolute characters": Late Local Items, *Chicago Tribune*.

"two filthy wretches": City Criminal Record, *Daily Inter Ocean*.

"old men": Untitled notice, *Daily Inter Ocean*, June 22, 1880, 6.

"attempting to commit": Amusements, *Daily Inter Ocean*, June 29, 1880, 6.

"engaged in disgusting": Ibid.

"committing a nameless crime": "Late Arrests," *Daily Inter Ocean*.

"the professors": Amusements, *Daily Inter Ocean*, June 29, 1880, 6.

"Chicago," an 1891 article: "Chicago's Dark Places," *Deseret Weekly*.

3. We Never Liked His Species

"Erotic imagery": Ullman, "'Twentieth Century Way,'" 589.

"gloves and silk": "Clever Method of Shoplifting," *Chicago Tribune*.

"one of the cleverest": Ibid.

"most successful theater": Fosdick, "Hooley's Theater," 331.

"a variety of different types": Boyd, "Transgender and Gay Male Cultures," 29.

"earned the reputation": "A Frontier Mystery," *Daily Inter Ocean*.

"surprised and shocked": Ibid.

"There is some terrible": "Corporal Noonan," *Salt Lake Tribune*.

shot himself in "the heart": Ibid.

"thoughtfully pointed": Boag, *Re-dressing America's Frontier Past*, 90.

"Burt Shepherd": "Hooley's," *Chicago Tribune*.

"so decidedly bad": "Bliss Whitaker's Benefit Day," *Daily Inter Ocean*.

"first . . . to get": Footlight Notes, *Daily Inter Ocean*, July 3, 1879.

"He deserves": Footlight Notes, *Daily Inter Ocean*, July 5, 1879.

"callow youth": Amusements, *Daily Inter Ocean*, June 29, 1880.

"objectionable": Amusements, *Daily Inter Ocean*, January 18, 1893.

"featured over a score": Nickell, *Secrets of the Sideshow*, 49.

"wild abandon": Roth, "Jews on the Midway," 7.

"erotic imagery": Ullman, "'Twentieth Century Way,'" 589.

"played the part": Okihiro, *Common Ground*, 77.

4. A Fine Piece of Nude

"Sieveking likes": "Strongest Man in the World," *New York World*.

"A sculptress has created": Kasson, *Tarzan*, 25.

"happy domesticity": Chapman, *Sandow the Magnificent*, 51.

"great and inseparable friend": Ibid.

"Sandow is a truly": "Strongest Man in the World," *New York World*.

"the particular attraction": Sandow, "My Reminiscences," 147.

"a fine piece of nude": A. Callen, "Doubles and Desire," 688.

"a beautiful set": Chapman, *Sandow the Magnificent*, 34.

"The Sandow photographs": Symonds, *Letters of John Addington Symonds*, 3:436.

"little how much": "How the World," *Literary Digest*, 46.

"nude portrait": Carlton, *Looking for Little Egypt*, 81.

"white silk trunks": "He Is a Man," *Chicago Tribune*.

"stroked Sandow's": Kasson, *Tarzan*, 56.

"a dangerously handsome": Ibid., 53.

"One thing seems": Chapman, *Sandow the Magnificent*, 75.

"Rape, sodomy": Daniel, "Castration of Sexual Perverts," 267.
"tall, slender, exquisitely": Chapman, *Sandow the Magnificent*, 92.
"a sub-culture": Scupham-Bilton, "Body of a God."
"modeling himself": Todd, "Bernarr Macfadden," 66.
"a great success": Bennett, "Weakness—a Crime!"
"of him in classic poses": Black, "Charles Atlas."
"the qualities of Adonis": Kasson, *Tarzan*, 46.
"actor representing": Moriarty, "Sandow—Gay Strongman," 31.

5. My Vileness Is Uncontrollable

"Last summer": H. Ellis, *Studies in the Psychology of Sex*, 2:171.
"loins": Ibid., 169.
"Lynch him!": Ibid.
"the arrival of a dozen": "Almost a Lynching," *New York Times*.
"attempted lynching": Hirschfeld, *Homosexuality in Men and Women*, 41.
"fell in love": H. Ellis, *Studies in the Psychology of Sex*, 2:169.
"at least ten years": Ibid., 170.
"indulge in": Reckless, "Natural History of Vice Areas," 133–34.
"sex perverts": Ibid., 134.
"a rather dark": C. Shaw, *Jack-Roller*, 97.
"as I'd walk": Ibid., 85–86.
"young boy": Thrasher, *Gang*, 96.
"developed a passion": H. Ellis, *Studies in the Psychology of Sex*, 2:170.
"to undergo medical treatment": Ibid.
previous lover's life "miserable": Ibid.
"so frightened, hurt": Ibid., 172.
group of "passionate" letters: Ibid., 170.
"hysterical melancholia": Ibid.
"I might as well": Ibid., 171.
"decent creature": Ibid.
"doctors knew": Ibid.
"this disease": Talbot and Ellis, "Case of Developmental Degenerative Insanity," 343.
"I am utterly incorrigible": H. Ellis, *Studies in the Psychology of Sex*, 2:171.
even a "monster": Ibid.
"born in me": Talbot and Ellis, "Case of Developmental Degenerative Insanity," 343.
rid himself of the "monster": H. Ellis, *Studies in the Psychology of Sex*, 2:171.
"Fearing that my": Ibid.
"butting his head": "Olmstead Takes a Dose," *Chicago Tribune*.

"improvement": H. Ellis, *Studies in the Psychology of Sex*, 2:172.

"consider sexual perversion": Ibid., 173.

"insane criminal": Akin, letter to John T. Peters, January 29, 1900.

"A scandal is said": "Shot Down on the Streets," *Utica Daily Observer*.

"He is probably insane": "Tried to Kill a Letter Carrier," *Elkhart Daily Review*.

"It is evident": "Great New Chance," *Chicago Tribune*.

"Olmstead shot a man": Ibid.

6. The Hottest Show on Earth!

"Chicago ain't no sissy": Sawyers, "Hinky Dink."

"impersonating a female": "2 Park Arrests," Clippings on Vice in Chicago.

"The indecent show": "Bad Park Show to Go," *Chicago Record-Herald*.

"female minstrels": "Minstrel," *Billboard*.

"The Hottest Show": Duncan Clark's Female Minstrels, advertisement, *Chicago Tribune*.

"This co. is": "Nebraska," *New York Dramatic Mirror*.

"artfully dressed": "2 Park Arrests, " Clippings on Vice in Chicago.

"the most reprehensible": Dressler, "Burlesque as a Cultural Phenomenon," 54.

"If any person": Chicago Municipal Code §1603 (1851).

"on the charge": "'Attractions' Go into Court Today," *Chicago Tribune*.

"impersonating a female": "2 Park Arrests," Clippings on Vice in Chicago.

"We arrest men": "Says Bad Shows Gain," *Chicago Record-Herald*.

"case against Bertha Faulk": "'Attractions' Go into Court Today," *Chicago Tribune*.

"vulgar" performance: "Acquit Bronze Beauty," *Chicago Record-Herald*.

"dance for the benefit": Ibid.

"her 'scant' costume": Ibid.

"was nothing if not": Ibid.

"Twice beaten": "Boys, Girls, Vice," *Chicago Record-Herald*.

"Ladies and gentlemen": "Reform of Parks," *Chicago Tribune*.

"illicit sexuality": Sprague, "Chicago Sociologists," 13.

"rampant vice": Ibid.

"sex education": Ibid., 15.

"an elite group": Ibid.

"to protect children": Ibid.

"about $50,000": Reckless, "Natural History of Vice Areas," 78.

"the old Custom House Place": Kendall, "First Ward Ball."

"If a great disaster": Griffin, "Sin Drenched Revels," 56.

"Guests not contributing": McCutcheon, "Grand March."

"'These reform guys'": "Craig 'Belle' of the Ball." *Chicago Tribune*.

"It was surprising": Riis, "Sociologist at a Dance."
"female impersonators": Griffin, "Sin Drenched Revels," 54.
"unbelievably appalling": de la Croix, *Chicago Whispers*, 23.
"debauch, which reminds": "Sees Pagan Rome," *Chicago Tribune*.
"with batteries of cameras": "Cameras to Aid," *Chicago Tribune*.
"reformers of a certain": "Bomb Explodes," *New York Times*.
"Chicago ain't no sissy": Sawyers, "Hinky Dink."
"the female impersonator" also "received": "Threaten Bomb," *Chicago Tribune*.
"the first male": Ibid.
"superintendent of the Chicago": "Describe Orgy," *Chicago Tribune*.
"Two women and their male companions": Ibid.

7. A Sodomist Is One Who Enlarges the Circles of His Friends

"Though one might": Spring, *Secret Historian*, loc. 246–52.
"wore extravagant clothes": S. L. Lewis, "Gay Masquerade," 40.
"roving lecture forum": Heap, *Slumming*, 236.
"the second floor": Drury, *Dining in Chicago*, 186.
"was a sodomist": S. L. Lewis, "Gay Masquerade,"40.
"mostly sandwiches": Drury, *Dining in Chicago*, 186.
"a truly bohemian atmosphere": Ibid., 78.
"only the most daring": S. L. Lewis, "Gay Masquerade,"40.
"a point of entry": Ibid., 214.
"owners of . . . rooming": Sprague, "On the 'Gay Side,'" 11.
"the wealthy Gold Coast": Gapp, "Death of Bohemia."
"reading tournaments": Smith, *Chicago's Left Bank*, 9.
"the geographical center": Brown and Brown, *Biography of Mrs. Marty Mann*, 19.
"near-naked male": Oatman-Stanford, "Before Rockwell."
"the icon": Ibid.
"kitchens and baths": Gazell, "High Noon," 61.
"nearby teashops": Ibid.
"distorted forms of sex": Zorbaugh, *Gold Coast*, 100.
"the apartment area": Reckless, "Natural History of Vice Areas," 161.
"Midwest American": Spring, *Secret Historian*, loc. 246–52.
"bohemians willingly": Heap, *Slumming*, 164.
"The homosexual group": Reitman, "Homosexuality," 1.
"In bohemia": Ibid., 1–2.
"female impersonator": G.A.D., "Such Is Life in Chicago."
"On any night": Bruns, *Damndest Radical*, 224.

"On galactic Summer": Heap, *Slumming*, 64.

"crime of Oscar": T. M. Anderson, unpublished autobiography, 77.

"I soon found": Ibid.

"Later I happened": Ibid.

"largely responsible": Reitman, "Homosexuality," 4.

"unconventional reputation": BLR, "Collection Summary."

"lost hands down": S. L. Lewis, "Gay Masquerade,"41.

"certain churches": Sprague, "On the 'Gay Side,'" 7.

"debates on free": Zorbaugh, *Gold Coast*, 98.

"semi-private club": S. L. Lewis, "Gay Masquerade,"92.

"affluent Chicagoans": Heap, *Slumming*, 155.

"men were smoking": Zorbaugh, *Gold Coast*, 100.

"men . . . fondling": Ibid.

"Why I thought": Ibid.

"combined literary": Kissack, *Free Comrades*, 174.

"a hermaphrodite violinist": Ibid.

"At a bar": S. L. Lewis, "Gay Masquerade,"93.

"a group of male": Zorbaugh, *Gold Coast*, 100.

"warm summer evenings": Ibid.

"From bench to bench": Ibid.

"Broads on the make": Schweik, "Chicago World Fairies," 13.

"whole groups": Vice Commission of Chicago, *Social Evil in Chicago*, 296.

"Everywhere I go": S. L. Lewis, "Gay Masquerade," 90.

"on an unloading": S. Anderson, *Memoirs*, 339.

"The men who": Ibid., 339–340.

"sissies": Ibid., 150.

"What did it all": Ibid., 340.

"prick lickers": "Conversation with Edwin Teeter," EWB, 4.

"the queen type": "Queen's Jealousy," EWB, 1.

"marihuana, acrobatic": Schweik, "Chicago World Fairies," 13.

"Gin, din": Living History of Illinois and Chicago, "Towertown."

"quite a scene": Berton, *Remembering Bix*, 216.

"He zings": Ibid., 217.

"somewhat made up": Ibid.

"some WAN": Ibid., 218.

"men in girls' costumes": "2 Views of Night Life," *Chicago Tribune*.

"My Lord—ain't": Ibid.

"indecent poetry": "35 'Bohemians' Seized," *Chicago Tribune*.

"English basement": Rexroth, "Kenneth Rexroth's Autobiography."
"the bark": Schweik, "Chicago World Fairies," 16.
"some 35": "Pansy Parlors," *Variety*.
"*finocchio*": Crawford, "David Petillo."
"and [Charles] Gagliodoto": US Department of Justice, "David Petillo," 12.
"Professor Lant": Beck, *Hobohemia*, 86–87.
"his all-out-sexy": Ibid., 87.
"57 saloons": Heap, *Slumming*, 65.
"singing and dancing": N. Anderson, "Cabaret."
"any pros": Ibid.
"a man, garbed": Heap, *Slumming*, 65.
"an atmosphere of abandonment": S. L. Lewis, "Gay Masquerade," 95.
"A group of 'homos'": Zorbaugh, *Gold Coast*, 96.
"A white male": Heap, *Slumming*, 356n57.
"at 'certain cafes'": Ibid., 254.

8. They're Regular He-Whores

"Unusually well developed": Vollmer, "Vagabond Boy," 1.
"used to be a tramp": N. Anderson, *On Hobos*, 112.
"I never saw": Ibid., 111.
"either the female": Ibid., 112.
"Inspired by dime": Salerno, *Sociology Noir*, 89.
"home trouble": N. Anderson, "Juvenile and the Tramp," 301.
"headquarters for thousands": Sprague, "On the 'Gay Side,'" 14.
"backwash of flotsam": Beck, *Hobohemia*, 15.
"two types of perverts": N. Anderson, *Hobo*, 144.
"situational homosexuality": Gianoulis, "Situational Homosexuality," 1.
"kid": N. Anderson, "Chronic Drinker," 1.
"as long as there": Ibid., 3.
"there were hundreds": Ibid.
"natural": Ibid., 4.
"take a crack": Ibid.
"We'll freeze": Ibid., 5.
"coffee and": Ibid.
"men and boys": N. Anderson, "Evening Spent on the Benches," 1.
"I'm getting a little": Ibid.
"punks in": Ibid.
"Any of you": Ibid., 2.

"runaways" who thought: N. Anderson, "Juvenile and the Tramp," 301.

"predatory" in nature: DePastino, *Citizen Hobo*, 87.

"Coercing, cajoling": Ibid.

"a club": N. Anderson, "Juvenile and the Tramp," 303.

"lump," a handout: Sandburg, *Always the Young Strangers*, 383.

"was hardly twelve": Reitman, "Homosexuality," 3.

"a mob of crooks": Ibid.

"fell prey": DePastino, *Citizen Hobo*, 90.

"rival jockers": Ibid., 89.

"worked on a boat": N. Anderson, *Hobo*, 146.

"thirty-six boys": N. Anderson, "Juvenile and the Tramp," 306.

"very intense": Ibid.

"stealing, begging": DePastino, *Citizen Hobo*, 89.

"hug and kiss him": N. Anderson, "Boy Tramp," 2.

"an intelligent, handsome ":Ibid.

Calling Tramp a "punk": N. Anderson, "Case of Boy in Teens," 1.

"for about half an hour": Ibid., 2.

"Take it from me": N. Anderson, "Case of Boy in Teens," 4.

"boyish looking": Vollmer, "Vagabond Boy," 1.

"hesitant": Ibid.

"he needed money": Ibid., 2.

"slim" but "muscular": Vollmer, "Boy Hustler," 1.

"declined to talk": Ibid., 2.

"make some easy": Ibid.

"I didn't like": Ibid., 3.

"get a job": Ibid., 4.

"kiss" the men: Ibid., 3.

"very much.": Ibid., 4.

"Ya' know": Ibid., 5–6.

"pal around": Ibid., 6.

9. A Man Will Do When There Is Nothing Else in the World

"I would like": "Leo. Age 18," EWB, 2.

"'bright light' district": Stanford University Libraries, "Swinging on the South Side."

"high-pitched, feminine": Oliver, *Blues Fell*, 98.

"freakish man": Hannah, "Freakish Man Blues."

"the outstanding favorite": Edwards, "Antonio (Tony) Junius Jackson."

"When Tony Jackson walked": Lomax, *Mister Jelly Roll*, 43.

"dark-skinned": Reed, *Hot from Harlem*, 195.

"the Dago, Russell's": Sprague, "Jackson, Tony (Anthony)."

"a pearl gray derby": Rose, *Storyville*, 91.

"If you can't play": Ibid.

"tall skinny young man": Sprague, "Jackson, Tony (Anthony)."

"only received": "Gets Pittance for Great Song Hit," *Kansas City Sun*.

"thousands of dollars": Ibid.

"he saw grown up": Nosey Sees All, *Chicago Whip*.

"a man attired": Heap, *Slumming*, 85–86.

"were insertive" Drexel, "Before Paris Burned," 125.

"a real bitch": Ibid.

"girlish looking boy": "Leo. Age 18," EWB, 2.

"deceived": Ibid., 10.

"The black and tan": Hal, "Plantation, Chicago."

"by the 'fruits'": Heap, *Slumming*, 45.

"At these disreputable": Curon, *Chicago*, 146.

"the uninformed observer" Ibid., 147.

"a silver cigarette": "Grand Masque Ball," *Chicago Defender*.

"Come, bring your children": "Mask Dance at Masonic Hall," *Chicago Defender*.

"world's toughest town": "Pansy Parlors," *Variety*.

10. Hell, I Wish They'd Give Me a Safety Razor and a Shot of Gin

"A lot of": "'Husband' of Sex Hoaxer," *Chicago Tribune*, 12.

"I'd hate to tell you": "Hold Man as 'Girl Slayer,'" *Chicago Tribune*.

an occupation: "singer": "1910 United States Federal Census," Ancestry.com.

"singer" as his occupation: "U.S. City Directories, 1822–1995," Ancestry.com.

"well built athletes": "Queens Galore," *Labor World*.

"Herculean marvels": "Washington," *Spokane Press*.

"models in classical": "Last Week of Music," *San Francisco Call*.

"theater patron": "Man Poses as Woman," *Chanute Daily Tribune*.

"Peeping Tom": "Youth Who Grew," *Syracuse Herald*.

"May Belmont": Ibid.

"May or Harry": Ibid.

"a woman or": Ibid.

"eradicator": Ibid.

"so strenuously": "'May Belmont' Jumps," *Syracuse Herald*.

"the caged songbird": Ibid.

"masquerading in public": Ibid.

"searched by police matrons": "Man Poses as Woman," *Chanute Daily Tribune.*

"a murmur of attention": "May Belmont Before Justice Shove," *Syracuse Herald.*

"They made a striking": Ibid.

"ostrich feathers": Ibid.

"Her architecture": Ibid.

"beauty doctors": "They All Want to Know," *Syracuse Journal.*

"she had discovered": Ibid.

"an evil, leering": "Unmask 'Girl Slayer,'" *Chicago Herald-Examiner.*

"whose name police": "'Blue Eyes' Doff Rouge," *Chicago Tribune.*

"kicking, screaming oaths": "Hold Man as 'Girl Slayer,'" *Chicago Tribune.*

"My God! That": "Unmask 'Girl Slayer,'" *Chicago Herald-Examiner.*

"discussed the possibility": "'Husband' of Sex Hoaxer," *Chicago Tribune,* 12.

"A lot of prominent": Ibid.

"The Shaving": "The Shaving Grace," *Chicago American.*

"winked coquettishly": "'Man-Girl' Is Bored," *Chicago Herald-Examiner.*

"duplex psychology": "'Husband' of Sex Hoaxer," *Chicago Tribune,* 12.

"psychic hermaphrodites": Brill, "Conception of Homosexuality," 336.

"I'm gonna fight": "Hold Man as 'Girl Slayer,'" *Chicago Tribune,* 12.

"smoothed 'her' henna": Ibid., 1.

"rubbed stubby fingers": Ibid., 12.

"squirmed": "'Husband' of Sex Hoaxer," *Chicago Tribune,* 1.

"We'd 'a' known": "Trail Pal of 'Bandit Girl,'" *Chicago Tribune.*

"man-girl": "'Man-Girl' Faces Tesmer," *Chicago Tribune.*

"cake eating type": Lesy, *Murder City,* 164.

"didn't have": "Trail Pal of 'Bandit Girl,'" *Chicago Tribune.*

"held that the fact": "Thompson Is Recognized," *Chicago Herald-Examiner.*

"precedent-making": "Thompson Pleads for Dress," *Chicago American.*

"jury box": "'Man-Girl' Is Acquitted," *Chicago Herald-Examiner.*

"Everybody's been swell": Lesy, *Murder City,* 167.

"wanted to live": "'Man-Girl' Is Acquitted," *Chicago Herald-Examiner.*

"nude photos": Shteir, *Striptease,* 83.

"such a person": "Police Prohibit Man-Girl," *Chicago Tribune.*

"I shall halt": Ibid.

"Shock and hemorrhage": Ohio Department of Health, death certificate for Fred Thompson.

11. Used as a Pimp for Others to Get Their Meat

"To hell with": Dececco, *Behind the Mask,* 2172–79.

"practiced 'friction'": Ibid., 1540–47.

"Krafft-Ebing": Ibid., 1242–49

"slave pen": Ibid., 1247

"boy prostitutes": Ibid., 1249–56.

"romantic type": Ibid.

"B—L—": Zorbaugh, *Gold Coast*, 100.

"squirrel": Dececco, *Behind the Mask*, 2410–15.

"intimate with a perfect": Ibid., 1957–64.

"quite a lot": Ibid., 2304–10.

nicknamed the "young tenor": Ibid., 1249–56.

"direct relationship": Hatheway, *Gilded Age Construction*, 84.

"a characteristic": Hagenbach, "Masturbation," 603.

men's and boy's "vigor": Mumford, "'Lost Manhood' Found", 33.

"women . . . in their": Beard, *Sexual Neurasthenia*, 106.

"only $18.00": Sears, Roebuck and Company, "Our $18.00 Giant," 476.

"enemy alien": Kepner and Murray, "Henry Gerber (1895–1972)," 24.

"officers and enlisted": Cornebise, *"Amorac News,"* 2.

"as many as twenty-five": Dececco, *Behind the Mask*, 1316.

"tonsillitis": "File Memorandum Re: Henry Gerber," GAS, 1.

"diagnosis of 'secondary'": Ibid., 2.

between men "'immoral'": Gerber, "Society for Human Rights."

"anything so rash": Ibid.

"nude sepia photographs": Dececco, *Behind the Mask*, 572.

"The average homosexual": Gerber, "Society for Human Rights."

"that as long as": Ibid.

"men of good reputation": Ibid.

"plumper" in a shop: "1920 United States Federal Census," Ancestry.com.

"job with the railroad": Gerber, "Society for Human Rights."

"racial prejudices": Dececco, *Behind the Mask*, 1264–71.

"an article on 'self-control'": National Park Service. "Henry Gerber House," 16.

"intended to use": Ibid.

"paper" written and published: Heap, *Slumming*, 176n28.

"picks up all the Dirt!": Reitman, "Homosexuality," 10.

phony "program": Ibid.

"Maxine . . . and Rose": Reitman, "Homosexuality," 11.

"sauntering / Along": Ibid.

"exclude the much larger": Gerber, "Society for Human Rights."

"a visit downtown": Ibid.

"Where's the boy?": Ibid.

"strange rites": "Girl Reveals Strange Cult," *Chicago American.*

"an indigent laundry queen": Gerber, "Society for Human Rights."

"powder puff": Sprague, "60th Anniversary."

"It was admitted": Gerber, "Society for Human Rights."

"heavy makeup": King, "'Latin Lover.'"

"face-powder dispenser": Ibid.

"two 'men'": Ibid.

"to meet me": Ferguson, *Idol Worship*, 25.

"beating" and taunted: King, "'Latin Lover.'"

"a hatchet-faced female": Gerber, "Society for Human Rights."

"I love Karl": Ibid.

"'shyster' lawyer": Ibid.

"two postal inspectors": "File Memorandum Re: Henry Gerber," GAS, 2.

"and that was the end": Gerber, "Society for Human Rights."

"everything had been 'arranged'": Ibid.

"an outrage": Ibid.

"I had nothing": Ibid.

"What was the idea": Ibid.

"for conduct unbecoming": "File Memorandum Re: Henry Gerber," GAS, 3.

"Unholy Inquisition": Gerber, "Society for Human Rights."

"To hell": Ibid.

"punk" Gerber had propositioned: Dececco, *Behind the Mask*, 2069.

"former Major General": Gerber, "Society for Human Rights."

"screwballs": Dececco, *Behind the Mask*, 2006.

"NYC Male": Ibid., 1987–94.

"Young college graduate": Box 593-D, personals ad, unidentified newspaper.

"used as a pimp": Dececco, *Behind the Mask*, 2199.

"Section VIII board": National Park Service, "Henry Gerber House," 20.

"investigator's limited understanding": Ibid.

"only practiced mutual": Ibid.

"weekend orgies": Dececco, *Behind the Mask*, 2243.

"haven" as well as: Ibid., 2385.

"environment of old": Henry Gerber to Manuel boyFrank, February 18, 1946, 2.

"sex laws" Dececco, *Behind the Mask*, 2468.

"the lavender curtain": Ibid., 6636.

"nine out of ten": Ibid., 2385.

"I once lost": Ibid., 2468.

sanctified "monogamy": Ibid., 2278.

"secret underground": Ibid., 2448.

"better sort of homosexuals": Ibid., 2455.

"$200 mustering": Ibid., 2527.

"practical" in love: Henry Gerber to Manuel boyFrank, February 18, 1946, 2.

"If I were a fairy": Dececco, *Behind the Mask*, 2317.

12. All Have Waitresses Who Are Lads in Gal's Clothing

"Either put on": Heap, *Slumming*, 95.

"the street corner": Drexel, "Before Paris Burned," 127.

"quite a few": See, "'Female Impersonators' Rule."

"a dress not": Drexel, "Before Paris Burned," 127.

"literally entertained": Heap, *Slumming*, 256.

"male 'hostess'": Ibid., 90.

"spectacles of perversion": Ibid.

"strange and little known": "Seek to Make City," *Chicago Tribune*.

"Welcome all": Ibid.

"McKinlock campus": Ibid.

"pansy parlors": "Pansy Parlors," *Variety*.

"former quarters": Heap, *Slumming*, 237.

"odd sort of place": Ibid.

"an eccentric night life": "Launch Tavern Cleanup War," *Chicago Sunday Tribune*, 1.

"femme impersonators": Heap, *Slumming*, 90.

"she intended": "Case Is a Rather Well Built," EWB, 1.

"impersonators" and "male hostesses": Heap, *Slumming*, 90.

to get "rid": Ibid.

"obnoxious" and its performances: "Launch Tavern Cleanup War," *Chicago Sunday Tribune*, 1.

"either put on pants": Heap, *Slumming*, 95.

"After two years": "Chi Lily-White," *Variety*.

"more and more vulgar": Rexroth, "Kenneth Rexroth's Autobiography."

"immoral practices": "Revoke License of Bathhouse," *Chicago Tribune*.

"rare quality": McMillan, "Chicagoan in Harlem."

an "entertainer": "1940 United States Federal Census," Ancestry.com.

"the South Side's Oddest Nite Club": Tovey, "Down at the Cabin Inn," 203.

"producin' a show": Ibid., 207.

"elderly" man dressed: "Goblins," EWB.

"the sidewalks and entrance": Vollmer, "New Year's Eve Drag," 1.

"uniformed guards": Ibid.

"heavily powdered: Ibid., 2.

"wrong" bathroom: Ibid., 4.

"in street clothes": Ibid., 2.

"Young effeminate lads": Ibid., 2–3.

"well known tradesman": Ibid., 3.

the only "meat" available: Heap, *Slumming*, 271.

"a man hanging": Ibid.

"Negroes": Vollmer, "New Year's Eve Drag," 4.

"a preponderance of Jews": Ibid.

"enabled people": Wilson, "Gay Life in Chicago."

"at the Halloween": Rofes, "Steward on Sex," 88.

"double wedding": Zagria, "Cabin Inn, Chicago."

"eccentric midget": Abbott, "Dusky Singer Scores Hit."

"comedian and acrobatic dancer": "'Scandals' End," *Rockford Morning Star.*

"very handsome": de la Croix, *Chicago Whispers*, 146.

"owners Nat Ivy": Ibid., 147.

"obscenity": de la Croix, Ibid.

"The testimony does not": Ibid.

"in the basement": Cabello, "Queer Bronzeville: The Drag Balls."

"they'd just pick": Ibid.

"a seven or eight": Ibid.

"tall and languorous": "Cocktails Get Female Impersonator," *Chicago Defender.*

"displaying conduct": Ibid.

"notorious varietarists": Heap, *Slumming*, 259.

"one of the best": "Chicago Has Pansies," *Afro-American.*

"entertainment by female impersonators": Ibid.

"Several weeks ago": Ibid.

"rid the district": "Southside Wars on 'Pansies,'" *Afro-American.*

"CABARETS": Heap, *Slumming*, 316n39.

"ebony and white": Ibid., 190.

"young white girl": "Southside Wars on 'Pansies,'" *Afro-American.*

"Censoring seems": Heap, *Slumming*, 323n65.

"'white slave' traffic": Barnes, "Story of the Committee of Fifteen," 146.

"targeting the Cabin": Heap, *Slumming*, 95.

"standing in front": Bruns, *Damndest Radical*, 279.

"undercover white anti-vice": Heap, *Slumming*, 263.

"still in the entrance": "Club on Study Tour," *Chicago Tribune.*

"negroid temperament": Ibid.

"is devoted to": Ibid.
"enormous three-story": Cabello, "Queer Bronzeville: Bronzeville's Vice Dictrict."
"How naked it": Heap, *Slumming*, 318n44.

13. Play It, Whip It, Pat It, Bang It

"Mr. and Mrs. Frankie": McMillan, "47th Street."
"Frankie has": "Frankie Jaxon on Tour," *Chicago Defender*.
"one of the greatest": "Sunset," *Chicago Defender*.
"a big-time ofay act": "Frankie at It," *Chicago Defender*.
"over some very treacherous": "Frankie Jaxon in Chi," *Chicago Defender*.
"he had to have special": Ibid.
"clever little entertainer": "Frank's Fixed," *Chicago Defender*.
"lose little Frankie": "Frankie Jaxon Air Feature," *Chicago Defender*.
"play it, whip it": Jaxon, "Hannah Fell in Love."
"Palais de Danse": Jaxon, "I'm Gonna Dance."
"I'm gonna dance wit": Ibid.
he can "operate": Jaxon, "Operation Blues."
"Right there!": Jaxon, "My Daddy Rocks Me."
"more heat": "My Daddy Rocks Me," advertisement, *Chicago Defender*.
"nudie chump": Jaxon, "Willie the Weeper."
"brownskin": Jaxon, "Chocolate to the Bone."
"talkie": "Frankie Jaxon in Talkies," *Chicago Defender*.
"The show is": Ibid.
"a brusque and spirited": Parth, "Editorial Review."
"Mr. and Mrs. Frankie": McMillan, "47th Street."
"actor" in a "theater": "1930 United States Federal Census," Ancestry.com.
abandoned "hat factory": First Church of Deliverance, "Church History."
"nine thousand congregants": Pinder, *Painting the Gospel*, 53.
"200-member choir": Stribling, "Three Bronzeville Churches."
"by state's attorney's police": Orro, "Six Sleuths."
"a travesty": de la Croix, *Chicago Whispers*, 157.
"I am full man": Orro, "Six Sleuths."
"unsavory incident": de la Croix, *Chicago Whispers*, 156.
"careful" because of the political: Jaxon, "Be Your Natural Self."

14. Once a Bitch, Always a Bitch

"Queers were born": "Even Thought," EWB, 3.

"social disorganization": University of Chicago Library, "Guide to the Ernest Watson Burgess Papers."

"acted upon": "Case of Herman," EWB.

"I do not care": "H" ["I knew 'hell'"], EWB.

"doctor and nurse": "Herman" ["I liked my mother best"], EWB, 1.

"in a more friendly": "H. 28," EWB.

"I did not care": "H." ["I did not care to go"], EWB.

"You are getting": "H. 28," EWB.

"I met a fellow": "Three Children," EWB, 6.

"he had a high-pitched": "Alexander Stahl," EWB, 30.

"'punk' around": Ibid., 31.

"a beautiful young girl": Ibid.

"laid her on the bed": Ibid., 32.

"This guy told": Ibid., 33.

"poked fun": "Carl's Experience," EWB, 1.

"busy section": Ibid., 2.

"Queen Racket": "The Racketeering, EWB, 1

"aloof" and "pretend": Ibid., 2.

"playing trade": "As Told to Me by Mr. H.," EWB.

"report him": "Under Hypnosis," EWB, 19.

"$5.00 or more": "At Thompson's," EWB, 1.

"jump him": Ibid.

"I stripped": Ibid., 2.

"Harold was picked up": "As Told to Larry," EWB.

1940 federal census as "artist": "1940 United States Federal Census," Ancestry.com.

"kick Nazi ass": Meredith, e-mail to Roland Derylo, May 2, 2016.

"loud, expressive": Ibid.

"from social security check": Ibid.

"unabashedly erotic": Hines, "Photography," 218.

"the glinting torso": Cox, "Edmund Teske," 6.

"bare-chested and grease-covered": Kaczorowski, "Teske, Edmund," 3.

"Although Soakup is engaged": Ibid., 2–3.

"asocial tendencies": Ibid., 16.

"there is an obvious": Ibid.

"accept the facts": Ibid., 17.

"nice looking clean": "H. [I knew "hell"], EWB.

"What is the matter": "Even Thought," EWB, 1.

"loads of Jewish friends": Ibid.

"took a liking": Ibid.

"fellows fell in love": Ibid., 2.

he called "friendship": Ibid., 1.

"fellow [who] eyed": Ibid., 2.

"many of his friends": Ibid.

"affair" lasted nine months: "Herman's Diary," EWB, 1.

"who were very": Ibid.

"many wonderful times": Ibid., 2.

"an accomplished musician": Ibid.

"a perfectly legitimate": "Even Thought," EWB, 2.

"art and music": "As Told to Me by Herman," EWB.

"His interest": "Even Thought," EWB, 3.

"I like a person": ["He opened my pants"], EWB, 1.

"I love Lipson": "As Told to Me by Herman," EWB.

"fell for Harry": "As Told to Harry by Herman," EWB, 1.

"began to bandage": Ibid.

"How is Harry": Ibid.

"gifts and clothes": Ibid.

"Don't see Clarence": Ibid.

"very effeminine": Ibid.

"rather manly": "As Told to Me by Max," EWB, 1.

"Queens will not": Ibid.

"kissing": Ibid., 2.

"feeling up one another": Ibid., 1.

called Herman "vulgar": Ibid., 2.

"acted very effeminate": "Told to Me by Herman," EWB.

"When Herman walks": "As Told to Me by Harry," EWB.

"queers were born": ["He opened my pants"], EWB, 3–4.

"homosexuals are born": "Even Thought," EWB, 3.

"My opinion": "Robert—Age 33 Years," EWB, 9.

"One day": ["He opened my pants"], EWB, 3–4.

"is not wise": "H" ["I knew 'hell'"], EWB.

"get married": ["He opened my pants"], EWB, 2.

"feminine role": ["After failing in the experience"], EWB.

"Once a bitch": Ibid.

acted as "feminine" as possible: Ibid.

"wished that I": "Case of James," EWB, 1.

"I have always wished": "Charles, Age Twenty-Three," EWB, 4–5.

"I never wished": "Mr. C.," EWB.

"When I was 23": Ibid., 1.

"the same type": "Mr. P.," 6.

of being "queer": "Jimmy—Age," EWB, 6.

"dirtier": Ibid.

"I used to go": ["My mother told me"], EWB, 2.

"who is jam": "Told to Me by Clarence," EWB.

"What are you": "Clarence: Additional Material," EWB.

"a girl who knew": "Another Incident at the Ballyhoo," EWB.

"good looking woman": "Wednesday Nov. 22nd, 1933," EWB, 1.

"about six foot": Ibid.

"In my sweet": "Songs," EWB.

"made gestures toward": "Wednesday Nov. 22nd, 1933," EWB, 2.

"drag parade": Ibid.

15. A Nudist Club for Boys and Young Men

"Why they don't": Freedman, "'Uncontrolled Desires,'" 94.

"youth who had visited": "Police Arrest Man," *Rockford Morning Star.*

"a nudist club": Ibid.

"members" of the club: Ibid.

"implicated" him "in immoral": Ibid.

"as long as four": "Expect Grand Jury," *Rockford Morning Star.*

"morals charges": "Moral Probe Is Planned," *Lincoln Evening Journal.*

"immoral activities": "Jail Two More," *Rockford Morning Star.*

"nudist club": "Police Arrest Man," *Rockford Morning Star.*

"the activity": "Moral Probe Is Planned," *Lincoln Evening Journal.*

"In cases of small": Ibid.

"series of immoral acts": "Arrest Fifth Man," *Rockford Morning Star.*

"Terrible Swen": *Rockford High School Annual: 1912,* 27.

"The original": Editorials, *Rockford High School Annual: 1912,* 124.

"informal supper party": "Social Functions," *Rockford Register-Gazette.*

committing "immoral activities": "Jail Two More," *Rockford Morning Star.*

"I never had any man": "Sentence U.S. Art Teacher," *Rockford Register-Republican,* 1.

"put on probation": Ibid.

"had any contact": Ibid., 2.

"the judge wasn't paying": Mavigliano and Lawson, *Federal Arts Project in Illinois,* 43.

"immoral activities" and despite: "Jail Two More," *Rockford Morning Star.*

wasn't Carlson's "first offense": "Sentence U.S. Art Teacher," *Rockford Register-Republican*, 2.

"butt-ends of humanity": Beck, *Hobohemia*, 15.

"14 years" earlier: "Sentence U.S. Art Teacher," *Rockford Register-Republican*, 2.

"nudist club for boys": "Police Arrest Man," *Rockford Morning Star*; .

dropped "young men": "Moral Probe Is Planned," *Lincoln Evening Journal*.

Carlson to the "penitentiary": "Sentence U.S. Art Teacher," *Rockford Register-Republican*, 2.

"Ray said to me": Mavigliano and Lawson, *Federal Arts Project in Illinois*, 43.

"given anyone permission'": "Suicide Verdict," *Rockford Register-Republican*.

"nudist club" roundup: "Police Arrest Man," *Rockford Morning Star*.

"on the complaint": "Probation Hearing Set," *Rockford Register-Republican*.

"regretted that 'Illinois'": "Regrets Lack of Whipping," *Rockford Morning Star*.

Wright had a "good record": "Wright Released," *Rockford Morning Star*.

"This man is no": "Nudist Case Defendant," *Rockford Register-Republican*.

"degenerate sex offenders": Lave, "Only Yesterday," 549.

"every 43 minutes": Ibid., 550.

"sex killers are psychopathic": Ibid., 551.

"degenerate": Ibid., 549.

"psychopathic": Ibid., 551.

"sex moron": "Life Sentence," *Chicago Tribune*, 1.

"sexual psychopath": Lave, "Only Yesterday," 549.

"nuisances" because of the "scandal": Ibid., 563.

"thousands" of monsters: Ibid., 562.

"potential murderers": Heap, *Slumming*, 281.

"to search for sexual": Ibid., 280.

"sex moron": "Life Sentence," 1.

"post-pansy panic": Morris, "Pink Herring," 233.

"sex in its abnormalities": Ibid., 234.

"innocuous pansy": Ibid.

"about the kidnapping": Freedman, "'Uncontrolled Desires,'" 94.

16. Thank God I Got Only 60 Days and a Small Fine

"If there were more": J.D. to Alfred C. Kinsey, June 26, 1940.

"post-pansy panic": Morris, "Pink Herring," 233.

"repressed culture": Gathorne-Hardy, *Kinsey*, 136.

"You are a distinctive": Alfred C. Kinsey to R.J.B., November 1, 1939.

"You are an outstanding": Alfred C. Kinsey to E.B., June 17, 1940.

"Folk as intelligent": Ibid.

"made more tolerant": Jones, *Alfred C. Kinsey: A Public/Private Life*, 375.

"depraved human beings": Lave, "Only Yesterday," 549.

"You had 'T.E.'s'": Alfred C. Kinsey to T.K., July 6, 1939.

"I appreciate very much": Alfred C. Kinsey to R.B., December 14, 1939.

"If there were more people": J.D. to Alfred C. Kinsey, June 26, 1940.

"understanding of the problem": Jones, *Alfred C. Kinsey: A Public/Private Life*, 372.

"sexual diary": Ibid., 374.

"Your capacity for love": Ibid., 375.

"The stuff of which": Alfred C. Kinsey to P."B."J., December 14, 1939.

"Thank God I got only": P."B."J. to Alfred C. Kinsey, February 13, 1940.

"the confidence gained": D.M. to Alfred C. Kinsey, June 24 ,1940.

"had done little": H.B. to Alfred C. Kinsey, July 17, 1939.

"brief but intense": Jones, *Alfred C. Kinsey: A Public/Private Life*, 382.

"Sometime I want": Alfred C. Kinsey to T.K., July 6, 1939

"various gay cocktail": T.K. to Alfred C. Kinsey, November 15, [1939].

"I've been thinking": T.K. to Alfred C. Kinsey, November 20, [1939].

"There is so much ripened": T.K. to Alfred C. Kinsey September 13, 1943.

"I was glad": Alfred C. Kinsey to J.J., November 1, 1939.

one "community" but two: Jones, *Alfred C. Kinsey: A Public/Private Life*, 384.

"a haven" from the "social isolation": Ibid., 379.

"married and single men": Ibid., 384–85.

"brief, anonymous": Ibid., 385.

"did not really know": Ibid., 384.

"his private guide": Ibid., 379.

"while preserving the perfect": Ibid., 385.

"it makes us home-sick": Alfred C. Kinsey to J.F., October 14, 1949.

Bibliography

ACK   Alfred C. Kinsey Correspondence Collection, Archives, Kinsey Institute for Research in Sex, Gender, and Reproduction, Indiana University, Bloomington

BLR   Ben Lewis Reitman Papers, Special Collections and University Archives, University of Illinois at Chicago

EWB   Ernest Watson Burgess Papers, Special Collections, Regenstein Library, University of Chicago

GAS   Gregory A. Sprague Papers, Chicago History Museum

JA   John Applegate Papers, Gerber/Hart Library and Archives, Chicago, Illinois

JDH   John Daniel Hagenhofer Papers, Gerber/Hart Library and Archives, Chicago, Illinois

JMW   John M. Wing Papers, Newberry Library, Chicago, Illinois

JPA   Juvenile Protective Association Papers, Special Collections and University Archives, University of Illinois at Chicago

MbF   Manuel boyFrank Papers, Coll2013-028, ONE National Gay & Lesbian Archives, USC Libraries, University of Southern California, Los Angeles

MSJ   Marjorie Stewart Joyner Papers, Vivian G. Harsh Research Collection, Woodson Regional Library, Chicago, Illinois

TMA   Tennessee Mitchell Anderson Papers, Newberry Library, Chicago, Illinois

PLEASE NOTE: *Some of the sources used in this book were never given a title. For the sake of clarity, I've used the first few words of the text surrounded by brackets as their title.*

Abbott, Keene. "Dusky Singer Scores Hit." *Omaha (NE) World-Herald*, January 2, 1935, 14.

Abrams, Brett L. *Hollywood Bohemians: Transgressive Sexuality and the Selling of the Movieland Dream*. Jefferson, NC: McFarland, 2008.

Adam, Barry D. *Rise of a Gay and Lesbian Movement*. Boston: Twayne, 1995.

Afro-American (Baltimore, MD). "Chicago Has Pansies on the Run." December 14, 1935, 9.

———. "Southside Wars on 'Pansies' in Vice Cleanup." December 24, 1932, 6.

Akin, Edward C. Letter to John T. Peters, January 29, 1900. In *Biennial Report of the Attorney General of the State of Illinois*. Springfield, IL: State Printers, 1900.

Allman, Jas. "Moral Dancers." *Day Book* (Chicago, IL), February 23, 1916, 24.

Ancestry.com. "1860 United States Federal Census." Database. Provo, UT: Ancestry. com Operations, 2010.

———. "1870 United States Federal Census." Database. Provo, UT: Ancestry.com Operations, 2010.

———. "1880 United States Federal Census." Database. Provo, UT: Ancestry.com Operations, 2010.

———. "1900 United States Federal Census." Database. Provo, UT: Ancestry.com Operations, 2010.

———. "1910 United States Federal Census." Database. Provo, UT: Ancestry.com Operations, 2010.

———. "1920 United States Federal Census." Database. Provo, UT: Ancestry.com Operations, 2010.

———. "1930 United States Federal Census." Database. Provo, UT: Ancestry.com Operations, 2002.

———. "1940 United States Federal Census." Database. Provo, UT: Ancestry.com Operations, 2010.

———. "New York, Passenger Lists, 1820–1957." Database. Provo, UT: Ancestry.com Operations, 2010.

———. "U.S. City Directories, 1822–1995." Database. Provo, UT: Ancestry.com Operations, 2011.

———. "U.S., Find a Grave Index, 1600s–Current." Database. Provo, UT: Ancestry. com Operations, 2012.

———. "U.S., School Yearbooks, 1880–2012." Database. Provo, UT: Ancestry.com Operations, 2010.

———. "U.S., World War I Draft Registration Cards, 1917–1918." Database. Provo, UT: Ancestry.com Operations, 2005.

———. "U.S., World War II Army Enlistment Records, 1938–1946." Database. Provo, UT: Ancestry.com Operations, 2005.

——. "U.S., World War II Draft Registration Cards, 1942." Database. Provo, UT: Ancestry.com Operations, 2010.

Anderson, Eric. "Prostitution and Social Justice: Chicago, 1910–15." *Social Service Review* 48 (1974): 203–28.

Anderson, Nels. "Boy Tramp, Great Wanderer, Homosexual, Intelligent, Two Years on Road." Unpublished typescript, n.d. Box 127, folder 4, EWB.

——. "Cabaret." December 7, 1923. Folder 93, JPA.

——. "Case of Boy in Teens, Tramp, 'Flirting' with Men in Grant Park." Typescript, n.d.. Box 127, folder 2, EWB.

——. "Chronic Drinker, Stockyards Worker, Seldom Migrates, Many Arrests Away from Wife Twelve Years: 'Shorty.'" Unpublished typescript, n.d. Box 127, folder 1, EWB.

——. "An Evening Spent on the Benches of Grant Park." Unpublished typescript, n.d. Box 127, folder 4, EWB.

——. *The Hobo: The Sociology of the Homeless Man.* Chicago: University of Chicago Press, 1923.

——. "The Juvenile and the Tramp Problem." *Journal of Criminal Law and Criminality* 14 (1923–1924): 290–312.

——. *On Hobos and Homelessness.* Edited by Raffaele Rauty. Chicago: University of Chicago Press, 1998.

Anderson, Sherwood. *Sherwood Anderson's Memoirs: A Critical Edition.* Edited by Ray Lewis White. Chapel Hill: University of North Carolina Press, 1969.

Anderson, Tennessee Mitchell. Unpublished autobiography. September 3, 1928. Box 96, folder 3101, TMA.

Austin, Roger. *Genteel Pagan: The Double Life of Charles Warren Stoddard.* Amherst: University of Massachusetts Press, 1991.

Baldwin, Peter C. *In the Watches of the Night: Life in the Nocturnal City, 1820–1930.* Chicago: University of Chicago Press, 2012.

Ball, B. L. "Auto-surgical Operation." *Boston Medical and Surgical Journal* 30 (1844): 82–83.

Barnes, Clifford W. "The Story of the Committee of Fifteen of Chicago." *Journal of Social Hygiene* 4 (April 1918): 145–156.

Barry Singer Gallery. "Edmund Teske." Barry Singer Gallery website, accessed March 5, 2017. www.singergallery.com/bio.cfm?artistID=209.

Baylen, Joseph O. "A Victorian's 'Crusade' in Chicago, 1893–1894." *Journal of American History* 51 (1964): 418–34.

Beard, George M. *Sexual Neurasthenia: Its Hygiene, Causes, Symptoms and Treatment.* Repr. ed. New York: Arno, 1972.

Beck, Frank O. *Hobohemia*. Rindge, NH: Smith, 1956.

Bekken, Jon. "Crumbs from the Publishers' Golden Tables: The Plight of the Chicago Newsboy." *Media History* 6 (2000): 45–57.

Belvidere (IL) Daily Republican. "Operator of Nudist Club Gets 10 Years." December 9, 1937, 2.

Bennett, Jim. "Weakness—a Crime!" BernarrMacfadden.com, accessed June 11, 2016. www.bernarrmacfadden.com/macfadden3.html.

Berger, Brian. "Frankie Jaxon." HiLoBrow, February 3, 2013. http://hilobrow .com/2013/02/03/frankie-jaxon/.

Berger, Mark. "Biography." The Julian Eltinge Project (website), accessed March 20, 2014. www.julianeltinge.com.

——. "Julian Eltinge: The Fascinating Widow: A Film Documentary." The Julian Eltinge Project (website), accessed March 14, 2014. www.julianeltinge.com/project .html.

Berton, Ralph. *Remembering Bix: A Memoir of the Jazz Age*. New York: DaCapo, 1974.

Billboard. "Minstrel." October 10, 1908, 17.

Binford, Jessie F. *The Year's Work: 1925*. Chicago: Juvenile Protective Association, 1926.

Black, Jonathan. "Charles Atlas: Muscle Man." *Smithsonian Magazine*, August 2009. www.smithsonianmag.com/history/charles-atlas-muscle-man-34626921/.

Blair, Cynthia M. "Prostitution." *Encyclopedia of Chicago*, accessed February 5, 2013. www.encyclopedia.chicagohistory.org/pages/1015.html.

Blanchard, Mary W. "The Soldier and the Aesthete: Homosexuality and Popular Culture in Gilded Age America." *Journal of American Studies* 30 (1996): 25–46.

Blinstrub, Benjamin. "Follow-Up Work on Mr. Kinsie's Investigation." Unpublished typescript, December 27, 1923. Box 6, folder 96, JPA.

BLR. "Collection Summary." University of Illinois at Chicago official website, accessed February 24, 2014. http://findingaids.library.uic.edu/sc/MSReit71.xml.

Boag, Peter. *Re-dressing America's Frontier Past*. Berkeley: University of California Press, 2011.

Bogdan, Robert. *Freak Show: Presenting Human Oddities for Amusement and Profit*. Chicago: University of Chicago Press, 1988.

Bostonian. Players and Plays. May 1895, 205.

Box 593-D. Personals ad. Unidentified newspaper, n.d. Box 1, folder "French," JA.

Boyd, Nan Alamilla. "Transgender and Gay Male Cultures from the 1890s Through the 1960s." In *Wide-Open Town: A History of Queer San Francisco to 1965*, by Nan Alamilla Boyd, 25–62. Berkeley: University of California Press, 2005.

Bram, Christopher. *Art of History: Unlocking the Past in Fiction and Nonfiction*. Minneapolis: Graywolf, 2016.

Brickell, Chris. "A Symbolic Interactionist History of Sexuality?" *Rethinking History* 10 (2006): 415–32.

Brill, A. A. "The Conception of Homosexuality." *Journal of the American Medical Association* 61 (1913): 335–40.

Brown, Sally, and David R. Brown. *A Biography of Mrs. Marty Mann: The First Lady of Alcoholics Anonymous.* Center City, MN: Hazelden, 2013.

Bruce, Earle Wesley. "Comparison of Traits of the Homosexual from Tests and from Life History Materials." MA thesis, University of Chicago, Department of Sociology, Chicago, 1942.

Bruns, Roger A. *The Damndest Radical: The Life and World of Ben Reitman, Chicago's Celebrated Social Reformer, Hobo King, and Whorehouse Physician.* Urbana: University of Illinois Press, 1987.

Bullough, Vern L. "Challenges to Societal Attitudes Toward Homosexuality in the Late Nineteenth and Early Twentieth Centuries." *Social Sciences Quarterly* 58 (1977): 29–44.

———. "Commentary." *Medical Aspects of Human Sexuality* 7 (1973): 49.

Bullough, Vern L., and Martha Voght. "Homosexuality and Its Confusion with the 'Secret Sin' in Pre-Freudian America." *Journal of the History of Medicine* 28, no. 2 (1973): 143–55.

Burnham, John. "Early References to Homosexual Communities in American Medical Writings." *Medical Aspects of Human Sexuality* 7 (1973): 34, 40–41, 46–49.)

Cabello, Tristan. "Queer Bronzeville: Bronzeville's Vice District." Outhistory.org, accessed April 1, 2014. http://outhistory.org/exhibits/show/queer-bronzeville/part-1/vice-district.

———. "Queer Bronzeville: The Drag Balls." Outhistory.org, accessed April 1, 2014. http://outhistory.org/exhibits/show/queer-bronzeville/part-2/drag-balls.

———. "Queer Bronzeville: A History of African American LGBTs." Pt. 2. *Windy City Times*, March 14, 2012, 44–45.

———. "'The White Queens Got Scared!'": The Making of an African American Gay Nightlife in Bronzeville (1935–1965)." Paper presented at the annual convention of the Association for the Study of African American Life and History, Birmingham, AL, October 1, 2008.

Cadagin, Joe. "Michigan Men in Corsets: How a Cross-Dressing Opera Troupe Built the Union." *Michigan Daily* (Ann Arbor, MI), October 13, 2011. www.michigandaily.com/arts/michigan-union-operas.

Callen, Anthea. "Doubles and Desire: Anatomies of Masculinity in the Later Nineteenth Century." *Art History* 26 (2003): 669–99.

Callen, Jeffrey. "Gender Crossings: A Neglected History in African American Music." In *Queering the Popular Pitch*, edited by Sheila Whiteley and Jennifer Rycenga, 185–98. New York: Routledge, 2006.

Cambridge (MA) Chronicle. "Columbia—Burlesque." February 6, 1909, 13.

Carlton, Donna. *Looking for Little Egypt.* Bloomington, IN: IDD Books, 1994.

Casey, Kathleen Bridget. "Cross-Dressers and Race-Crossers: Intersections of Gender and Race in American Vaudeville, 1900–1930." PhD diss., University of Rochester, Department of History, Rochester, NY, 2010.

Castenholz, Bill. "The Great Crosby Opera House Lottery." *Check Collector,* March 1997. www.ascheckcollectors.org/subpage14.html.

C.C. "Bernie Ready to Go on Tour." *Chicago Tribune,* October 1, 1933, E5.

Chanute (KS) Daily Tribune. "Man Poses as Woman for 27 Years." June 1913, 4.

Chapman, David L. *Sandow the Magnificent: Eugen Sandow and the Beginnings of Bodybuilding.* Urbana: University of Illinois Press, 1994.

Chase, Al. "Dill Pickles Sour Over Sale of Their Club." *Chicago Tribune,* January 21, 1926, 28.

Chauncey, George. *Gay New York: Gender, Urban Culture, and the Making of the Gay Male World, 1890–1940.* New York: Basic, 1994.

Chicago American. "Girl Reveals Strange Cult Run by Dad." July 13, 1925, 11.

———. "Poem Born at 'Green Mask' Saves Angie." September 6, 1922, 3.

———. "The Shaving Grace." June 20, 1923, 1.

———. "Thompson Pleads for Dress." October 3, 1923, 1.

Chicago Civil Service Commission. *Police Investigation, 1911–1912: Final Report.* Chicago: Chicago Civil Service Commission, 1912.

Chicago Defender. "Alpha to Stage Show." March 30, 1918, 9.

———. "'The Brute,' a Strong Drama, at Avenue; 'Who's Stealin', a Scream, at the Grand." January 10, 1920, 6.

———. Cabarets. August 18, 1934, 8.

———. Chicago Theatrical News. January 14, 1928, 7.

———. Chicago Theatrical News. December 29, 1928, 7.

———. Chicago Theatrical News. March 30, 1929, 6.

———. Chicago Theatrical News. May 18, 1929, 6.

———. "Chicagoans Pleased with All-Star Xmas Matinee." December 12, 1925, 4.

———. "Cocktails Get Female Impersonator in 'Dutch.'" July 15, 1939, 24.

———. "Crowd Jams Cabin Inn at Its Opening." October 22, 1938, 19.

———. "Dixie Jean Has Party at Creole." October 1, 1938, 18.

———. "Earl Hines to Go Back on Air Late in Season." July 15, 1933, 5.

———. "'Female Impersonators' Rule Many Floor Shows." September 12, 1936, 21.

———. "Frankie at It." January 31, 1925, 6.

———. "Frankie Jaxon." June 16, 1928, 7.

———. "Frankie Jaxon Air Feature to Stay for While." July 8, 1933, 5.

———. "Frankie Jaxon and 8 Try Out." June 18, 1932, 5.

———. "Frankie Jaxon Back." April 25, 1925, 6.

———. "Frankie Jaxon in Chi." October 17, 1925, 7.

———. "Frankie Jaxon in Talkies for Tricolor." August 10, 1929, 6.

———. "Frankie Jaxon on Tour." September 8, 1933, 5.

———. "Frankie Jaxon's Line." March 21, 1925, 8.

———. "Frank's Fixed." January 24, 1925, 6.

———. "Gloria Goes to 101 Ranch." January 29, 1938, 19.

———. "'Gloria' Off for the East." January 21, 1933, 5.

———. "Gloria's Back." July 21, 1934, 8.

———. Going Backstage with the Scribe. October 14, 1933, 5.

———. Going Backstage with the Scribe. July 21, 1934, 8.

———. "Grand Masque Ball." November 30, 1912, 5.

———. "'Half-Pint' Jaxon Heads Big Show at 'The Bowery.'" May 12, 1938, 19.

———. "Half-Pint Jaxon Opens Gary Spot." December 18, 1937, 18.

———. "'Half Pint' Jaxon Returns to Discs." June 15, 1940, 21.

———. Hits and Bits. June 8, 1929, 7.

———. Hits and Bits. December 17, 1932, 5.

———. "Irvin Mills Signs Jaxon to Contract." September 9, 1933, 5.

———. "Mae West Is Back from Coast Trip." September 12, 1936, 20.

———. "Mask Dance at Masonic Hall." February 23, 1918, 5.

———. The Monogram. December 23, 1911, 7.

———. The Monogram. August 2, 1913, 6.

———. "My Daddy Rocks Me (with One Steady Roll)," by Frankie Jaxon. Advertisement. July 6, 1929, 6.

———. New Jersey. July 28, 1917, 12.

———. "New York Police Launch Drive on Harlem Cafes." March 17, 1934, 5.

———. "Nite Spotting in Bronzeville." May 1, 1937, 20.

———. "North Shore Dancing Class." February 16, 1918, 10.

———. A Note or Two. September 4, 1920, 5.

———. A Note or Two. September 6, 1924, 6.

———. A Note or Two. February 21, 1925, 6.

———. A Note or Two. December 29, 1928, 7.

———. A Note or Two. June 1, 1929, 7.

———. "Old Monogram." April 24, 1915, 6.

———. "On the Stage." October 7, 1933, 5.

———. "Patrons See Smart Revue at Cabin Inn." February 11, 1939, 18.

———. "Radio Pastor Sues Defender for $250,000." December 9, 1939, 9.

———. "Reed-Middleton Wedding." March 21, 1914, 4.

———. "Rev. Cobbs Halts Service to Oust Defender Scribe." October 26, 1940, 7.

———. "Rose Morgan Tops Cabin Inn Bill." August 26, 1939, 21.

———. "Sam Fouche in City." November 9, 1935, 8.

———. "Stars, Stars, and Still More Stars for Our Show." December 26, 1936, 20.

———. "The Sunset." September 23, 1922, 6.

———. Theatrical Review. January 26, 1918, 4.

———. "To Invade the Coast." October 19, 1935, 9.

———. "A Unique Show at Cozy Cabin." September 1, 1934, 8.

———. "Weber's Theatre; 19th and Wabash Ave." February 18, 1911, 4.

Chicago Eagle. "Barney and Bob." February 28, 1914, 1.

———. "Let the College Be Kept Clean." April 17, 1909, 6.

———. "The Lunch Route." January 21, 1911, 1.

———. "Some More Action by Council Needed." July 6, 1912, 4.

Chicago Evening American. "Aged Kidnaper Lures Boy of 15 from Dixieland." July 10, 1909, 2.

Chicago Evening Post. "Washburn's Figures." June 24, 1873, 4.

Chicago Herald-Examiner. "'Man-Girl' Is Acquitted as Tesmer Testifies." October 4, 1923, 1.

——— "'Man-Girl' Is Bored as Death Trial Opens." October 2, 1923, 6.

———. "Thompson Is Recognized as Wife by Court." October 3, 1923, 1.

———. "Unmask 'Girl Slayer' as Man." June 26, 1923, 1, 3.

Chicago Historical Society. "Col. Wood's Museum." The Great Chicago Fire & the Web of Memory, accessed February 16, 2014. www.greatchicagofire.org/landmarks /col-woods-museum/.

Chicago Hush. "Pansy Blackmailing Plan Fails to Frighten Prof." October 8, 1932, 2.

Chicago Imagebase. "Chicago Growth 1850–1990." University of Illinois at Chicago official website, accessed December 23, 2013. http://tigger.uic.edu/depts/ahaa /imagebase/chimaps/mcclendon.html (site discontinued).

Chicago Municipal Code §1603 (1851).

Chicago Record-Herald. "Acquit Bronze Beauty." July 20, 1909, 4.

———. "Bad Park Show to Go." July 7, 1909, 10.

———. "Boys, Girls, Vice, Police, Sloth and Hypocrisy." August 5, 1909, 8.

———. "Close Parks, Demand." July 12, 1909, 2.

———. "Says Bad Shows Gain by Public Exposure." July 18, 1909, 9.

———. "Vile Shows Must Go." July 8, 1909, 10.

———. "Wants Vice in Bounds." May 31, 1905, 7.

———. "Will Indecency Win?" July 19, 1909, 6.

Chicago Sunday Tribune. "Launch Tavern Cleanup War to Stamp Out Vice." December 9, 1934, 1, 9.

Chicago Tribune. "Actor Dies, Widow Arrested." November 6, 1911, 2.

———. "An Ancient Seat of Learning." December 18, 1940, 14.

———. "Another Jolt for Levee." August 24, 1901, 2.

———. "Another Levee Must Go." December 28, 1904, 5.

———. "Art Concern Leases Space in Dill Pickle Property." April 9, 1944, 1.

———. "At Last the Cabaret Has Arrived to Gladden Chicago's 'Bohemians.'" June 30, 1912, A6.

———. "'Attractions' Go into Court Today." June 15, 1909, 3.

———. "Big Dance Is a 'Sizzler.'" January 7, 1903, 3.

———. "'Blue Eyes' Doff Rouge for Tests as Girl Slayer." June 16, 1923, 7.

———. "Cameras to Aid Reformers' Work." September 30, 1908, 9.

———. "Chicago Man Satisfied on a Roof." June 22, 1902, 51.

———. "Clever Method of Shoplifting." November 22, 1892, 1.

———. "Club on Study Tour Freed in Morals Court." November 18, 1930, 5.

———. "Collins Takes Charge of Hunt for Girl Slayer." June 10, 1923, 6.

———. "Coroner's Jury Holds Man-Girl for Murder After Mrs. Tesmer Repeats Her Identification at Inquest." June 28, 1923, 36.

———. "Coughlin Yields; Orgy Called Off." December 10, 1909, 3.

———. "Craig 'Belle' of Ball." December 23, 1903, 3.

———. "Crowds Rush to Congratulate 'Man-Girl' upon Acquittal." October 4, 1923, 34.

———. "Dean Takes Hope to Levee." December 25, 1907, 1.

———. "Democracy Again in Society." February 8, 1909, 11.

———. "Derby Dance Hall in Peril by Bomb." December 14, 1908, 1.

———. "Describe Orgy of New Year Eve as Blow to City." January 2, 1913, 1.

———. "Dill Pickle Proprietor Held to Federal Jury." October 29, 1930, 17.

———. "Dr. Ben Reitman Dead." November 17, 1942, 18.

———. "Dry Raiders Seize 1,200 Bottles of Home Brew." August 26, 1931, 4.

———. Duncan Clark's Female Minstrels. Advertisement. October 29, 1893, 28.

———. "Even in 'Cotton' Stockings." December 2, 1923, 1.

———. "First Ward Ball? Say 'Sure.'" November 27, 1908, 1.

———. "First Ward Democrats Dance." February 15, 1900, 1.

———. "First Ward in Annual Orgy." December 10, 1907, 5.

———. ". . . For the Stage." November 9, 1887, 7.

———. "Fun Behind the Masks." February 16, 1890, 1.

———. "Grand Jury Gets Case of Thompson, Man-Girl." July 11, 1923, 1.

———. "A Great New Chance for the Judges." March 29, 1894, 2.

———. "He Is a Man of Mighty Muscle." August 11, 1893, 9.

———. "His 'Hot Air Balloon' Burst." April 21, 1901, 62.

———. "Hold Five for Trying to Seize Control of Club." January 4, 1932, 4.

———. "Hold Man as 'Girl Slayer.'" June 20, 1923, 1.

———. "Hooley's." June 24, 1879, 5.

———. "How a Man Makes Himself a Beautiful Woman." September 27, 1908, F6.

———. "'Husband' of Sex Hoaxer, Prey of Dope, Goes Mad." June 22, 1923, 1.

———. Inquiring Reporter. June 7, 1923, 21.

———. Late Local Items. June 7, 1880, 3.

———. Law Intelligence. February 12, 1864, 4.

———. Law Intelligence. February 16, 1864, 4.

———. Law Intelligence. March 8, 1864, 4.

———. Law Intelligence. March 18, 1864, 4.

———. "'Leading Lady.'" December 20, 1922, 223.

———. "Levee's Hordes Storm Coliseum." December 15, 1908, 1.

———. "Life Sentence Starts Court Moron Drive." February 5, 1937, 1, 6.

———. "Man, Posing as Woman, Held for Tesmer Murder." June 20, 1923, 40.

———. "Man-Girl Denied Bail Must Doff Garb of Woman." July 3, 1923, 8.

———. "'Man-Girl' Faces Tesmer Murder Hearing Today." June 23, 1923, 3.

———. "'Man-Girl' in Murder Case Is Woman, Claim." October 3, 1923, 5.

———. "Man-Girl Made Man Again." June 24, 1923, 2.

———. "'Man Girl' on Trial Today for Tesmer Murder." October 1, 1923, 4.

———. Meetings and Lectures. April 9, 1927, 12.

———. Meetings and Lectures. October 29, 1927, 16.

———. Meetings and Lectures. January 11, 1930, 11.

———. Meetings and Lectures. March 7, 1931, 10.

———. "Mollycoddle Gets Blame." June 24, 1907, 1.

———. "Mr. D. Finucane Aspires to the Bohemian Life." March 28, 1933, 2.

———. Music and Drama. August 26, 1890, 4.

———. "Nab Girl as Tesmer Slayer." June 15, 1923, 1.

———. "New Chicago." April 14, 1872, 5

———. "Olmstead Takes a Dose of Poison." March 30, 1894, 8.

———. "On with Dance, O'Malley." November 26, 1909, 1.

———. "'Petting Parties' in Wind Blew Inn? No, Youths Aver." February 15, 1922, 17.

———. "Police Prohibit Man-Girl Going on Stage Here." October 7, 1923, 3.

———. "Ready for Frolic." August 18, 1916, 2.

———. "Rebuilding Burnt Chicago." January 14, 1872, 3.

———. "Reform of Parks Is Only a Spasm." August 5, 1909, 38.

———. "Revoke License of Bathhouse." March 13, 1936, 4.

———. "A Revolting Crime." August 17, 1864, 1.

———. "'Revelers' Sure to Revel." December 7, 1908, 1.

———. "Seek to Make City Conscious of 'Little Paris.'" March 6, 1932, F3.

———. "Seek to Put Stop to 1st Ward Balls." September 29, 1908, 5.

———. "Sees Pagan Rome in 1st Ward Ball." October 6, 1908, 7.

———. "Seven Arts Cub to Offer Varied Program Tonight." March 16, 1935, 17.

———. "Sex Hoaxer Held as Slayer When Again Identified." June 28, 1923, 2.

———. "Shot in Broad Day." March 29, 1894, 2.

———. "16 Men and Women Taken in Green Mask Raid." September 5, 1922, 3.

———. "Slave-Driving." July 29, 1928, F3.

———. "South Side and Illinois Win." May 25, 1896, 8.

———. "Stagg Expels Track Stars." May 24, 1908, 1.

———. "They Want the 'Levee' Purified." August 10, 1890, 3.

———. "35 'Bohemians' Seized in Raid on 'Green Mask.'" January 11, 1923, 1.

———. "Those Beautiful Women of Chicago Are Boys—Every One of Them!" December 8, 1907, G4.

———. "Threaten Bomb for Orgy." December 4, 1909, 1.

———. "To Clean Wabash Avenue." May 6, 1903, 3.

———. "Trail Pal of 'Bandit Girl.'" June 21, 1923, 1.

———. "2 Views of Night Life." March 21, 1920, 3.

———. "Weil's Sponsor in Lecture Freed on Lack of Permit." December 16, 1942, 23.

———. What's Doing Today. April 12, 1930, 16.

———. What's Doing Today. May 24, 1930, 14.

———. What's Doing Today. October 10, 1931, 18.

———. "W. H. Schmedtgen Is Dead." December 30, 1936, 14.

———. "Wind Blew Inn Is Now Green Mask." July 22, 1922, 11.

Chicago Whip. Nosey Sees All Knows All. November 6, 1920, 2.

Chillicothe (MO) Constitution-Tribune. "Girl Bandit Unmasked Today by Physicians." June 20, 1923, 1.

City of Chicago. "First Church of Deliverance." Official website, accessed August 28, 2015. http://webapps.cityofchicago.org/landmarksweb/web/landmarkdetails.htm?lanId=1302.

Clippings on Vice in Chicago. "2 Park Arrests Made." Unsourced newspaper clipping, n.d. Vol. 4. Crerar MS 234, Special Collections Research Center, University of Chicago Library.

Clopper, Edward N. Child Labor in City Streets. New York: Macmillan, 1912.

Cocca, Carolyn. Jailbait: The Politics of Statutory Rape Laws in the United States. Albany, NY: SUNY Press, 2004.

Columbia Spectator (New York, NY). "University of Michigan Will Present Production at Metropolitan Tonight." December 18, 1923, 1.

Columbus, OH, city directory. Polk, OH: 1912.

Conzen, Michael P. "Progress of the Chicago Fire of 1871." *Encyclopedia of Chicago*, accessed June 1, 2009. www.encyclopedia.chicagohistory.org/pages/3710.html.

Cornebise, Alfred E. *The "Amaroc News": The Daily Newspaper of the American Forces in Germany, 1919–1923*. Carbondale, IL: Southern Illinois University Press, 1981.

Cornell Daily Sun. "Jury Now Selected for Chicago Slayer's Trial." October 3, 1923, 2

Cox, Julian. "Edmund Teske: Intimate Visions." In *Spirit into Matter: The Photographs of Edmund Teske*. Los Angeles: J. Paul Getty Museum, 2004.

Crawford, Phillip, Jr. "David Petillo Did It in Drag." The FBI Files (website), accessed February 1, 2013. http://bitterqueen.typepad.com/friends_of_ours/2010/12/the -fbi-files-david-petillo-did-it-in-drag.html.

Cressey, Paul G. *The Taxi-Dance Hall: A Sociological Study in Commercialized Recreation and City Life*. Rept. Montclair, NJ: Patterson Smith, 1969.

Crosby, Josiah. "Seminal Weakness—Castration." *Boston Medical Surgical Journal* 29 (1843): 10–11.

Cullen, Frank. "Julian Eltinge." In *Vaudeville Old and New: An Encyclopedia of Variety Performances in America*, 353–55. New York: Routledge, 2007.

Curon, L. O. *Chicago: Satan's Sanctum*. Chicago: Phillips, 1899.

Current Literature. "Organized Vice as a Vested Interest." March 1912, 292–94.

Daiches, Eli. Plays and Players. *Sentinel* (Chicago, IL), April 7, 1911, 14–15.

Daily Inter Ocean (Chicago, IL). Amusements. June 23, 1877, 6.

———. Amusements. June 29, 1880, 6.

———. Amusements. January 18, 1893, 12.

———. "Before Judge Collins." October 12, 1888, 9.

———. "Bliss Whitaker's Benefit Day." December 20, 1878, 8.

———. "Bridge-End Dens." May 22, 1879, 4.

———. The Calls for To-day. September 3, 1890, 11.

———. The Calls for To-day. September 30, 1890, 11.

———. City Criminal Record. May 15, 1880, 8.

———. "Clifford Held Without Bail." April 1, 1894, 5.

———. "The County Building." July 28, 1881, 10.

———. "Figures on Crime." May 20, 1892, 5.

———. Footlight Notes. July 3, 1879, 3.

———. Footlight Notes. July 5, 1879, 6.

———. "A Frontier Mystery." November 9, 1878, 4.

———. "Illinois Cyclist Club's Show." March 26, 1896, 4.

———. Late Arrests. July 21, 1880, 6.

———. Midway Plaisance. Advertisement. January 21, 1894, 31.

———. Miscellaneous. November 22 1892, 7.

———. Miscellaneous. November 23, 1892, 7.

———. "Olmstead Held Without Bail." April 1, 1894, 5.

———. Police Courts. September 22, 1870, 4.

———. "Shot on the Street." March 29, 1894, 4.

———. "Six Years for Harry Mortimer." October 19, 1895, 6.

———. Untitled notice. June 22, 1880, 6.

———. "Who Runs the House?" August 7, 1888, 6.

Daley, Bill. "A City Tour of LGBT History." *Chicago Tribune*, July 26, 2013. www
.chicagotribune.com/lifestyles/books/ct-prj-chicago-whispers-delacroix-story.html.

Daniel, F. E. "Castration of Sexual Perverts." *Texas Medical Journal* 9 (1893): 255–71.

Day Book (Chicago, IL). "'Nameless Crimes' Occur in South Parks Due to Improper
Police Protection." November 25, 1914, n.p.

———. "War on Hotel Lobby Dope Fiends." November 26, 1912, 4.

———. "War Stocks Bring Hootch Dance to Loop Hotel." January 2, 1917, 5.

———. The World's News in Brief. May 21, 1913, 3.

de la Croix, St. Sukie. *Chicago Whispers: A History of LGBT Chicago Before Stonewall.*
Madison: University of Wisconsin Press, 2012.

Dececco, John. *Behind the Mask of the Mattachine: The Hal Call Chronicles and the Early
Movement for Homosexual Emancipation.* Kindle ed. New York: Routledge, 2011.

Decency. "Look Under the Bridges, Officers." *Chicago Tribune*, May 18, 1879, 6.

Dedmon, Emmett. *Great Enterprises: 100 Years of the YMCA of Metropolitan Chicago.*
Chicago: Rand McNally, 1957.

D'Emilio, John. *In a New Century: Essays on Queer History, Politics, and Community
Life.* Madison: University of Wisconsin Press, 2014.

DePastino, Todd. *Citizen Hobo: How a Century of Homelessness Shaped America.* Chicago: University of Chicago Press, 2003.

Deseret Weekly (Salt Lake City, UT). "Chicago's Dark Places." September 12, 1891, 352.

DiGirolamo, Vincent. "Newsboy Funerals: Tales of Sorrow and Solidarity in Urban
America." *Journal of Social History* 36 (2002): 5–30.

D.M. Letter to Alfred C. Kinsey. June 24, 1940. ACK.

Doyle, David D., Jr. "'A Very Proper Bostonian': Rediscovering Ogden Codman and
His Late-Nineteenth-Century Queer World." *Journal of the History of Sexuality*
13 (2004): 446–76.

Dressler, David. "Burlesque as a Cultural Phenomenon." Diss., New York University,
1937.

Drexel, Allen. "Before Paris Burned: Race, Class, and Male Homosexuality on the Chicago South Side, 1935–1960." In *Creating a Place for Ourselves: Lesbian, Gay, and Bisexual Community Histories*, edited by Brett Beemyn, 119–44. New York: Routledge, 1997.

Drucker, A. P. *On the Trail of the Juvenile-Adult Offender: An Intensive Study of 100 County Jail Cases.* Chicago: Juvenile Protective Association, 1912.

Drury, John. *Dining in Chicago.* New York: Day, 1931.

Duffy, John. "Sex, Society, Medicine: An Historical Comment." *Philosophy and Medicine* 23 (1987): 69–85.

Duis, Perry R. *Challenging Chicago: Coping with Everyday Life, 1837–1920.* Chicago: University of Illinois Press, 1998.

Durden, Michelle. "Not Just a Leg Show: Gayness and Male Homoeroticism in Burlesque, 1868–1877." *Thirdspace* 3 (2004): 8–26.

Eaklor, Vicki Lynn. *Queer America: A GLBT History of the 20th Century.* Westport, CT: Greenwood, 2008.

Edwards, Bill. "Antonio (Tony) Junius Jackson." Ragpiano.com, accessed September 14, 2014. http://ragpiano.com/comps/tjackson.shtml.

Elkhart (IN) Daily Review. "Tried to Kill a Letter Carrier." March 29, 1894, 1.

Elledge, Jim. "'Artfully Dressed in Women's Clothing:' Drag Queens on Chicago's Burlesque Stage, an Account from the Summer of 1909." In *Queers in American Popular Culture*, edited by Jim Elledge, 2:211–28. New York: Praeger, 2010.

———. "Chicago's Man-Girl Trial." *Windy City Times*, August 24, 2001, 15

———. "Eugen Sandow's Gift to Gay Men." *Gay and Lesbian Review Worldwide* 18, no. 4 (2011): 14–17.

———. *Henry Darger, Throwaway Boy: The Tragic Life of an Outsider Artist.* New York: Overlook, 2013.

———. "'It Is Just Something Greek; That's All': Eugen Sandow—Queer Father of Modern Body Building." In *Queers in American Popular Culture*, edited by Jim Elledge, 3:117–43. New York: Praeger, 2010.

———. "Lovers' Quarrel, 1890s Style." *Gay and Lesbian Review Worldwide* 17, no. 6 (2010): 14–15.

———. "When 'The Love That Dare Not Speak Its Name' Did." *Windy City Times*, January 19, 2011, 14.

Ellis, Havelock. "A Note on the Treatment of Sexual Inversion." *Alienist and Neurologist* 17 (1896): 257–64.

———. *Studies in the Psychology of Sex.* Vol. 2, *Sexual Inversion.* 3rd ed. Philadelphia: Davis, 1915.

Ellis, Jack. The Orchestras. *Chicago Defender*, October 1, 1932, 5.

———. The Orchestras. *Chicago Defender*, November 19, 1932, 5.

———. The Orchestras. *Chicago Defender*, August 12, 1933, 5.

Eltinge, Julian. "From the Players' Point of View Why I Do It." *Chicago Tribune*, December 11, 1910, 1.

Emanon. "Some Movement, This Dance!" *Day Book* (Chicago, IL), October 27, 1915.

Epstein, Joseph. "The Secret Life of Alfred Kinsey." *Commentary*, January 1, 1998.

Erenberg, Lewis A. "Ain't We Got Fun?" Chicago History 14, no. 4 (Winter 1985): 4–21.

———. "Entertaining Chicagoans." *Encyclopedia of Chicago*, accessed February 5, 2013. www.encyclopedia.chicagohistory.org/pages/428.html.

Eskridge, William N., Jr. "Hardwick and Historiography." Yale Law School Faculty Scholarship Series 3808 (1999). http://digitalcommons.law.yale.edu/cgi/viewcontent.cgi?article=4794&context=fss_papers.

———. "Law and the Construction of the Closet: American Regulation of Same-Sex Intimacy, 1880–1946." Yale Law School Faculty Scholarship Series 3804 (1997). http://digitalcommons.law.yale.edu/cgi/viewcontent.cgi?article=4798&context=fss_papers.

———. "Privacy Jurisprudence and the Apartheid of the Closet, 1946–1961." *Florida State University Law Review* 24 (Summer 1997): 703–840.

Evening World (New York, NY). "Novel Device of Shoplifters." November 22, 1892, 1.

EWB. ["After failing in the experience of being a woman . . ."] Typescript, n.d. Box 98, folder 11.

———. "Alexander Stahl." Unpublished typescript, n.d. Box 98, folder 5.

———. "Another Incident at the Ballyhoo." Unpublished typescript, n.d. Box 98, folder 3.

———. "As Told to Harry by Herman." Unpublished typescript, n.d. Box 98, folder 3.

———. "As Told to Larry by Harold about Max." Unpublished typescript, n.d. Box 128, folder 7.

———. "As Told to Me by Harry." Unpublished typescript, n.d. Box 98, folder 3.

———. "As Told to Me by Herman." Unpublished typescript, n.d. Box 98, folder 3.

———. "As Told to Me by Max." Unpublished typescript, n.d. Box 98, folder 11.

———. "As Told to Me by Mr. H Who Now Hustles." Unpublished typescript, June 1930. Box 98, folder 4.

———. "At the Age of Six." Unpublished typescript, n.d. Box 98, folder 4.

———. "At Thompson's Restaurant Randolph St." Unpublished typescript, n.d. Box 98, folder 11.

———. "Ballyhoo Café." Unpublished typescript, September 24, 1933. Box 98, folder 2.

———. "Carl's Experience." Unpublished typescript, n.d. Box 98, folder 2.

———. "Case Is a Rather Well Built Young Girl." Unpublished typescript, n.d. Box 98, folder 6.

——. "Case of Herman." Unpublished typescript, n.d. Box 98, folder 2.

——. "Case of James." Unpublished typescript, n.d. Box 98, folder 11.

——. "Charles, Age Twenty-Three." Unpublished typescript, n.d. Box 128, folder 9.

——. "Clarence: Additional Material." Unpublished typescript, June 1925. Box 98, folder 2.

——. "Conversation with Edwin Teeter." Unpublished typescript, n.d. Box 187, folder 6.

——. "Degeneracy." Unpublished typescript, n.d. Box 265, folder 27.

——. "Even Thought [sic] I Do Not Suck or Brown." Unpublished typescript, June 1, 1933. Box 98, folder 4.

——. "The Goblins." Unpublished typescript, October 30, 1932. Box 98, folder 11.

——. "H" ["I did not care to go"]. Unpublished typescript, n.d. Box 98, folder 4.

——. "H" ["I knew 'hell'"]. Unpublished typescript, n.d. Box 98, folder 2.

——. "H. 28." Unpublished typescript, n.d. Box 98, folder 3.

——. ["He opened my pants and just took it out"]. Unpublished typescript, n.d. Box 98, folder 2.

——. "Herman" ["I liked my mother best"]. Unpublished typescript, n.d. Box 98, folder 2.

——. "Herman" ["Up to the age of 16 years"]. Unpublished typescript, September 24, 1933. Box 98, folder 2.

——. "Herman's Diary." Unpublished typescript, September 1931. Box 98, folder 11.

——. "Jimmy—Age." Unpublished typescript, n.d. Box 128, folder 8.

——. "Johnny Ryan." Unpublished typescript, December 31, 1932. Box 98, folder 11.

——. "Leo. Age 18. Colored." Unpublished typescript, n.d. Box 98, folder 11.

——. "Mr. C." Unpublished typescript, n.d. Box 98, folder 11.

——. "Mr. X. 27 Also Two Brothers." Unpublished typescript, n.d. Box 128, folder 8.

——. ["My mother told me very little about sex"]. Unpublished typescript, n.d. Box 98, folder 4.

——. "Oldest Brother 40 Years. Leo 29 Jack. 26 Stoney 22." Unpublished typescript, n.d. Box 98, folder 4.

——. "Queen's Jealousy." Unpublished typescript, n.d. Box 98, folder 3.

——. "The Racketeering." Unpublished typescript, n.d. Box 98, folder 4.

——. "Robert—Age 33 Years." Unpublished typescript, n.d. Box 128, folder 9.

——. "Songs." Typescript, n.d. Box 187, folder 6.

——. "Three Children." Unpublished typescript, n.d. Box 98, folder 2.

——. "Told to Me by Clarence." Unpublished typescript, n.d. Box 98, folder 3.

——. "Told to Me by Herman." Unpublished typescript, n.d. Box 98, folder 3.

——. "Under Hypnosis." Unpublished MS, September 24, 1932. Box 22, folder 3.

——. "Visitors at the Subway Bar." Typescript, n.d. Box 98, folder 11.

——. "Wednesday Nov. 22nd, 1933." Unpublished typescript, n.d. Box 98, folder 3.

Falk, Candace, Stephen Cole, and Sally Thomas, eds. "Chronology, 1901–1919." In *Emma Goldman: A Guide to Her Life and Documentary Sources*. The Emma Goldman Papers (website), accessed February 15, 2014. www.lib.berkeley.edu/goldman /pdfs/EG-AGuideToHerLife_Chronology1901-1919.pdf.

FamilySearch. "Illinois. Cook County. Birth Certificates, 1871–1940." Database. Accessed February 23, 2017. www.familysearch.org/search/collection/1462519.

———. "Illinois. Cook County Deaths, 1878–1994." Database. Accessed February 23, 2017. www.familysearch.org/search/collection/1463134.

Ferguson, Michael. *Idol Worship: A Shameless Celebration of Male Beauty in the Movies*. 2nd ed. Sarasota, FL: Star Books, 2005.

FindAGrave.com. "Richard Martin Hooley." Accessed February 8, 2013. www.findagrave .com/memorial/5145883/richard-martin-hooley.

———. "Tony Jackson." Accessed April 1, 2013. www.findagrave.com/memorial /56879228/tony-jackson.

First Church of Deliverance. "Church History." Official website, accessed March 2, 2017. http://fcdchicago.org/about/ (page discontinued).

Fleeson, Lucinda. "The Gay '30s." *Chicago*, November 2005.

Fosdick, Scott. "Hooley's Theater." In *Cambridge Guide to American Theatre*, 2nd ed., edited by Don B. Wilmeth, 331–32. New York: Cambridge University Press, 2007.

Freedman, Estelle B. "'Uncontrolled Desires': The Response to the Sexual Psychopath, 1920–1960." *Journal of American History* 74 (1987): 83–106.

Friedman, Mack. *Strapped for Cash: A History of American Hustler Culture*. Los Angeles: Alyson, 2003.

G.A.D., "Such Is Life in Chicago." *New York Clipper*, March 14, 1914, 18.

Galveston (TX) Daily News. "A Contrivance by Store Thieves." November 23, 1892, 1.

Gapp, Paul. "Death of Bohemia." *Chicago Tribune*, February 14, 1988.

GAS. "File Memorandum Re: Henry Gerber Arrest (12 July 1925—Chicago)." Photocopy of typescript, n.d. Box 17, folder "Gerber, Henry," 1.

Gathorne-Hardy, Jonathan. *Kinsey: Sex the Measure of All Things*. Bloomington: Indiana University Press, 1998.

Gay, Gregory. Review of First Church of Deliverance Choir and Bishop Otto T. Houston III. Gospelflava.com, 2007. www.gospelflava.com/reviews/firstchurchdeliverance godcan.html.

Gazell, James Albert. "The High Noon of Chicago's Bohemias." *Journal of the Illinois State Historical Society* 65 (1972): 54–68.

Gehl, Paul F. "The Making of a Chicago Eccentric." In *The Chicago Diaries of John M. Wing, 1865–1866*, edited by Robert Williams, ix–xiii. Carbondale: Southern Illinois University Press, 2002.

Gentry, James J. "Bronzeville in Chicago." *Chicago Defender*, October 30, 1937, 19.

Gerber, Henry. Letter to Manuel boyFrank. February 18 1946. Box 1, folder 2, MbF.

———. "The Society for Human Rights—1925." *ONE*, September 1962. www.glapn.org /sodomylaws/usa/illinois/ilnews02.htm.

Gianoulis, Tina. "Situational Homosexuality." In *LGBTQ Encyclopedia*. GLBTQ Inc., 2015. www.glbtqarchive.com/ssh/situational_homosexuality_S.pdf.

Gibson, Campbell. "Population of the 100 Largest Cities and Other Urban Places in the United States: 1790 to 1990." US Bureau of the Census, June 1998; last rev. May 21, 2012. www.census.gov/population/www/documentation/twps0027/twps0027.html.

Gilbert, Rodney. "'Scout' Not Only Real Actor but Precocious Child Also." *Chicago Tribune*, February 12, 1911, B3.

Gillespie, Arthur. "The Evolution of Minstrelsy." *Green Book Magazine*, October 1909, 754–62.

Goldberg, Dan. "Chi's Nocturnal Side Roars Again After Slumbering for 10 Years." *Variety*, December 11, 1934, 47, 57.

Graham Journal of Health and Longevity. "Masturbation and Its Effect on Health." Vol. 2 (1838): 23–26.

Grant, Julia. "A 'Real Boy' and Not a Sissy: Gender, Childhood, and Masculinity, 1890–1940." *Journal of Social History* 37 (2004): 829–51.

Gregory, Terry. "First Ward Ball." Chicagology, accessed January 12, 2014. https:// chicagology.com/notorious-chicago/firstwardball/.

Griffin, Richard T. "Sin Drenched Revels at the Infamous First Ward Ball." *Smithsonian*, November 1976, 52–61.

Gustav-Wrathall, John Donald. *Take the Young Stranger by the Hand: Same-Sex Relations and the YMCA*. Chicago: University of Chicago Press, 1998.

Hagenbach, Allen W. "Masturbation as a Cause of Insanity." *Journal of Nervous and Mental Disease* 6, no. 4 (1879): 603–12.

Hal. "Plantation, Chicago." *Variety*, April 21, 1926, 45.

Hall, Bob. "Lewis, Meade 'Lux.'" In *Blues Encyclopedia*, edited by Edward Komaara, 1:600. New York: Routledge, 2006.

Haller, Mark. "Urban Vice and Civic Reform: Chicago in the Early Twentieth Century." In *Cities in American History*, edited by Kenneth T. Jackson and Stanley K. Schultz, 290–305. New York: Knopf, 1972.

Hannah, George. "Freakish Man Blues." Paramount L-562-1, 1930.

Harris, Robert E. "A University Competes with Ziegfeld." *Vagabond* (Bloomington, IN), February 1924, 33–35.

Hartland, Claude. *The Story of a Life*. Repr. ed. San Francisco, CA: Gray Fox Press, 1985; orig. publ. 1901.

Hatheway, Jay. *Gilded Age Construction of Modern American Homophobia*. New York: Palgrave, 2003.

Hayes, Bob. "Cabin Inn Show Has Plenty Songs, Dances." *Chicago Defender*, March 25, 1939, 19.

———. Here and There. *Chicago Defender*, December 15, 1928, 6.

———. Here and There. *Chicago Defender*, September 21, 1929, 7.

———. Here and There. *Chicago Defender*, December 6, 1940, 5.

———. Here and There. *Chicago Defender*, May 16, 1942, 22.

———. Here and There. *Chicago Defender*, September 4, 1943, 10.

H.B. Letter to Alfred C. Kinsey, July 17, 1939. ACK.

Healy, William. *The Individual Delinquent: A Text-Book of Diagnosis and Prognosis for All Concerned in Understanding Offenders*. Boston: Little, Brown, 1915.

Heap, Chad. "The City as Sexual Laboratory: The Queer Heritage of the Chicago School." *Quantitative Sociology* 26 (Winter 2003): 457–87.

———. *Slumming: Sexual and Racial Encounters in American Nightlife, 1885–1940*. Chicago: University of Chicago Press, 2009.

Held, William. *Crime, Habit or Disease? A Question of Sex from the Standpoint of Psycho-Pathology*. Chicago: William Held, 1905.

Henry, George W. *Sex Variants: A Study of Homosexual Patterns*. One-vol. ed. New York: Hoeber, 1948.

Herring, Scott. "Introduction." In *Autobiography of an Androgyne*, by Ralph Werther, edited by Scott Herring, ix–xxxiv. New Brunswick, NJ: Rutgers University Press, 2008.

Hines, Thomas S. "Photography, Architecture, and the Coming to Oneself: Edmund Teske and Frank Lloyd Wright." In *Looking for Los Angeles: Architecture, Film, Photography, and the Urban Landscape*, edited by Charles G. Salas and Michael S. Roth, 211–46. Los Angeles: Getty, 2001.

Hirschfeld, Magnus. *Homosexuality in Men and Women*. Translated by Michael A. Lonbardi-Nash. Amherst, NJ: Prometheus, 2000.

History Channel. "Prohibition." Official website, accessed April 12, 2014. www.history.com/topics/prohibition.

Hull, William I. "The Children of the Other Half: Their Homes, Their Lives, Their Perils, the Helping Hands Held Out to Them." *Arena* 85 (December 1896): 1039–51.

Illinois State Register (Springfield, IL). "Dr. Clemenson Denied Pardon." November 28, 1914.

Internet Broadway Database. "*The Fascinating Widow*." IBDB.com, accessed March 14, 2014. www.ibdb.com/broadway-show/the-fascinating-widow-3478.

Isaak, Abe, Jr. "Report from Chicago: Emma Goldman." *Free Society*, June 9, 1901, 3.

James, George Wharton. *Chicago's Dark Places: Investigations by a Corps of Specially Commissioners*. Chicago: Craig Press, 1891.

Jaxon, Frankie. "Be Your Natural Self." On *Frankie "Half-Pint" Jaxon: Complete Recorded Works in Chronological Order*, vol. 3, *22 July 1937–17 April 1940*. Document Records DC5258, 1994.

———. "Chocolate to the Bone (I'm So Glad I'm Brownskin)." DECCA 7360, 1937.

———. "Hannah Fell in Love with My Piano." On *Frankie "Half-Pint" Jaxon: Complete Recorded Works in Chronological Order*, vol. 1, *14 May 1926–22 July 1929*. Document Records DC5258, 1994.

———. "I'm Gonna Dance wit de Guy Wot Brung Me." On *Frankie "Half-Pint" Jaxon: Complete Recorded Works in Chronological Order*, vol. 1, *14 May 1926–22 July 1929*. Document Records DC5258, 1994.

———. "My Daddy Rocks Me (with One Steady Roll)." On *Copulatin' Blues*. Stash Records ST-101, 1976.

———. "Operation Blues." On *Frankie "Half-Pint" Jaxon: Complete Recorded Works in Chronological Order*, vol. 1, *14 May 1926–22 July 1929*. Document Records DC5258, 1994.

———. "Willie the Weeper." On *Frankie "Half-Pint" Jaxon: Complete Recorded Works in Chronological Order*, vol. 1, *14 May 1926–22 July 1929*. Document Records DC5258, 1994.

J.D. Letter to Alfred C. Kinsey. June 26. 1940. ACK.

Jewett, Eleanor. "Three Exhibits Get Attention of Art Critic." *Chicago Tribune*, March 16, 1935, 17.

Johnson, David K. "The Kids of Fairytown: Gay Male Culture on Chicago's Near North Side in the 1930s." *Creating a Place for Ourselves: Lesbian, Gay, and Bisexual Community Histories*, edited by Brett Beemyn. New York: Routledge, 1997.

Joiner, Thekla Ellen. *Sin in the City: Chicago and Revivalism, 1880–1920*. Columbia: University of Missouri Press, 2007.

Jones, James H. *Alfred C. Kinsey: A Life*. New York: Norton, 1997.

———. *Alfred C. Kinsey: A Public/Private Life*. New York: Norton, 1997.

JPA. "Follow-Up Work on Mr. Kinsie's Investigation." Typescript, December 27, 1923.

Junger, Richard. *Becoming the Second City: Chicago's Mass News Media, 1833–1898*. Urbana: University of Illinois Press, 2010.

Juvenile Protective Association. "[Untitled List of Houses of Prostitution.]" Typescript, n.d. JPA.

Kaczorowski, Craig. "Teske, Edmund (1911–1996)." In *LGBTQ Encyclopedia*. GLBTQ Inc., 2015. www.glbtqarchive.com/arts/teske_edmund_A.pdf.

Kansas City (MO) Sun. "Gets Pittance for Great Song Hit." February 17, 1917, 1.

Kansas Historical Society. "Hattie McDonald." Kansapedia, May 2009. www.kshs.org /kansapedia/hattie-mcdaniel/12146.

Kaplan, Arielle. "Sex, Love and Science." *812*, Winter/Spring 2017. www.812magazine .com/article/2017/03/sex-love-science.

Kaplan, Jacob. "Disused Police Stations." Forgotten Chicago, December 13, 2008. http:// forgottenchicago.com/articles/disused-police-stations/.

Kasson, John F. Houdini. *Tarzan, and the Perfect Man: The White Male Body and the Challenge of Modernity in America*. New York: Hill and Wang, 2001.

Katz, Jonathan Ned. "Coming to Terms: Conceptualizing Men's Erotic and Affectional Relations with Men in the United States, 1820–1892." In *A Queer World: The Center for Lesbian and Gay Studies Reader*, edited by Martin Duberman, 216–35. New York: New York University Press, 1997.

Kelley, Florence. "A Boy Destroying Trade." *Charities*, July 4, 1903, 14–19.

Kendall, Todd D. "First Ward Ball." *Chicago Crime Scenes Project* (blog). May 9, 2009. http://chicagocrimescenes.blogspot.com/2009/05/first-ward-ball.html.

———. "Under the Willow." *Chicago Crime Scenes Project* (blog), August 30, 2008. http://chicagocrimescenes.blogspot.com/2008/08/under-willow.html.

Kepner, Jim, and Stephen O. Murray. "Henry Gerber (1895–1972): Grandfather of the American Gay Movement." In *Before Stonewall: Activists for Gay and Lesbian Rights in Historical Context*, edited by Vern Bullough, 24–34. New York: Haworth, 2002.

Kerber, K. L. *Sexual Inversion*. New Delhi, India: Global Vision, 2005.

Kerwin, Kaye. "Male Prostitution in the Twentieth Century." *Journal of Homosexuality* 46 (2003): 1–77.

Kiernan, James G. "Classification of Homosexuality." *Urologic and Cutaneous Review* 20 (1916): 348–50.

———. "Increase of American Inversion." *Urologic and Cutaneous Review* 20 (1916): 44–48.

———. "Psychical Treatment of Congenital Sexual Inversion." *Review of Insanity and Nervous Disease* 4 (1894): 293–95.

———. "Responsibility in Sexual Perversion." *Chicago Medical Recorder* 3 (May 1892): 185–210.

Kimmel, Michael. *Manhood in America: A Cultural History*. New York: Free Press, 1996.

King, Gilbert. "The 'Latin Lover' and His Enemies." *Smithsonian*, June 13 2012. www .smithsonianmag.com/history/the-latin-lover-and-his-enemies-119968944/.

Kinsey, Alfred C. Letter to Earle Bruce. October 22 1943. ACK.

———. Letter to E.B. June 17 1940. ACK.

———. Letter to J.F. October 14, 1949. ACK.

———. Letter to J.J. November 1, 1939. ACK.

———. Letter to J.P.B. December 23, 1939. ACK.

———. Letter to P."B."J. December 14, 1939. ACK.

———. Letter to P."B."J. March 2, 1940. ACK.

———. Letter to R.B. December 14, 1939. ACK.

———. Letter to R.J.B. November 1, 1939. ACK.

———. Letter to T.K. July 6, 1939. ACK.

Kissack, Terence. *Free Comrades: Anarchism and Homosexuality in the United States, 1895–1917.* Oakland, CA: AK Press, 2008.

Kurda, Marie J. "Early 1900s: A Woman's Place." In *Out and Proud in Chicago: An Overview of the City's Gay Community,* edited by Tracy Baim, 19. Chicago: Agate, 2008.

———. "The 1893 World's Fair." In *Out and Proud in Chicago,* edited by Tracy Baim, 18. Chicago: Surry, 2008.

———. "World War II's Impact on Gay Chicago." In *Out and Proud in Chicago: An Overview of the City's Gay Community,* edited by Tracy Baim, 53. Chicago: Agate, 2008.

Labor World (Duluth, MN). "Queens Galore." November 3, 1906, 5.

Langer, Carol. "Lady Bill . . . the Story of Julian Eltinge." New York Foundation for the Artsa accessed March 14, 2014. www.nyfa.org/ArtistDirectory/ShowProject/9259b64d-4006-4b64-ad1d-f09c1838fa6f.

Langston, Tony. Musical and Dramatic. *Chicago Defender,* February 6, 1915, 6.

———. "'Players' in New Show at Avenue." *Chicago Defender,* February 17, 1923, 6.

Lave, Tamara Rice. "Only Yesterday: The Rise and Fall of Twentieth Century Sexual Psychopath Law." *Louisiana Law Review* 69 (2008–2009): 549–91.

Lebergott, Stanley. "Labor Force, Employment, and Unemployment, 1929–39: Estimating Methods." *Monthly Labor Review,* July 1948. www.bls.gov/opub/mlr/1948/article/pdf/labor-force-employment-and-unemployment-1929-39-estimating-methods.pdf.

Lesy, Michael. *Murder City: The Bloody History of Chicago in the Twenties.* New York: Norton, 2007.

Levitt, Aimee. "The Migration of the Hipster: A Chicago History, 1898–Present." *Chicago Reader,* October 2, 2013. www.chicagoreader.com/chicago/hipster-history-of-gentrification-bohemians-logan-square/Content?oid=11117198.

Lewis, Arthur H. *La Belle Otero.* New York: Trident, 1967.

Lewis, Steven L. "Gay Masquerade: Male Homosexuals in American Cities, 1910 to 1940." Thesis, Department of History, Western Michigan University, 1988.

Lincoln (NE) Evening Journal. "Moral Probe Is Planned." December 3, 1937, 5.

Linehan, Mary. "Vice Commissions." *Encyclopedia of Chicago*, accessed February 19, 2014. www.encyclopedia.chicagohistory.org/pages/1303.html.

Literary Digest. "How the World Went Mad over Sandow's Muscles." October 31, 1925, 46, 48.

Little, Richard Henry. Around Chicago. *Chicago Tribune*, September 20, 1910, 10.

Living History of Illinois and Chicago. "Towertown: A Chicago Neighborhood." Digital Research Library of Illinois History, accessed February 22, 2016. http://livinghis toryofillinois.com/pdf_files/Towertown%20Neighborhood%20of%20Chicago.pdf.

Lomax, Alan. *Mister Jelly Roll: The Fortunes of Jelly Roll Morton, New Orleans Creole and "Inventor of Jazz."* 2nd ed. Berkeley: University of California Press, 1950.

Lopata, Jim. "Prescott Townsend: One of Most Influential Boston Gay Rights Pioneers You've Never Heard Of." *Boston Spirit* (blog), September 3, 2013. http://archive .boston.com/lifestyle/blogs/bostonspirit/2013/09/prescott_townsend_one_of_most .html.

Louisville (KY) Daily Journal. "Locofocoism in Illinois." June 15, 1843, 2.

Lydston, G. Frank. *Impotence and Sterility with Aberrations of the Sexual Function and Sex-Gland Implantation*. Chicago: Riverton, 1917.

———. "Sexual Perversion, Satyriasis and Nymphomania." *Medical and Surgical Reporter* 61 (1889): 253–85.

Lyons, George R. "Cause for the Mollycoddle." *Chicago Tribune*, April 18, 1909, E9.

Matta, Christina. "Ambiguous Bodies and Deviant Sexualities: Hermaphrodites, Homo-sexuality, and Surgery in the United States, 1850–1904." *Perspectives in Biology and Medicine* 48 (2005): 74–83.

Matthews, Franklin. "'Wide-Open' Chicago." *Harper's*, February 12, 1898, 88–91.

Maudsley, Henry. "Illustrations of a Variety of Insanity." *Journal of Mental Science* 14 (1868): 149–62.

Mavigliano, George J., and Richard A. Lawson. *The Federal Arts Project in Illinois, 1935–1943*. Carbondale: Southern Illinois University Press, 1990.

Mayne, Xavier. *The Intersexes: A History of Similisexualism as a Problem in Social Life*. Repr. ed. New York: Arno, 1975.

McClure's. "Chicago as Seen by Herself." May 1907, 67–73.

McCutcheon, John T. "The Grand March at Bathhouse John's Ball." Cartoon, 1908. *Encyclopedia of Chicago*, accessed December 26, 2013. www.encyclopedia .chicagohistory.org/pages/3822.html.

McGill, Nettie P. *Children in Street Work*. Washington, DC: Government Printing Office, 1928.

McKee, J. H. "George Ade Reports the World's Fair." *Nieman Reports*, September 1964, 18-22.

McMillan, Allan. "A Chicagoan in Harlem." *Afro-American* (Baltimore, MD), May 12, 1934, 8

———. "47th Street—Chicago." *Chicago Defender*, July 1, 1933, 15.

Medical and Surgical Reporter. "Cosmetics of Castration." October 24, 1896, 543.

Melody, Michael Edward, and Linda M. Peterson. *Teaching American About Sex: Marriage Guides and Sex Manuals from the Late Victorians to Dr. Ruth.* New York: New York University Press, 1999.

Meredith, Eva Hagenhofer. E-mail to Roland Derylo, May 2, 2016.JDH.

Metzger, Richard. "Julian Eltinge: America's First Drag Superstar." Dangerous Minds, July 22, 2013. http://dangerousminds.net/comments/julian_eltinge_americas_first _drag_superstar.

Meyerowitz, Joanne. "Sexual Geography and Gender Economy: The Furnished Room Districts of Chicago, 1890–1930." *Gender and History* 2 (1990): 274–96.

Miami (FL) News-Metropolis. "'Man-Woman' Takes Stand." October 3, 1923, 1.

Miller, Donald L. *City of the Century: The Epic of Chicago and the Making of America.* New York: Simon and Schuster, 1996.

MilitaryBases.com. "Great Lakes Training Center Navy Base, North Chicago, IL." Accessed March 4, 2014. http://militarybases.com/illinois/great-lakes/.

Moffett, Nancy. "Repairing the Ravages of Time." *Chicago Sun-Times*, November 6, 2002, 26.

Moriarty, J. "Sandow—Gay Strongman of Gay '90s." *Advocate*, March 14, 1973, 30–31.

Morning Oregonian. "Playhouse Revue Has Half in Cast." August 22, 1933, 4.

Morris, Charles E., III. "Pink Herring and the Fourth Persona: J. Edgar Hoover's Sex Crime Panic." *Quarterly Journal of Speech* 88 (2002): 228–44.

Moscato, Marc. *Brains Brilliancy Bohemia: Art and Politics in Jazz-Age Chicago.* Exhibition catalog. Chicago: n.p., 2009.

"Mr. P." Unpublished typescript, n.d. Box 128, folder 7, EWB.

Mumford, Kevin J. "'Lost Manhood' Found: Male Sexual Impotence and Victorian Culture in the United States." *Journal of the History of Sexuality* 3 (1992): 33–57.

Murray, Stephen O. *Homosexualities.* Chicago: University of Chicago Press, 2002.

Museum of Modern Art. "Prize Pictures in P.M. Competition." In *PM Competition: "The Artist as Reporter" Master Checklist.* Typescript, n.d. Museum of Modern Art official website. www.moma.org/documents/moma_master-checklist_325170.pdf.

My Al Capone Museum. "Hinky Dink and Bathhouse John: Chicago's Infamous Aldermen." June 2008. www.myalcaponemuseum.com/id147.htm.

National Archives and Records Administration. *Passport Applications, 1795–1905*, roll no. 263: April 1, 1884–April 30, 1884. NARA Series. Washington, DC: National Archives and Record Administration.

National Archives at St. Louis. *Draft Registration Cards for Fourth Registration for Illinois, 04/27/1942–04/27/1942.* NAI no. 623284. Record group title: "Records of the Selective Service System." Record group no. 147. St. Louis, MO: National Archives at St. Louis.

National Medical Association. Sketches from Life. *Journal* 6 (1914): 112.

National Park Service. "Henry Gerber House." National Historic Landmark Nomination registration form. National Park Service, US Department of the Interior, 2014. www.nps.gov/nhl/news/LC/fall2014/HenryGerberHouse.pdf.

National Police Gazette (New York, NY). "The Ladies Idolize Sandow." January 27, 1894, 6.

——. "Oscar Wilde Gets a Reception." January 21, 1882, 8.

——. "Too, Too, Utterly Utter." January 2, 1882, 8.

Newberry Library. "A Night in Bohemia: Dill Pickle Masked Ball." Frontier to Heartland, Newberry Library official website, accessed September 1, 2012. http://publications.newberry.org/frontiertoheartland/items/show/179.

New York Dramatic Mirror. "Nebraska." August 20, 1890, 10.

New York Times. "Acquits Man-Wife of Murder Charge." October 4, 1923, 12.

——. "Alleged 'Gun Woman' a Man in Disguise." June 20, 1923, 21.

——. "Almost a Lynching in Chicago." March 29, 1894, 1.

——. "Bomb Explodes, Aimed at Coliseum." December 14, 1908, 1.

——. "Chicago's Reform Wave." December 2, 1900, 15.

——. "The Strongest Man in the World." June 20, 1893, 8.

Nickell, Joe. *Secrets of the Sideshow.* Lexington: University of Kentucky Press, 2005.

Norton, W. B. "Church Women Reveal Suggestive." *Chicago Tribune,* March 12, 1917, 7.

Oakland Tribune. "Actor Has Gone Always as Girl." June 8, 1913, 1.

Oatman-Stanford, Hunter. "Before Rockwell, a Gay Artist Defined the Perfect American Male." *Collectors Weekly,* August 28, 2012. www.collectorsweekly.com/articles/the-perfect-american-male/.

Ohio Department of Health. Death certificate for Fred Thompson, April 8, 1953.

Okihiro, Gary Y. *Common Ground: Reimagining American History.* Princeton, NJ: Princeton University Press, 2001.

Oliver, Paul. *Blues Fell This Morning: Meaning in the Blues.* New York: Cambridge University Press, 1960.

——. *The Story of the Blues.* Rev. ed. Boston: Northeastern University Press, 1997.

O'Neal, Jim, and Amy van Singel. "Georgia Tom Dorsey." In *The Voice of the Blues: Classic Interviews from "Living Blues" Magazine,* edited by Jim O'Neal and Amy van Singel, 1–41. New York: Routledge, 2002.

Orro, David H. "Six Sleuths Put on Trail of Shocking Rumors in Rev. Cobbs 'Scandal.'" *Chicago Defender,* December 2, 1939, 12.

Osborne, A. E. "Castrating to Cure Masturbation." *Pacific Medical Journal* 38 (March 1895): 151–53.

Padgett, Ken. "Minstrel Show Female Impersonators." Blackface! (website), accessed February 8, 2013. http://black-face.com/minstrel-female-impersonators.htm.

Painter, George. "The History of Sodomy Laws in the United States: Illinois." GLAPN, 1991–2002. www.glapn.org/sodomylaws/sensibilities/illinois.htm.

Parth, Johnny. "Editorial Review." In *Complete Recorded Works*, vol. 2, *1929–1937*. Document Records DOCD-5259, 1994.

P."B."J. Letter to Alfred C. Kinsey. February 13, 1940. ACK.

Pettey, Tom. "Atlantic City Hands Chicago Wide Open Grin." *Chicago Tribune*, May 17, 1928, 1.

Peyton, Dave. "Geo. Walker Benefit an Artistic Success." *Chicago Defender*, July 3, 1926, 6.

Pinder, Kymberly. *Painting the Gospel: Black Public Art and Religion in Chicago.* Urbana: University of Illinois Press, 2016.

Plaindealer (Kansas City, KS). "We Become a Dancer." October 25, 1935, 7.

Printer's Ink. Miscellaneous. July 8, 1896, 28.

Provines, June. Front Views and Profiles. *Chicago Tribune*, October 12, 1940, 17.

Quincy Daily Whig. Crime. August 28, 1868, 1.

Rambling Reporter. "Seen and Heard at the Fair." *Chicago Defender*, June 10, 1933, 12.

Reckless, Walter. "Natural History of Vice Areas." PhD diss., University of Chicago, 1925.

Reed, Bill. *Hot from Harlem: Twelve African American Entertainers, 1890–1960.* Jefferson, NC: McFarland, 2010.

Reitman, Ben. "Homosexuality." *Living with Social Outcasts.* Unpublished typescript, n.d. Box 3, folder 50, BLR.

Rexroth, Kenneth. "Kenneth Rexroth's Autobiography." Bureau of Public Secrets, accessed September 10, 2014. www.bopsecrets.org/rexroth/autobio/.

Rice, Edward Le Roy. *Monarchs of Minstrelsy from "Daddy" Rice to Date.* New York: Kenny, 1911.

Riis, Jacob A. "Sociologist at a Dance." *Chicago Tribune*, February 8, 1901, 1.

Rockford (IL) Daily Register-Gazette. Holiday Personals. December 29, 1924, 14.

Rockford (IL) Morning Star. "Army, Navy Sign 11 New Recruits." June 25, 1942, 7.

———. "Arrest Fifth Man in Probe of Nudist Club." December 11, 1937, 1.

———. "Coronado Stage to Present New Revue Thursday." June 3, 1934, 15.

———. "Ethel M. Davis Wed to Ralph S. Wright." March 16, 1938, 4.

———. "Expect Grand Jury to Hear Boys' Stories." November 14, 1937, 4.

———. "Host to Denishawns." February 10, 1927, 8.

———. "Jail Two More in 'Nudist Club' Quiz." November 30, 1937, 3.

———. "Police Arrest Man as Leader of Nudist Club." November 13, 1937, 1.

———. "Ralph Wright to Celebrate 80th Birthday." February 14, 1960, 8.

———. "Raymond Carlson Leaves Rockford." June 16, 1925, 6.

———. "Regrets Lack of Whipping Post as He Releases Tobin." March 5, 1938, 1.

———. "'Scandals' End Coronado Stage Showing Tonight." June 9, 1934, 12.

———. "Wright Released on Probation by Court." January 28, 1938, 17.

Rockford (IL) Register. "Mustered Out." November 8, 1945, 4.

Rockford (IL) Register-Gazette. "Social Functions Are Announced for Rockford Players." November 6, 1926, 14.

Rockford (IL) Register-Republic. "Men and Women in the Armed Forces." April 27 1943, 11.

———. "Nudist Case Defendant Admitted to Probation." January 27 1938, 1.

———. "Probation Hearing Set in Party Youth's Case." May 4 1938, 1.

———. "Sentence U.S. Art Teacher on Morals Charges." December 13 1937, 1.

———. "Suicide Verdict in Ray Carlson Death." December 16 1937, 14.

Rockford (IL) Republic. "Country Club Dinner Dance Friday Eve." July 29 1926, 4.

———. "Pecatonica M.E. Church Names Heads." September 25, 1926, 5.

Rockford High School Annual: 1912. Rockford, IL: Rockford High School, 1912.

———. Editorials, 124. Rockford, IL: Rockford High School, 1912.

Rofes, Eric E. "Steward on Sex." Advocate, December 11, 1984, 88–90.

Rohm, Harland. "Breezes from the Lake." Chicago Tribune, February 6 1927, F2.

Romesburg, Don Alan. "Arrested Development: Homosexuality, Gender, and American Adolescence, 1890–1930." Diss., University of California, Berkeley, 2006.

Rose, Al. Storyville, New Orleans: Being an Authentic, Illustrated Account of the Notorious Red Light District. Tuscaloosa: University of Alabama Press, 1978.

Roth, Walter. "Jews on the Midway." Chicago Jewish History 25, no. 1 (Spring 2001): 1, 4, 6–7.

Roy, Rob. "Billy Mitchell, Comedy Star, to the Annex Club." Chicago Defender, January 19, 1935, 9.

———. "Earl Hines Is One Up on Jim Lunceford Now." Chicago Defender, August 24, 1935, 7.

Rydell, Robert W. "World's Columbian Exposition." Encyclopedia of Chicago, accessed April 29, 2017. www.encyclopedia.chicagohistory.org/pages/1386.html.

Rye, Howard. "Can't You Wait till You Get Home?" Sleeve notes. Can't You Wait Till You Get Home? Collectors Items, 1984.

Salerno, Roger A. Sociology Noir: Studies at the University of Chicago in Loneliness, Marginality and Deviance, 1915–1935. Jefferson, NC: McFarland, 2007.

Salt Lake Tribune. "Corporal Noonan." January 4, 1879, 5.

San Francisco Call. "Last Week of Music Plays at American." November 28, 1909, 28.

Sandburg, Carl. *Always the Young Strangers.* New York: Harcourt, 1953.

Sandow, Eugen. "My Reminiscences." *Strand Magazine* 39 (March 1910): 147.

Sawyers, June. "Hinky Dink and Bathhouse John's 'Carnival of Evil.'" *Chicago Tribune,* January 25, 1987.

Scheck, E. H. "Offers Thanks." *Day Book* (Chicago, IL), September 23, 1916, 23–24.

Schwarzlose, Richard A. "Newspapers in Jack Wing's World." In *The Chicago Diaries of John M. Wing, 1865–1866,* edited by Robert Williams, xv–xlviii. Carbondale: Southern Illinois University Press, 2002.

Schweik, Schwanda. "Chicago World Fairies." *Brevities,* December 7, 1931, 16, 13, 12.

Scupham-Bilton, Tony. "The Body of a God: Part 3." *Queerstory Files* (blog), September 27, 2013. http://queerstoryfiles.blogspot.com/2013/09/the-body-of-god-part-3.html.

Sears, Roebuck and Company. "Our $18.00 Giant Power Electric Belt." *Sears, Roebuck Catalogue* 112 (1902): 476.

See, Hilda. "'Female Impersonators' Rule Many Floor Shows.'" *Chicago Defender,* September 11, 1936, 21.

Seligman, Amanda. "Towertown." *Encyclopedia of Chicago,* accessed April 1, 2010. www.encyclopedia.chicagohistory.org/pages/1265.html.

Senelick, Laurence. "Boys and Girls Together." In *Crossing the Stage: Controversies on Cross-Dressing,* edited by Lesley Ferris, 80–95. New York: Routledge, 1993.

———. "Transvestism, Theatrical." In *Encyclopedia of Homosexuality,* edited by Wayne Dynes, 1314–1322. New York: Garland, 1990.

Shaw. "Who's a Fairy?" Cartoon. Unidentified newspaper, n.d. Box 1, folder "Newspaper Cuttings," JA.

Shaw, Clifford. *The Jack-Roller: A Delinquent Boy's Own Story.* Repr. ed. Chicago: University of Chicago Press, 1966; orig. publ. 1930.

Shteir, Rachel. *Striptease: The Untold History of the Girlie Show.* New York: Oxford University Press, 2004.

Smith, Alson J. *Chicago's Left Bank.* Chicago: Henry Regnery, 1953.

Spitzka, E. C. "Cases of Masturbation (Masturbic Insanity)." *Journal of Mental Science* 33 (1887): 57–78, 238–54.

Spokane (WA) Press. "Washington." September 25, 1909, 3.

Sprague, Gregory. "Chicago Sociologists and the Social Control of Urban 'Illicit' Sexuality, 1892–1918." Typescript, n.d. Box 5, folder 12, GAS.

———. "Chicago's Past: A Rich Gay History." *Advocate,* August 18, 1983, 28.

———. "Discovering the Thriving Gay Male Subculture of Chicago During 1920s and 1930s." MS, n.d. Box 5, folder 12, GAS.

———. "Gay Balls, an Old Chicago Tradition." *Gay Life*, November 14, 1980, 3, 8.

———. "Jackson, Tony (Anthony)." Typescript, n.d. Box 17, "Reference Articles on Homosexuality, 1920s & 1930s," GAS.

———. "Male Homosexuality in Western Culture: The Dilemma of Identity and Sub-culture in Historical Research." *Journal of Homosexuality* 10 (Winter 1984): 29–43.

———. "On the 'Gay Side' of Town: The Nature and Structure of Male Homosexuality in Chicago, 1890–1935." Typescript, n.d. Box 5, folder 12, GAS.

———. "60th Anniversary of the First U.S. Gay Rights Organization." Unpublished typescript, n.d. Box 17, folder "Gerber, Henry," GAS.

———. "Urban Male Homosexuality in Transition: The Characteristics and Structure of Gay Identities in Chicago, 1920–1940." Typescript, n.d. Box 5, folder 12, GAS.

Spring, Justin. *Secret Historian: The Life and Times of Samuel Steward, Professor, Tattoo Artist, and Sexual Renegade.* Kindle ed. New York: Farrar, Straus, Giroux, 2010.

Stanford University Libraries. "Swinging on the South Side: The Heartbeat of Chicago Jazz." Jim Cullum Riverwalk Jazz Collection, Stanford University Libraries, accessed September 1, 2013. http://riverwalkjazz.stanford.edu/bonus-content /swinging-south-side-heartbeat-chicago-jazz.

Stead, William. *If Christ Came to Chicago: A Plea for the Union of All Who Love in the Service of All Who Suffer.* London: Review of Reviews, 1894.

Stribling, Dees. "Three Bronzeville Churches." *Been There, Seen That* (blog), November 4, 2014. www.dees-stribling.com/2014/11/04/two-bronzeville-churches/.

Suisman, David. "(Black Swan 14127) Trixie Smith, 'My Man Rocks Me." DavidSuis-man.net, accessed April 1, 2013. http://davidsuisman.net/?page_id=437.

Sunday Times (Chicago, IL). Personal. July 30, 1876, 2.

Survey. "Relentless War Against Vice in Chicago." June 9, 1917, 249.

Sutherland, Sidney. "'Medutations' of Yellow Kid Run Lyle Out." *Chicago Tribune*, January 17, 1926, 1.

Swinnerton, Frank. "Viola Meynell's New Novel Wins Praise in Britain." *Chicago Tribune*, December 3, 1927, 15.

Symonds, John Addington. *The Letters of John Addington Symonds.* Vol. 3, *1885–1893*. Edited by Herbert M. Schueller and Robert L. Peters. Detroit: Wayne Stare University Press, 1969.

Syracuse (NY) Herald. "'May Belmont,' a Singer in Concert Halls, Is a Man." June 7, 1913, 6.

———. "May Belmont Before Justice Shove." June 9, 1913, 11.

———. "'May Belmont' Jumps His Bail." June 11, 1913, 3.

———. "Only Concert Hall Where They Never Sold Liquor Will Soon Be No More." April 10, 1914, 18.

———. "Youth Who Grew Up Masqued as Girl Held by Police." June 8, 1913, 1.

Syracuse (NY) Journal. "They All Want to Know How 'Miss Belmont' Shaved." June 27, 1913, 2.

Talbot, E. S., and Havelock Ellis. "A Case of Developmental Degenerate Insanity, with Sexual Inversion, Melancholia Following Removal of Testicles, Attempted Murder and Suicide." *Journal of Medical Science* 42 (1896): 340–46.

Taylor, Troy. "Bath House John, Hinky Dink and Others: Chicago's History of Graft and Corruption." Weird & Haunted Chicago, accessed November 13, 2013. www .prairieghosts.com/graft.html.

Telegraph (Nashua, NH). "Cut Nude Dances at Chicago Fair." August 2, 1933, 4.

Terman, Lewis M., and Catharine Cox Miles. *Sex and Personality: Studies in Masculinity and Femininity.* New York: McGraw-Hill, 1936.

Terry. "J. C. Leyendecker." *Gay Influence: Gay & Bisexual Men of Importance* (blog), August 11, 2012. http://gayinfluence.blogspot.com/2012/08/jc-leyendecker.html.

Thomas de la Peña, Carolyn. "Designing the Electric Body: Sexuality, Masculinity and the Electric Belt in America, 1880–1920." *Journal of Design History* 14 (2001): 275–89.

Thrasher, Frederic M. *The Gang: A Study of 1,313 Gangs in Chicago.* Edited by Piers Beirne. Chicago: University of Chicago Press, 2006.

T.K. Letter to Alfred C. Kinsey. November 15 [1939]. ACK.

———. Letter to Alfred C. Kinsey. November 20 [1939]. ACK.

———. Letter to Alfred C. Kinsey. September 13, 1943. ACK.

Todd, Jan. "Bernarr Macfadden: Reformer of Feminine Form." *Journal of Sport* History 14 (Spring 1987): 61–75.

Tovey, Michael. "Down at the Cabin Inn: The Oddest Night Club in Chicago." *Storeyville* 144 (1990): 203–13.

Townsend, Kim. *Sherwood Anderson.* Boston: Houghton Mifflin, 1987.

Ullman, Sharon. "'The Twentieth Century Way': Female Impersonation and Sexual Practice in Turn-of-the-Century America." *Journal of the History of Sexuality* 5 (1995): 573–600.

University of Chicago Library. "Guide to the Ernest Watson Burgess Papers 1886–1966." University of Chicago Library official website, 2009. www.lib.uchicago.edu/e/scrc /findingaids/view.php?eadid=icu.spcl.burgess.

University of Chicago Magazine. News from the Classes. November 1911, 50.

University of Kentucky Libraries. "Andrew Tribble." Notable Kentucky African Americans Database, accessed November 13, 2013. https://nkaa.uky.edu/nkaa/items/show/59.

US Department of Justice. "David Petillo." FBI field office file, September 27, 1963. File no. New York 92-02915.

US Department of Labor. "CPI Inflation Calculator." Bureau of Labor Statistics official website, accessed September 2, 2013. www.bls.gov/data/inflation_calculator.htm.

Utica (NY) Daily Observer. "Shot Down on the Streets." March 29, 1894, 2.

Vadeboncoeur, Jim, Jr. "Illustrators: J.C. Leyendecker." JVJ Publishing, accessed February 21, 2017. www.bpib.com/illustrat/leyendec.htm.

Van Duzer, Winifred. "Why 'Iron Mike' Became 'Miss Fluffy Ruffles.'" *Sarasota (FL) Herald-Tribune,* October 4, 1925, 65.

Variety. "Black and Tan Raids on Chi's Mixed Places." January 19, 1927, 47.

———. "Chi Lily-White in Sudden Morals Drive, While Philly Is Livening Up." January 8, 1935, 51.

———. "Pansy Parlors." December 10, 1930, 1.

———. "Police O-Oing Unlicensed Niters." February 11, 1931, 77.

Vice Commission of Chicago. *The Social Evil in Chicago.* Chicago: City of Chicago, 1911.

Vollmer, Myles. "Boy Hustler: Chicago." Unpublished typescript, 1933. Box 145, folder 8, EWB.

———. "The New Year's Eve Drag." Unpublished typescript, n.d. Box 140, folder 2, EWB.

———. "Vagabond Boy—Chicago." Unpublished typescript, n.d. Box 145, folder 8, EWB.

Webster, Ronald. "The Harmless Sexuality of Syncopated Music. *Chicago Tribune,* February 7, 1915, E1, E3.

Wendt, Lloyd. "John the Bath and the First Ward Ball." *Chicago Tribune,* December 15, 1940, 2.

Wertheim, Elsa. *Chicago Children in the Street Trades.* Chicago: Juvenile Protective Association, 1917.

Whiteley, Sheila, and Jennifer Rycenga. *Queering the Popular Pitch.* New York: Routledge, 2006.

Williams, Robert. Introduction to *The Chicago Diaries of John M. Wing, 1865–1866.* Edited by Robert Williams, xlix–lxiii. Carbondale: Southern Illinois University Press, 2002.

Willrich, Michael. *City of Courts: Socializing Justice in Progressive Era Chicago.* Cambridge: Cambridge University Press, 2003.

Wilson, Terry. "Gay Life in Chicago." *Chicago Tribune,* October 21, 1997, http://articles.chicagotribune.com/1997-10-21/features/9710210045_1_lesbian-bisexual-veterans-gay-george-chauncey.

Wing, John M. *The Chicago Diaries of John M. Wing, 1865–1866.* Edited by Robert Williams. Carbondale: Southern Illinois University Press, 2002.

———. Pocket diary for 1858. MS ES, W72, JMW.

——. Pocket diary for 1859. MS 15, no. 219, JMW.

——. Pocket diary for 1860. MS 150, vol. 3, JMW.

——. Pocket diary for 1861. MS 150, JMW.

Winters, Christopher. "Before and After the Fire: Chicago in the 1860s, 1870s, and 1880s." University of Chicago Library official website, accessed February 5, 2013. www.lib.uchicago.edu/e/collections/maps/chifire/.

Woman's Medical Journal. Items of Interest. Vol. 11 (April 1901): 145.

Yates, Ted. "Harlem Denies Love Story in Suicide Leap." *Chicago Defender*, May 16, 1936, 8.

Young, Al. "'John Henry' Is Plenty Good in Southern Yarn." *Chicago Defender*, July 1, 1933, 5.

Zagria. "Cabin Inn, Chicago." *A Gender Variance Who's Who* (blog), August 5, 2013. https://zagria.blogspot.com/2013/08/the-cabin-inn-chicago.html.

Zorbaugh, Harvey Warren. *The Gold Coast and the Slum: A Sociological Study of Chicago's Near North Side.* Chicago: University of Chicago Press, 1929; repr. 1976.

Index

Page numbers in italics refer to illustrations.

H- 8/18
O 3/19
W 10/19
H 5/20